Parapsychology
and
the Skeptics

A Scientific Argument for the Existence of ESP

Chris Carter

SterlingHouse Publisher, Inc.   Pittsburgh, PA

Parapsychology
and
the Skeptics

Chris Carter

P A J A BOOKS

ISBN-10: 1-58501-108-8
ISBN-13: 978-1-58-501108-7
Trade Paperback
© Copyright 2007 Chris Carter
All Rights Reserved
Library of Congress #2007923559

Requests for information should be addressed to:
SterlingHouse Publisher, Inc.
7436 Washington Avenue
Pittsburgh, PA 15218
info@sterlinghousepublisher.com
www.sterlinghousepublisher.com

Paja Books
is an imprint of SterlingHouse Publisher, Inc.

SterlingHouse Publisher, Inc.
is a company of CyntoMedia Corporation.

Cover Design: Brandon M. Bittner
Interior Design: Kathleen M. Gall
Images provided by iStockphoto.com

Printed in U.S.A.

Dedicated to the memories of
Curt Ducasse, Frederic Myers, and Karl Popper,
three remarkable individuals who never let fashion dictate their opinions.

ALL TRUTH PASSES THROUGH THREE STAGES:
First, it is ridiculed.
Second, it is violently opposed.
Third, it is accepted as self-evident.

Arthur Schopenhauer

Table of Contents

Foreword

By Rupert Sheldrake

This is an important book. It deals with one of the most significant and enduring fault-lines in science and philosophy. For well over a century, there have been strongly divided opinions about the existence of psychic phenomena such as telepathy. The passions aroused by this argument are quite out of proportion to the phenomena under dispute. They stem from deeply held world-views and belief systems. They also raise fundamental questions about the nature of science itself. This debate, and the present state of parapsychology are brilliantly summarised in this book. Chris Carter puts his argument in a well-documented historical context, without which the present controversies make no sense.

The kind of skepticism Carter is writing about is not the normal healthy kind on which all science depends, but arises from a belief that the existence of psychic phenomena is impossible; they contradict the established principles of science, and if they were to exist they would overthrow science as we know it, causing chaos and confusion. Therefore anyone who produces positive evidence supporting their reality is guilty of error, wishful thinking, self-delusion or fraud. This belief makes the very investigation of psychic phenomena taboo and treats those who investigate them as charlatans or heretics.

Although some committed skeptics behave as if they are engaged in a holy war, in this debate there is no clear correlation with religious belief or lack of it. Among those who investigate psi phenomena are atheists, agnostics and followers of religious paths. But the ranks of committed skeptics also include religious believers, agnostics and atheists.

As Carter shows so convincingly in this book, the question of the reality of psi phenomena is not primarily about evidence, but about the interpretation of evidence; it is about frameworks of understanding, or what Thomas Kuhn, the historian of science, called paradigms. I am sure Carter is right.

I have myself spent many years investigating unexplained phenomena such as telepathy in animals and in people. At first I naively believed that this was just a matter of doing properly controlled experiments and collecting evidence. I soon found that for committed skeptics this is not the issue. Some dismiss all the evidence out of hand, convinced in advance that it must be flawed or defective. Those who do look at the evidence have the intention of finding as many flaws as they can, but even if they can't find them, they brush aside the evidence anyway, assuming that fatal errors will come to light later.

The most common tactic of committed skeptics is to try to prevent the evidence from being discussed in public at all. For example, in September 2006, I presented a paper on telephone telepathy at the Annual Festival of the British Association for the Advancement of Science. Our controlled experiment had shown that people could, before answering the phone, correctly identify who was calling (from a choice of four people) over 40% of the time, when a success rate of 25% would be expected by chance alone. The following day, in *The Times* and other leading newspapers, several prominent British skeptics denounced the British Association for "lending credibility to maverick theories on the paranormal" by allowing this talk to take place. One of them, Professor Peter Atkins, a chemist at Oxford University, was quoted as saying, "There is no reason to suppose that telepathy is anything more than a charlatan's fantasy." (*The Times*, September 6, 2006). Later the same day, he and I took part in a debate on BBC Radio. He dismissed all the evidence I presented as "playing with statistics". I then asked him if he had actually looked at the evidence, and he replied, "No, but I would be very suspicious of it".

As Carter shows, conflicts about frameworks of understanding are inherent within science itself. Since its beginnings in the sixteenth century, science grew through a series of rebellions against established worldviews. The Copernican revolution in astronomy was the first. The mechanistic revolution of the seventeenth century, with its dismissal of souls in nature, as previously taught in all the medieval universities, was another great rebellion. But what started as rebel movements in turn became the orthodoxies, propagated by scholars, and taught in universities. Subsequent revolutions, including the theory of evolution in the nineteenth century, and the relativity and quantum revolutions in physics of the twentieth century again broke away from an older orthodoxy to become a new orthodoxy in turn.

There is a similar tension within the Christian religion, which provided the cultural background to the growth of Western science. Christianity itself began as a rebellion. Jesus rejected many of the standard tenets of the Jewish religion into which he was born. His life was one of rebellion against the established religious authorities, the scribes and Pharisees, the chief priests and the elders. But the religion established in his name in its turn became orthodox, rejecting and persecuting heresies, only to be disturbed by further rebellions, most notably the Protestant Reformation. In the debate that Carter documents, the skeptics are the upholders of the established mechanistic order, and help maintain a taboo against "the paranormal". They come in various kinds, and it would probably not be too difficult to find parallels to the chief priests and elders, concerned with political power and influence, and to the scribes and Pharisees, the zealous upholders of righteousness.

This struggle has a strong emotional charge in the context of western religious and intellectual history. But now, in the twenty-first century, there are many scientists of non-western origin, including those from India, China, Africa and the Islamic world. Western history is not their history, nor are the strong emotions aroused by psi phenomena ones with which they can easily identify. In most parts of the world, even including western industrial societies, most people take for granted the existence of telepathy and other psychic phenomena, and are surprised to discover that some people deny them so vehemently.

From my own experience of talking to scientists and giving seminars in scientific institutions, dogmatic skeptics are a minority within the scientific community. Many scientists are curious and open-minded, if only because they themselves or people they know well have had experiences that suggest the reality of psi phenomena. Nevertheless, almost all scientists are aware of the taboo, and the open-minded tend to keep their interests private, fearing scorn or ridicule if they discuss them openly with their colleagues.

I believe that for the majority of the scientific community, in spite of the appearances created by vociferous skeptics, what counts more than polemic is evidence. In the end, the question of whether or not psi phenomena occur, and how they might be explained, depends on evidence and on research.

No one knows how this debate will end or how long it will take for parapsychological investigations to become more widely known and accepted. No one knows how big a change they will make to science itself, or how far they will expand its framework. But the conditions are good, and an intensifying debate about the nature of consciousness makes the evidence from parapsychology more relevant than ever before.

This is one of the longest running debates in the history of science, but changes could soon come faster than most people think possible. *Parapsychology and the Skeptics* is an invaluable guide to what is going on. It is essential reading for anyone who wants to be part of a scientific revolution in the making.

Introduction

In 1772 the prestigious French Academy of Science appointed a committee to investigate reports of what are now called meteorites. After long deliberations and examination of much evidence, the conclusion reached by the committee was that with which they started: There are no such things as hot stones that have fallen from the sky because there are no stones in the sky to fall. Reports of the phenomena must have other explanations—delusionary "visions," stones heated after being struck by lightning, stones borne aloft by whirlwinds or volcanic eruptions, and so forth. So great was the prestige of the committee and so convincing its arguments that museums all over Western Europe threw away their meteorite specimens. As a result, today there are very few preserved meteorite specimens that date prior to 1790.

Meteorites were dismissed as superstitions lingering from a time when Jove was thought to punish errant mortals by hurtling his thunderbolts at them. But when evidence of their reality was eventually conceded—in 1803, following another report from the Academy—scientists did not learn humility. They merely congratulated themselves for correcting the errors of their predecessors.[1]

In 1831 the French Academy appointed another committee, this one to investigate reports of what is now called clairvoyance—correct perception of objects or events not accessible to one's sense organs at the time of apprehension. Much to the surprise of many Academy members, the committee reported that clairvoyance had in fact been satisfactorily demonstrated.[2] But unlike meteorites, the Academy did not finally concede that clairvoyance was more than just silly superstition. The mechanistic science of Galileo and Newton simply could not accommodate such phenomena. So the report was set aside and ignored.

The Strange Trials of Henry Slade

Forty-five years later, a bizarre trial divided London and attracted international attention. It all started in the summer of 1876 when the American psychic Henry Slade visited some friends in London and held séances with several prominent townspeople. At these séances Slade would demonstrate his apparent psychic powers, which would include the movement of untouched objects, the disappearance and reappearance of objects, and the tying of knots in untouched endless cords.

But what got Slade into trouble was his most popular skill: that of seemingly producing automatic writing on a slate. Slade would take a child's slate, put a crumb of pencil lead on it, and hold it face upwards under the flap of a table, with his fingers under the back of the slate, and his thumb on top of the table flap. After a few seconds scraping noises would be heard, and a scrawled message would be found on the slate. Slade had been tested in America by Robert Collyer, and although Collyer found the messages often trivial and sometimes ridiculous, he was satisfied that they could not have been produced by any trick.

Shortly after arriving in England, Slade was tested by August Cox on behalf of the Psychological Society he had founded. Although anxious to expose cheats, Cox was also unable to find any fault with Slade. The room, he reported, was sunlit; in addition to slate writing, the inexplicable movement of large and small objects was said to have occurred. A few days later Slade was tested by Dr. Carter Blake, the former Secretary of the Anthropological Society, who also pronounced that he considered Slade genuine.

All of this was too much for Edwin Ray Lankester, the young laboratory assistant to the famous zoologist and skeptic Thomas Henry Huxley. Apparently eager to impress his heroes Darwin and Huxley, Lankester and his fellow medical student Horatio Donkin visited Slade, pretending to be believers. During a séance, Lankester claimed that he had suddenly snatched a slate out of Slade's hands before the "spirit" could begin to write, and had found a message on it. Slade claimed in a letter to *The Times* that the writing had in fact been heard before the slate was snatched away. But Donkin denied this, and Slade was charged with violating the Vagrancy Act, an old law designed to protect the public from traveling palm readers and sleight-of-hand artists.

Throughout the fall of 1876, London buzzed with talk of the Slade trial. The courtroom was packed with Slade's supporters and detractors, and *The Times* carried trial transcripts day after day. The trial also divided the scientific community: Charles Darwin contributed 10 pounds to the prosecution (a substantial sum in those days), while his co-founder of the theory of evolution, Alfred Russell Wallace, was set to testify as star witness for the defense.

By common consent, the legal evidence against Slade was weak. Even a historian favorably disposed toward Lankester and Donkin wrote that:

> Both scientists turned out to be terrible witnesses; their observational
> skills, developed in anatomy and physiology labs, were useless in
> detecting fraud by professional cheats. ...Indeed, Lankester and
> Donkin apparently could not agree on anything much beyond their
> charge that Slade was an imposter.[3]

The two had to admit they could not explain how Slade's tricks were accomplished. All they were prepared to assert with confidence was that they *must* have been tricks, because the conjuror John Maskelyne had shown them how the table had been designed for that purpose. It had specially constructed flaps, movable bars, and wedges, specially designed to hold the slate, leaving Slade's fingers free to write on it, and to produce raps during the séances.

The table itself was then produced as an exhibit, and Maskelyne was called as a witness. He then proceeded to demonstrate how he thought the trick must have been done: With the aid of a pencil shaped like a thimble. The prosecution pointed out that the table had been constructed according to the specifications of Slade's assistant, who had been prosecuted with him, and so conspiracy was added to the charge of vagrancy.

This was a blow to the defense, but soon there was a new twist in the trial. The prosecution subpoenaed R.H. Hutton as a witness. Hutton was the shrewd, skeptical editor of the *Spectator*, a man with an unblemished reputation, who could be counted upon to testify accurately to whatever he had seen. He had attended séances, he told the court, and although he had doubts about some of the things he had seen, there were many that he could not account for by sleight-of-hand. The testimony of the foreman carpenter, on whose premises the table had been made, also turned out to be an embarrassment for the prosecution. He confirmed that the table had indeed been constructed to a particular specification—for instance, to have one support for each flap instead of two—but it was difficult to see how this could help a conjuror. What about the wedges, which Maskelyne alleged had been used to make the raps? The carpenter had to admit that these had not been in the specification, but had to be inserted after the table had been made, to compensate for some faulty workmanship.

The high point of the trial was the testimony of Wallace for the defense. His integrity and candor were well-known. Wallace testified that the effects which he had observed could not have been produced by sleight-of-hand, although he refused to speculate on whether the slate-writings were caused by spirits.

In his summation, Slade's attorney argued that there was no convincing evidence against his client. The prosecution had not proved that the table was rigged, and Maskelyne's demonstrations of how the trick *could* have been done were irrelevant. The timing of the answer's appearance proved nothing about its origin, and Lankester and Donkin could not even agree on exactly what they had seen during the séance. Finally, the testimony of such an eminent scientist as Wallace should be considered at least as credible as that of young Lankester.

But nothing could save the accused. The judge ruled that Slade must be guilty, since "according to the well-known course of nature" there could be no other explanation. Three months hard labor was the sentence.

Two months later, the Court of Appeal rejected the verdict, because the words "by palmistry or otherwise" had inadvertently been omitted from the indictment. Lankester announced he would initiate a fresh prosecution, putting Slade in a difficult situation. If he left for Germany, accepting an invitation to visit, enemies would allege that he was a fugitive from justice. Before his trial, Slade had been urged by his friends to leave England, on the grounds that he would not receive a fair trial.

Slade had refused; but now he had been shown that an English court *could not* give him a fair trial, as a judge had ruled that regardless of the evidence, he *must* be guilty since the alleged phenomena were contrary to the laws of nature. Seeing no hope of escaping conviction, Slade left for Germany. He wrote to Lankester offering to come back to England to be tested, but only if Lankester would end his legal crusade. Lankester did not reply, and Slade did not return.

The physicists test Slade

This was not the end of Slade's story. He had been invited to Germany by Johann Zollner, professor of Physics and Astronomy. Zollner had heard of Slade's predicament, and of Slade's insistence that he could prove his innocence by duplicating his feats before a scientific body. Intrigued, Zollner decided to take up the challenge.

Although only in his early forties, Zollner had already acquired an international reputation for his work, some of which centered on the possibility of a fourth spatial dimension. Nothing in mathematics or theoretical physics excluded the possibility, but what Zollner needed was empirical evidence. The most convincing evidence, he thought, would be "the transport of material bodies from a space enclosed on every side."

To understand why, consider the analogy of beings existing on a flat plane, limited to a world of only two spatial dimensions. In such a world, a square or a circle would appear to be a sealed container. Once inside, it would seem impossible to the two-dimensional beings that an object would be able to escape, unless the square or circular-shaped container was opened. But if the enclosed object could move in the third spatial dimension, it could be raised perpendicularly to the plane, passed over and let down on the other side of the container. To the inhabitants of this flat land, it would appear as though the object suddenly vanished, and then reappeared outside of the container. The existence of a third spatial dimension would be, for such beings, as incomprehensible as a fourth spatial dimension seems to us.

Since Zollner wanted to find empirical evidence to support his theories, it could be argued that he was predisposed in Slade's favor, and therefore susceptible to his guile. But some of Zollner's best work had been done in research into sensory illusions, so he was no innocent. He shrewdly realized that he would need independent testimony, and so asked some of his colleagues to collaborate with him. These included Gustav Fechner, professor of physics and psychology, and Wilhelm Weber, who along with Gauss, had been one of the leading innovators in electro-magnetism. (Today, the official unit of magnetism is named the "weber" after him).

The tests began with slate writing, and then moved on to tests with a compass needle, which after some difficulty, Slade apparently caused to oscillate. Other phenomena reported included a string tying itself in knots, objects moving out of sealed containers, and a seashell passing through a table, after which it was found to be hot to the touch, almost too hot to hold.

But, critics pointed out that:

> Scientists, because they are trained to trust their senses, are the
> worst possible people to evaluate a magician. A magician is trained
> specifically to distract, deceive, and confuse those very senses. A
> scientist may carefully observe the magician's right hand, but it is the
> left hand that secretly performs the trick. …only another magician is
> clever enough to detect the sleight-of-hand tricks of a fellow magician.
> Only a thief can catch a thief.[4]

Accordingly, Slade was also tested by several professional magicians, the most
famous being Samuel Bellachini. After testing Slade in a series of sittings, Bellachini
provided Slade with a witnessed affidavit, claiming that the phenomena were
"impossible" to produce with sleight-of-hand.[5]

An astonishing number of the most prominent physicists of the day expressed
interest in Zollner's work with Slade, including: William Crookes, inventor of the
cathode ray tube, which until recently was used in television and computer moni-
tors; J.J. Thomson, who won the Nobel Prize in 1906 for the discovery of the electron; and Lord Rayleigh, considered one of the greatest physicists of the late
nineteenth century, and winner of the Nobel Prize in physics in 1904.

For their efforts in investigating these and other unusual phenomena, these
men were criticized and ridiculed mercilessly by their colleagues.[6] One particularly
savage piece of criticism, which appeared in the science quarterly *Bedrock*, was leveled at prominent physicists William Barrett and Oliver Lodge, for their work in
telepathy. In part, it read,

> It is not necessary either to regard the phenomena of so-called
> telepathy as inexplicable or to regard the mental condition of Sir W.F.
> Barrett and Sir Oliver Lodge as indistinguishable from idiocy. There is
> a third possibility. *The will to believe* has made them ready to accept
> evidence obtained under conditions which they would recognize to
> be unsound if they had been trained in experimental psychology.[7]

Of course, Barrett and Lodge could easily have retorted that *the will to disbelieve*
has made the critics ready to reject evidence obtained under conditions that they
would recognize to be sound if they had been trained in experimental physics *or*
psychology.

The New Quantum Controversy

One hundred twenty five years after Slade's trial, another storm was brewing. In the
intervening period physics had undergone two major revolutions. First, Einstein intro-

duced his theory of relativity; then, shortly afterward, came the even more fundamental revision known as quantum mechanics. Newtonian physics had been overthrown by two new upstarts, yet the subject matter of parapsychology was just as
controversial as ever. And a few daring physicists were still stirring up that controversy.

In September 2001 Britain's Royal Mail decided to honor the 100th anniversary
of the Nobel Prize by asking a British winner of each of the six different Nobel Prize
categories—physics, chemistry, medicine, peace, literature, and economics—to
write a small article about the implications of research in their field. Brian Josephson, who won the prize in 1973 for his work in quantum physics, contributed the
following short article:

> Physicists attempt to reduce the complexity of nature to a single
> unifying theory, of which the most successful and universal, the quan-
> tum theory, has been associated with several Nobel prizes, for example
> those to Dirac and Heisenberg. Max Planck's original attempts a
> hundred years ago to explain the precise amount of energy radiated
> by hot bodies began a process of capturing in mathematical form a
> mysterious, elusive world containing 'spooky interactions at a dis-
> tance', real enough however to lead to inventions such as the laser
> and transistor.
>
> Quantum theory is now being fruitfully combined with theories of
> information and computation. These developments may lead to an
> explanation of processes still not understood within conventional
> science such as telepathy, an area where Britain is at the forefront
> of research.[8]

The last sentence of this article ignited a firestorm of controversy. It had been
over a century since Zollner worked with Slade, but it was clear that even in the 21st
century a prominent scientist still could not endorse research into telepathy—the
direct communication between minds that is said to occur independently of the
sense organs—without arousing strong emotions in many of his colleagues. The
first to denounce Josephson in print was David Deutsch, quantum physics expert at
Oxford University. "It is utter rubbish," Deutsch spluttered to the London newspaper *The Observer*. "Telepathy simply does not exist. The Royal Mail has let itself be
hoodwinked into supporting ideas that are complete nonsense. The evidence for
the existence of telepathy is appalling." *

---

* *The Observer,* Sept 30, 2001. Deutsch embodies a curious double standard about the need for scientific evidence. He is a proponent of a theory that there are billions of parallel universes to our own, expounded
  in his book *The Fabric of Reality: The Science of Parallel Universes*. He also speculates freely on time travel,
  although there is not the slightest evidence for either of these phenomena.

The science editor of *The Observer* even suggested patronizingly that Josephson had "gone off the rails".[9]

The controversy was not confined to Britain. Professor Herbert Kroemer of Santa Barbara University, California, was quoted as saying:

> I am highly skeptical. Few of us believe telepathy exists, nor do we think physics can explain it. It also seems wrong for your Royal Mail to get involved. Certainly, if the U.S. postal services did something like this, a lot of us would be very angry.[10]

But in the controversy that followed, other prominent scientists were quoted as expressing opinions supporting Josephson's position. Bernard Carr, a cosmologist at the University of London, argued that even if one regards the probability of extrasensory perception being real as small, "its significance if established would be so immense that it is surely worth investing some effort into studying it."[11]

In an article in *Physics World*, Carr defended Josephson and other physicists interested in telepathy, explaining that the interaction between mind and matter is one of the main reasons why some physicists are interested in the paranormal.

> Quantum mechanics, after all, is the first theory in physics in which the role of the observer has to be taken into account. You cannot separate the observer from the system being observed, although the precise role of consciousness in this process remains controversial.[12]

A few weeks later Josephson defended himself in a letter to *The Observer*, in which he pointed out that complete skeptical denial regarding the existence of telepathy is by no means the rule among working scientists, contrary to what some skeptics would have us believe. In part, he wrote that:

> Surveys show that a large proportion of scientists accept the possibility that telepathy exists; if it appears that the contrary is the case, this is because such scientists wisely keep quiet about their opinions when in scientific company.

> The problem is that scientists critical of this research do not give their normal careful attention to the scientific literature on the paranormal: it is much easier instead to accept official views or views of biased sceptics.

> The CIA's Stargate Project provided clear evidence that people can intermittently pick up with their minds images of distant objects such as military installations, some times with striking accuracy. The research

arm of the project found that under controlled conditions the extent
to which this ability exceeded chance guessing was statistically highly
significant. There is much other supporting research: the views you
present are uninformed ones.

Recently Henry Stapp of the University of California has given strong
arguments for it being necessary to take mind into account in physics,
which opens up a whole field of possibilities; ironically, he also gives
strong arguments against Deutsch's many-worlds philosophy, which
has no experimental support whatever. My speculations in the bro-
chure are by no means incompatible with current science. My contacts
at Royal Mail do not consider they made an error in allowing the
statement to stand.

Brian Josephson
Department of Physics
University of Cambridge

In the same issue Phillip Parker of the Royal Mail defended the Post Office's
decision.

Royal Mail was fully aware that Professor Josephson's views in the
Nobel Stamps presentation pack could cause a debate among physicists.
This is why telepathy was referred to as an area 'not understood by
conventional science'. Six Nobel laureates were invited to write a
personal reflection. Professor Josephson ended his piece on Quantum
Theory with a few words speculating on the possible future direction
of this particular subject.

The Nobel Stamps issued on 2 October celebrate 100 years of Nobel
prizes. We are delighted that six laureates made unique contributions
to our pack.

Philip Parker
Royal Mail [13]

The controversy also played out over the airwaves. BBC radio confronted
Josephson with psychologist Nicholas Humphrey and conjuror James Randi, neither
of whom, it should be remembered, are Nobel laureates, Fellows of the Royal
Society, or even physicists.

Randi was first quoted, in part, as saying, "There is no firm evidence for the
existence of telepathy, ESP, or whatever we want to call it, and I think it is the refuge

of scoundrels in many respects for them to turn to something like quantum mechanics, which uses a totally different language from the regular English that we are accustomed to using from day to day."

Humphrey was more coherent: "Well, I think the idea that quantum physics explains the paranormal is an unnecessary idea, because there's nothing to explain. We haven't got any evidence."[14]

Since reports of telepathy, clairvoyance, and so forth date back over at least two thousand years, and since these phenomena have been studied experimentally for over one hundred years, the remark that "We haven't got any evidence" may seem somewhat surprising.

It may be even more surprising to learn that this remark came from a former holder of the Cambridge University Perrott-Warrick Fellowship for Psychical Research.[15]

Nothing of course was resolved in the brief exchange that followed. Humphrey patronizingly implied that Josephson "and other well-meaning physicists" are being fooled by conjuring tricksters if they believe in telepathy. In response, Josephson taunted Humphrey: "Now a few years ago he wrote a book...I looked at the book very carefully and I believe I disposed of all the arguments. I haven't heard any comeback from him."

"This isn't the time to review my book!" Humphrey squealed. The psychologist then proceeded to make some rather inaccurate remarks about the controversial role of consciousness in quantum physics, and time ran out on the talk show before Josephson was allowed to respond.

The issue was no more settled at the end of the radio talk show than it had been 125 years earlier, at the end of Slade's trial. Despite the fact that the controversy has now spanned three centuries, and has been carried on in scientific academies, courtrooms, academic journals, newspapers and radio stations, the opponents and proponents of parapsychology seem just as implacably opposed in the twenty-first century as they were in the nineteenth. Today, in the world of science, nothing seems more controversial than parapsychology.

Indeed, the story of parapsychology's struggle for legitimacy is an epic tale spanning centuries and continents, containing victories, sudden reversals, intrigue, scandals, heated arguments, wild accusations, ruined reputations and some of the most bizarre characters that have ever walked the earth. But *why* is parapsychology so controversial? *Why* has the controversy lasted centuries? And are we capable, at long last, of rationally resolving the issue?

In order to discover why parapsychology is so controversial, and why the controversy has lasted centuries, it is necessary to first understand the nature of the dispute. This is the key to a final rational resolution of the matter, a resolution that, by wide agreement, is long overdue.

1

Origins of the Debate

The question of whether paranormal phenomena actually exist probably divides educated members of modern Western civilization as sharply as any other single issue. [But] I do not believe the subject will make any progress unless we are sufficiently open-minded to accept the possibility of supernormal powers, and sufficiently critical to abandon claims shown to be false.

Horace Barlow
Physiologist
Cambridge, April 2000

The world is a battlefield of ideas, and the battle over the subject matter of parapsychology has been raging for centuries. The first shots of the war over the reality of the paranormal were fired almost three hundred years ago, and they signaled the opening rounds of an exchange that continues to this day. The skeptics often seem to be engaged in a kind of holy war, fueled by the belief that they alone are the last defenders of the citadel of science. This battlefield of ideas is murkier than most, as some of the disputants fight not only with logic and statistics but also with ridicule and charges of "pseudo-science", incompetence, and fraud. However, the smoke is finally clearing, and at last it is becoming possible to see what is left standing.

Skepticism, meaning the practice of doubt, is a crucial component of the practice of science. New and controversial claims must be subjected to critical, careful scrutiny before they are accepted into the "scientific worldview." Through the practice of conjecture, prediction, testing, analysis and debate, our scientific understanding of the universe continually evolves. Critical thinking is crucial if we are to minimize our chances of accepting unwarranted conclusions.

But skepticism is a double-edged sword that can be applied to any claim, including the claims of the skeptics. The philosopher Curt Ducasse made this point forcefully:

Although the evidence offered by addicts of the marvelous for the reality of the phenomena they accept must be critically examined, it is equally necessary on the other side to scrutinize just as closely and critically the skeptic's allegations of fraud, or of malobservation, or of misinterpretation of what was observed, or of hypnotically induced hallucinations. *For there is likely to be just as much wishful thinking, prejudice, emotion, snap judgment, naïveté, and intellectual dishonesty on the side of orthodoxy, of skepticism, and of conservatism, as on the side of hunger for and belief in the marvelous.*[16]

This book is a critical examination of skeptical claims regarding so-called paranormal phenomena. Paranormal phenomena include four other main categories of phenomena, as well as evidence for the survival of bodily death: 1) telepathy—a direct communication between minds that occurs independently of the sense organs and regardless of distance or obstacles; 2) clairvoyance—correct perception of objects or events not accessible to one's sense organs at the time of apprehension; 3) precognition—information perceived about future events without the use of ordinary means; and 4) psychokinesis—the direct action of mind upon matter, independently of muscles and limbs. The first three phenomena are referred to together as extra-sensory perception (ESP), and the last one is usually abbreviated to PK. All four are referred to collectively as *psi phenomena*, or simply as psi (pronounced "*sigh*")—the second last letter of the Greek alphabet.

Research into the question of survival is somewhat out of fashion in the parapsychology community today, as most researchers in the field spend their time designing and performing experiments in order to test theories of telepathy, clairvoyance, and psychokinesis. The evidence for survival will be assessed in a second book in this series, where the discussion of the survival hypothesis is defended on three grounds. The first is historical: The early psychic researchers were much more concerned about the survival question than with telepathy and other forms of psi. The second is psychological: Evidence for the survival of consciousness past the point of biological death is surely of great interest to most of mankind. And the third is simply the fact that the skeptics do not shy away from criticizing the claims of those who profess to offer evidence of survival, and so I consider the topic fair game.

Basis of the controversy

Webster's dictionary defines *prima facie* evidence as "evidence having such a degree of probability that it must prevail unless the contrary be proved." As we will see, in terms of sheer quantity and variety, the evidence in favor of the psi and survival hypotheses certainly does seem to provide strong *prima facie* cases in their favor. However, many alternative explanations have been proposed, explanations that account for this evidence in terms that do not require the existence of psi or the survival of bodily death. So, if we are to make up our minds about the reality of psi and survival on rational grounds, then we must demonstrate that one set of these explanations is more likely to be true than the other.

In order to understand the controversy, it is crucial to realize that many of the arguments about psi phenomena are not really about the evidence, as much as they are about the underlying preconceptions of the disputants. The fact that there *is* evidence in the form of numerous reports is not disputed by those who have taken the trouble to investigate these matters: what is disputed is the *interpretation* of this evidence. Believers and disbelievers tend to bring a different set of preconceptions to the table. Consequently, different people can examine the same evidence yet come to radically different conclusions—conclusions that usually support their initial preconceptions. When people are faced with seemingly compelling evidence that conflicts with long-held preconceived notions, they only rarely change their opinions with ease. This is because changing opinions would not merely mean accepting the reality of the phenomena in question: It would also mean changing one's deeply held preconceptions.

When people are faced with a conflict between belief and evidence, many are likely to enter into a state psychologists have termed *cognitive dissonance*. This is an uncomfortable state of tension that can only be relieved by changing one's preconceptions, or by dismissing the objectionable evidence. Needless to say, since the preconceived opinions we bring to the table are formed over a lifetime on the basis of our unique experiences, education, and personalities, changing them is rarely easy.

This means that any examination of the dispute over the reality of psi phenomena cannot simply be an examination of the evidence. As Professor Henry Bauer has written:

> In considering the available evidence we usually fail to make the crucially important distinction between weight of evidence adequate to support one's own belief and weight of evidence adequate to convince others. Since preconceptions vary, estimates of plausibility also vary: what seems likely to some seems quite unlikely to others. When something occurs that seems *to us* plausible, we accept it even on quite slender evidence; when however a thing seems implausible to us, we demand a mass of proof before accepting it and may even then remain unconvinced. [17]

In addition to examining the evidence, it is necessary to critically examine the different philosophic and scientific assumptions underlying acceptance and rejection of the evidence. It is really *these assumptions* that are in dispute, more so than the evidence itself. That a mass of favorable evidence exists can hardly be disputed if one has taken the trouble to look for it. Whether or not the conclusions to which the evidence seems to point should be accepted depends upon the validity of the skeptical objections, and by implication, of their underlying philosophic and scientific assumptions.

As Bauer points out, in order to make sense of the arguments over psi phenomena, "one needs to realize that the antagonists are always to a certain extent talking past one another: The manifest issue may be a proximate cause of the argument, but the real cause is a different set of preconceptions."[18] There are few subjects that generate as much passion among both scientists and laypersons as parapsychology. This is because an examination of the evidence the parapsychologists present brings us face to face with our most profound beliefs concerning the nature of human beings and our relationship with the world. The opinions we form on the subject of parapsychology have implications for our opinions concerning the relationship of mind with matter, and even the nature of reality itself. No small wonder then that the debate over parapsychology has been fought with the passion of a holy war.

It should also be stressed that just because the disputants are always to a certain extent "talking past one another", this does not mean that they cannot somehow understand each other, or that it is not possible to arrive at a rational conclusion to the debate. The idea that such opposing positions are somehow "equally valid" is one that should be soundly rejected. The philosopher of science Karl Popper called this idea the "Myth of the Framework", and dismissed as dangerous dogma the idea that we are hopelessly trapped in a prison built of our preconceptions:

> I do admit that at any moment we are prisoners caught in the framework of our theories; our expectations; our past experiences; our language. But we are prisoners in a Pickwickian sense; if we try, we can break out of our framework at any time. Admittedly, we shall find ourselves again in a framework, but it will be a better and roomier one; and we can at any moment break out of it again.[19]

The different preconceptions of researchers and skeptics may be thought of as "frameworks", but then the questions are: Have the scientists and philosophers who endorse psi research broken through into a better and roomier framework, one able to accommodate psi phenomena? Or, on the contrary, have the skeptics broken through to a framework that no longer has any place in it for psi phenomena, any more than it has a place for faeries and leprechauns? As we shall see, scientific theories (and the philosophical ideas that are always developed in their wake) have changed drastically over the last four hundred years. Our framework has been enlarged again and again. Some would argue that it is now large enough to accommodate the reality of psi; others would argue that these beliefs are relics from the past, and have no place in the current scientific worldview.

Origins of the Debate

Until the eighteenth century, the great majority of philosophers and scientists took for granted the existence of phenomena that could only be explained in terms of a spirit world. These phenomena might operate in accordance with God's will, or they might occur to serve the nefarious plans of Lucifer and his demons. A few individuals, such as witches, sorcerers, and alchemists, were thought to be able to induce these phenomena for better or for worse: to cure the sick, to see into the future, or to place a hex on someone. When these powers were wielded by a saintly individual, the results were deemed miraculous; on the other hand, the suspicion that these powers were being used for dark purposes could result in someone being burnt at the stake. Other sorts of phenomena, such as glimpses of the future in dreams, were considered too commonplace to be either miraculous or diabolic.

Among educated men, all of this changed with the dawn of the Scientific Revolution. This momentous mutation in human affairs spans the period between the birth of Galileo in 1564 and the death of Newton in 1727. Scientific advances during this period had the greatest impact on human affairs since the invention of agriculture and the dawn of civilization. And this period gave birth to a new worldview that drew a sharp distinction between the natural and the supernatural, between the normal and the paranormal.

The culmination of this revolution was surely the publication of Newton's *Principia* in 1687. Building upon the earlier works of Kepler and Galileo, Newton created a system that predicted the motions of the heavenly bodies with astonishing accuracy. No longer were comets considered portents of disaster: Newton and Halley calculated the orbits of certain comets and showed that they were as obedient as the planets to the law of gravitation. The universe was now viewed as a gigantic clockwork mechanism. There might still be a need for God to set the machine running—according to Newton the planets were originally hurled by the hand of God—but once started, the solar system was kept going by its own momentum, and operated as a self-regulating machine in accordance with inviolable laws. The rule of natural law had established its hold on men's imaginations, and there seemed to be no room left in the universe for magic and sorcery.

These views became prevalent in the eighteenth century, during what became known as the Enlightenment, which can be thought of as the ideological aftermath of the Scientific Revolution. Its most striking feature was the rejection of dogma and tradition in favor of the rule of reason in human affairs, and it was the precursor of modern secular humanism. Inspired by the dazzling success of the new physics, prominent spokesmen such as Diderot and Voltaire argued for a new worldview based upon an uncompromising mechanism or determinism that left no room for any intervention of mind in nature, whether human or divine. In the previous century, Descartes had written that the bodies of animals and men were machines, governed entirely by the laws of physics. Animals he regarded as mindless automata, but men, he maintained, had a soul and were thus the sole exceptions in an otherwise deterministic universe. But his successors during the Enlightenment did not hesitate to ask whether man himself might also be, in the final analysis, nothing more than a self-regulating machine.

One of the brightest stars of the Enlightenment was the Scottish philosopher David Hume, a contemporary of Diderot and Voltaire. As one biographer has remarked, the eighteenth century "must have seemed to Hume like the dawning of an era of opportunity: an age when human culture could at long last emerge from the darkness of superstition."[20] There were no miracles, Hume argued in 1748, because miracles were contrary to the uniform experience of mankind, "and as a uniform experience amounts to a proof, there is here a direct and full proof, from the nature of the fact, against the existence of any miracle."

Hume's criticism was directed specifically toward religious miracles, but his followers today apply this argument to those secular miracles that are today called paranormal events. In an earlier age, the fallacy of his argument would have been obvious: Miraculous events may not have been common, but they had been reported often enough to show that human experience had *not* been uniform. But by this time scientists longed for mechanistic certainties, and the assumption grew that there were natural laws that could not be broken and that *now* mankind knew these laws. Miraculous events did not fit into the new scientific worldview.

However, down through the ensuing centuries "miraculous" events such as thought transference, second sight, spiritual healing, hauntings and so forth continued to be reported. But the science of Newton, Galileo, and Kepler had given birth to a new *metaphysics*—philosophical assumptions about the nature of reality— which simply could not accommodate the reality of these phenomena. Skepticism based on the Humean model had taken hold, and so these reports were, for the most part, simply dismissed as incredible. Lingering widespread belief in the reality of these phenomena was considered to be the unfortunate legacy of a superstitious, irrational, pre-scientific era.

Parapsychology, which has its roots in the psychical research of the nineteenth century, is the scientific study of these "anomalous" phenomena, considered anomalous by some in the sense that they seem to defy a mechanistic explanation. However, parapsychologists part company with the astrologers, palm readers, and other practitioners of the occult arts in the manner in which they treat the evidence, a manner which they claim is scientific. But the claim that parapsychology is a science—or even that parapsychology has a subject matter to investigate—is of course controversial.

2

The Modern Critics

The opponents of parapsychology at the present time are those who see themselves as heirs of the Enlightenment, guardians of rationality who must at all costs discredit any dangerous backsliding into superstition. To this end, they even resort to mockery, the weapon Voltaire so-often wielded against his opponents. Although physics has changed in ways Newton could never have dreamed, and although the "laws of nature" have been rewritten several times since the publication of the *Principia*, the modern skeptics still invoke the principles of Newtonian physics and other arguments literally straight out of the eighteenth century—such as those of the skeptical philosopher David Hume—to argue against the claims of parapsychology.[21] They also occasionally blur the distinction between parapsychology and the various New Age cults, whose adherents, for the most part, are simply not interested in a careful and critical examination of the evidence.

Until the mid-1970's skeptics and debunkers of paranormal claims were disorganized, as they did not have a formal organization with which to advance their point of view. Serious skeptical opposition came almost entirely from freelance writers such as Martin Gardner, who wrote in the preface to his 1957 book *Fads and Fallacies in the Name of Science*: "Not many books have been written about modern pseudoscientists and their views." He knew of only two, with the most recent published in 1936. However, in the years following World War II, a number of books by authors with favorable views on the paranormal were published, and with what some have termed the "occult revival" of the early 1970's, the pace of publishing in this area accelerated.

This upsurge of interest in paranormal claims during the 1970's was not viewed favorably by several individuals in different quarters. One such individual who thought the growing interest signaled a rise in irrationality was Paul Kurtz, then a philosopher at the State University of New York at Buffalo and editor of *The Humanist* (the bi-monthly magazine of the American Humanist Association). Determined to do something about the rising popularity of astrology, Kurtz collected 186 scientist's signatures for a five-paragraph article titled "Objections to Astrology," which was published in the September-October 1975 issue of *The Humanist* and released with much fanfare to the press. In part, the statement read:

> One would imagine, in this day of widespread enlightenment and
> education, that it would be unnecessary to debunk belief based on
> magic and superstition. Yet, acceptance of astrology pervades modern
> society. We are especially disturbed by the uncritical dissemination of
> astrological charts, forecasts, and horoscopes by the media and by
> otherwise reputable newspapers, magazines, and book publishers.
> This can only contribute to the growth of irrationalism and obscuran-
> tism. We believe that the time has come to challenge directly, and
> forcefully, the pretentious claims of astrological charlatans.[22]

The statement, which also asserted that astrology has "no scientific foundation", was favorably reported in the nation's newspapers, with the *New York Times*
September 3rd edition giving the story front-page attention.

Less noted was the objection of one famous non-signer, celebrity-astronomer
Carl Sagan, who wrote in a letter to *The Humanist*:

> I find myself unable to endorse the "Objections to Astrology" state-
> ment…not because I feel that astrology has any validity whatever, but
> because I felt and still feel that the tone of the statement is authori-
> tarian. The fundamental point is not that the origins of astrology are
> shrouded in superstition. This is true as well for chemistry, medicine,
> and astronomy, to mention only three. To discuss the psychological
> motivations of those who believe in astrology seems to be quite
> peripheral to the issue of its validity. That we can think of no mechan-
> ism for astrology is relevant but unconvincing. No mechanism was
> known, for example, for continental drift when it was proposed by
> Wegener. Nevertheless, we see that Wegener was right, and those who
> objected on the grounds of unavailable mechanism were wrong.
>
> Statements contradicting borderline, folk, or pseudoscience that
> appear to have an authoritarian tone can do more damage than good.
> They never convince those who are flirting with pseudoscience but
> merely seem to confirm their impression that scientists are rigid and
> closed-minded.[23]

But the rhetoric of "Objections," with its warnings of "the growth of irrationalism and obscurantism," would sound familiar in future attacks on the paranormal
in which Kurtz would play a role. With Kurtz as editor, *The Humanist* vigorously criticized paranormal ideas of all kinds, defined as everything from religious faith to
popular occultism to the findings of academic parapsychology, and treated them all

as irrational superstition. Kurtz and his humanist associates believed interest in unorthodox claims was indicative of hostility to science and criticized favorable coverage of any such claims as dangerously promoting irrationality and primitive superstition.

However, there were other types of skeptics, such as sociologist of science Marcello Truzzi, publisher of *The Zetetic*, a newsletter that dealt with academic research into anomalies and the paranormal. Although a skeptic about the reality of many anomalous and paranormal phenomena, Truzzi did not regard interest in such matters as itself proof of irrationality or hostility to science. On the contrary, Truzzi stated in the September 1979 issue of *Fate* that some of those interested in unorthodox phenomena were presenting their arguments in ways "amenable to investigation and justification just like any scientific statement." He envisioned *The Zetetic* as a forum in which anomalous and paranormal claims could be debated in an intellectually responsible fashion, with fair representation given to all points of view.

Meanwhile, encouraged by the favorable media response to "Objections to Astrology," Kurtz began to explore the idea of founding an organization to challenge what he saw as the uncritical coverage of paranormal and occult ideas in television and print. One of the first prospective members he called was Truzzi, who expressed his opposition to "Objections" and made it clear that he was not a humanist. Nevertheless, Kurtz asked him if he would be co-chairman of the committee Kurtz was trying to organize, and even suggested that *The Zetetic* could be its official publication. Truzzi in turn sought assurances that the new organization would not simply be a debunking operation but would take a more open-minded approach than that of *The Humanist*. With Kurtz's reassurances that the group would separate itself from the magazine and have a diverse membership, Truzzi accepted the position of co-chairman.

The Committee for the Scientific Investigation of Claims of the Paranormal (CSICOP) was thus formed in 1976 at a meeting of the American Humanist Association. The expressed goals for CSICOP (pronounced *psi*-cop) were indeed laudable, as it pledged to "conduct objective and impartial inquiry" and stressed that "the purpose of the committee is not to reject on a priori grounds, antecedent to inquiry, any or all such claims, but rather to examine them openly, completely, objectively, and carefully."[24] No reasonable scientist could take issue with goals such as these, and CSICOP achieved considerable credibility by quickly attracting prominent figures in science and philosophy. Committee fellows included Antony Flew, philosopher; Carl Sagan, astronomer; B.F. Skinner, behavioral psychologist; W.V. Quine, Harvard philosopher; and others. Less prominent academics were put on a list of "scientific consultants." But with the exception of Sagan, who had undertaken some research on UFO sightings and had written a critique of the radical astrophysical theories of Immanuel Velikovsky, these eminent individuals had limited experience with anomaly research and little familiarity with the relevant literature.

In addition to scientists and philosophers, many of CSICOP's most active members were non-scientists. These members included the magician James Randi, who had made a career out of attempting to debunk metal-bender Uri Geller; Phillip Klass, aviation journalist and critic of UFOology; and of course Martin Gardner, columnist, author, and true godfather of the movement. These and other laypersons would write articles frequently in CSICOP's publications and help set the tone of the organization.

Over the next year, it became clear that Kurtz's plans for CSICOP were somewhat different from the professed goals of the organization. The committee came to be dominated by anti-paranormal hardliners who considered Truzzi, editor of CSICOP's official publication *The Zetetic*, too soft on CSICOP's intended targets. Truzzi, who had become increasingly uncomfortable with the crusading, inquisitional approach of the committee, resigned as co-chairman of the organization. Several other noted academics resigned shortly afterward for similar reasons. After Truzzi's departure, the name of CSICOP's official publication was changed to *Skeptical Inquirer*, and Kurtz appointed Kendrick Frazier as editor.

The Scientific Investigation of CSICOP

In spite of its name, CSICOP has engaged in only one case of scientific investigation. It concerned a neoastrological claim of French psychologists Michel and Francoise Gauquelin. Much of the Gauquelins' work has been aimed at debunking traditional astrology, but they have also gathered some of the most compelling scientific evidence in support of certain quasi-astrological ideas, namely, that the position of the planets at time of birth correlates with certain human characteristics. One of the Gauquelins' strongest claims has been for the so-called "Mars Effect": Although critical of traditional astrology, the Gauquelins had published statistical studies that seemed to show that significantly more world-class athletes were born when Mars was rising or transiting.

Gauquelin's results showed that 22 percent of European sports champions were born with Mars rising or transiting. Since Gauquelin divided the sky into 12 sectors, according to pure chance the probability of Mars being in any two sectors at time of birth is 2/12 or 17 percent, well below the 22 percent reported. With a sample size of 2088 sports champions, the odds are millions-to-one against these results occurring by chance.

The controversy started with an article by Lawrence Jerome that Kurtz had published in *The Humanist* along with his "Objections to Astrology." In his article, Jerome attacked the Mars Effect. When Gauquelin responded and turned out to be a more skilled statistician than his critic, and also intimated possible legal action, Kurtz reportedly became frantic to attack the Mars Effect in print.

Shortly before the formation of CSICOP, Kurtz began mailing articles relating to Gauquelin's claims to several of his fellow CSICOP members, including the statistician Marvin Zelen, and astronomers George Abell and Dennis Rawlins. In response,

Rawlins wrote a paper that first cautioned that *if* the European sample was unreliable, then no conclusions could be based upon it. He then wondered if there was a natural explanation, and proposed one: As seen from Earth, Mars appears near the sun more often than not. Since birth rates are higher at dawn, one would expect all births (not just sports champions) to be slightly higher with Mars rising (Sector 1) or transiting (Sector 4).

However, Rawlin's paper was not published in the January-February 1976 issue of *The Humanist*; instead, Kurtz published two other papers, one by Abell on astrology in general, and another by Zelen, "A Challenge" to Gauquelin.

Zelen's challenge was a proposal for a classic control experiment: Isolate the sports ability variable by comparing the position of Mars at the time Gauquelin's champions were born with the position in the sky at the time of birth of all other persons (*non*sports champions), the control group, defined as individuals born about the same time and place as the champions. If the 22 percent of the control group were also born when Mars was rising or transiting, then the Mars Effect would be shown to be due to entirely natural causes. This, of course, is the result Kurtz, Abell, and Zelen expected. If, however, only 17 percent of the control group's births occurred with Mars in these positions, then the results would be in Gauquelin's favor. As Zelen wrote, "If the sports figures' hours of birth fall into either of these sectors in greater proportion than do those on non-sports figures, we must accept Gauquelin's conclusions." The Challenge concluded with the words "We now have an objective way for *unambiguous corroboration or disconfirmation*."[25] Similarly, the astronomer Abell described it as a "very definitive test."[26]

The Gauquelins agreed to the terms of the test, and began to collect data on a large European sample of non-champions who were born about the same time and place as a smaller group of champions (chosen from their original sample). When ready, the data on the non-champions and the subset of champions was delivered to Committee members. The stage was now set for a decisive first encounter between CSICOP and the "astrological charlatans."

The results of the test did not appear in print for nearly two years. Finally, however, the results were published in two papers in the November-December 1977 issue of *The Humanist*. One paper, written by the Gauquelins, claimed that the results of the Zelen test supported the Mars Effect. The other paper, by Zelen, Kurtz, and Abell, questioned this interpretation. Zelen and his colleagues noted that when female athletes were dropped from the sample, the statistical significance of the results was reduced. They further argued that when the remaining sample was subdivided by geographical locale, the statistical significance of the results was further reduced. In order to gather enough birth records of non-champions born within one week of the champions in the same geographic locale, the Gauquelins had been forced to restrict their search to those born in large metropolitan areas. The Committee members noted that most of the significant effect came from one geographic region—Paris—and so argued that any evidence for the Mars Effect was really just a fluke: "In looking at many data sets one will occasionally conclude the existence of a real difference when in fact none really exists."[27]

The debate did not end there, and arguments continued back and forth. Two years later, in their new magazine the *Skeptical Inquirer,* the Committee published the results of their own study on an American sample which seemed to disprove the Mars Effect. The Gauquelins vigorously disputed the methodology used to gather the sample, arguing that it excluded "the very greatest" champions, and so diluted the effect. In response, they conducted their own study and reported positive results, which the Committee in turn refused to accept.

Fate intervenes

Shortly after the *Skeptical Inquirer* article concerning the American athletes, there was a change in the membership of CSICOP's ruling Executive Council. On December 15, 1979, Dennis Rawlins, astronomer, founding member of CSICOP and debunking hard-liner, was ejected from the council and replaced by Abell. The vote for expulsion was unanimous. The following October Rawlins was also removed from the list of Fellows. The significance of these events would not become known until a year later, when an extraordinary article appeared in the October 1981 issue of *Fate* magazine.

The article, titled "Starbaby," was Rawlins' inside account of CSICOP's investigation into the Mars Effect. Rawlins—the only planetary motions expert involved with the project—wrote that the CSICOP test on European athletes and non-champions had been botched from the beginning. According to Rawlins, Kurtz, Zelen, and Abell had repeatedly ignored his warnings; and when results came in supporting the existence of a Mars effect, the three CSICOP officials covered them up and so distorted them that it appeared that their results did not support the Mars Effect. The long delay between Zelen's Challenge and the publication of results Rawlins attributed to a frantic search by Kurtz for a way out of having to admit that the test results seemed to confirm an astrological claim.

When Rawlins alerted other CSICOP notables, including Gardner, Frazier, Randi, and Klass, he was shocked to learn that they were more interested in keeping him quiet than in facing up to the truth. When Rawlins refused to drop the issue, he was removed from the organization. In the opening paragraph of Starbaby he wrote, "I am still skeptical of the occult beliefs CSICOP was created to debunk. But I *have* changed my mind about the integrity of some of those who make a career of opposing occultism."[28]

Rawlins pointed out that the original purpose of the Zelen Challenge had been to examine the position of Mars in the sky at the time of birth of a group of non-sports champions born in about the same time and place as a sub-sample of Gauquelin's sports champions. Since Gauquelin had found that about 22 percent of the champions were born when Mars was in Sectors 1 and 4 (rising and transiting), and since pure chance would indicate that only 17 percent of births should occur at these times, the purpose of the test was to see if 22 percent of the non-champions were also born with Mars in Sectors 1 and 4. If so, then the position of Mars at time of birth would seem to have nothing to do with the ability to become a sports champion, and Gauquelin's claim for the Mars Effect would be refuted.

Rawlins had earlier warned Kurtz that as far he could tell, Gauquelin had performed his statistical analysis correctly, and so the whole analysis relied on the validity of Gauquelin's sampling method. Rawlins had repeatedly warned Kurtz, Zelen, and Abell that they were gambling CSICOP's reputation on the validity of the sample, but his warnings were ignored until results came in supporting Gauquelin's claims. Finally something had to be published. This is Rawlins' account of the November—December *Humanist* Control Test report, *Is There a Mars Effect?*:

> In the report KZA [Kurtz, Zelen, Abell] tried to obscure the clear success Gauquelin had scored. The Control Test had entailed analyzing 16,756 nonchampions born near (in time and space) 303 champions (a subsample of the original 2088 champions). KZA had believed that they too would score at 22 percent in key sectors (1 and 4) thus establishing that the champions' 22 percent hitrate was "natural."

> Instead, the nonchampions scored at exactly the chance-level (17 percent) that Gauquelin had predicted... Faced with this disaster KZA pulled a bait-and-switch. (Thus the report will be hereafter called the BS report.) Suddenly converting their *non*champions test into a *champions* test, they attacked the subsample of 303 champions![29]

As mentioned earlier, Kurtz, Zelen and Abell used various techniques to reduce the significance of the results from the sample of 303 champions, such as excluding female athletes and then sub-dividing the sub-sample of 303 (from the original 2088) by geographical locale, then arguing that the difference between the champions and non-champions was only significant for Paris. As will be discussed later, the smaller the sample the weaker its ability to prove anything statistically. But as Rawlins pointed out, all of this was completely beside the point. The whole purpose of the challenge was to see if the *non*-champions scored at the chance level of 17 percent, as Gauquelin had predicted. The sub-sample of champions was only used as a means of selecting the sample of non-champions. Since the non-champions' rate came out to be 17 percent, Rawlins was disgusted that Kurtz, Zelen, and Abell would not admit that the initial results had come out in Gauquelin's favor, but instead distorted the findings: "This is 'scientific investigation' which CSICOP claims as its middle name?"[30]

An independent investigation by Patrick Curry backed up Rawlins' charge that CSICOP had mishandled the investigation.[31] A similar conclusion was reached by psychologist and CSICOP fellow Richard Kammann, who was one of several members to resign in the wake of Rawlins statements.[32] Eventually, CSICOP acknowledged that mistakes had been made, although it did not directly address Rawlins' more serious charges that a Watergate-style cover-up had occurred. One immediate consequence of the Mars Effect scandal was the announcement that the Committee for the Scientific Investigation of Claims of the Paranormal would no longer conduct any more "scientific investigation," and this remains the official policy to this day.[33]

So, today most of the opposition faced by parapsychologists and other proponents of unusual claims comes from an organization that refuses to conduct any scientific research itself, and merely criticizes the work of others from the sidelines. The policy of no research has reduced the organization's vulnerability to criticism, for as George Hansen remarked, "If CSICOP had continued to undertake its own research, scientists might again point out errors in its procedures and ambiguities in its interpretations. That could threaten CSICOP's image of authority."[34] In their review of the Mars Effect controversy, sociologists of science T.J. Pinch and H.M. Collins concluded:

> As regards the Committee itself, and similar scientific-vigilante organizations, there are lessons to be learned. The Committee's main platform for attack upon parapsychology and astrology has been the standard, or canonical, model of science. This is a strategy that can only be used in complete safety by organizations that do not engage in controversial science themselves. ...The Committee's new position is that it will continue to fight the battle from the platform of the canonical version of science—preserving the ideology as it does so— while sensibly keeping its own hands clean and avoiding the risks of doing any experimental science itself.[35]

As for Rawlins, his experience did not change his skeptical views, but he did come to the conclusion that the leading members of CSICOP who tried to keep him quiet—including Kurtz, Randi, Gardner, Frazier, Klass, and others—were more concerned about publicity than in conducting open-ended scientific research. Shortly before he published his expose in Fate, Rawlins and James Randi had a couple of telephone conversations during which Randi suggested that CSICOP distance itself from the Gauquelin matter and not wash its dirty linen in public. Rawlins was "quite disgusted" when he hung up.

> I had asked Randi the big question, the question all CSICOPs will be asking themselves for years to come: Why? Why get involved in a conspiracy that was as stupid as it was low? Why do something that would mark him and CSICOP for the rest of their lives? The reply was ever the same: We can't let the mystics rejoice. A lifetime price—just to prevent a little transient cuckoo chirping.[36]

In due course the Starbaby scandal faded from the memories of all but those who were paying close attention, and through its magazine *Skeptical Inquirer* CSICOP went on to address a growing audience. Backed by an aggressive marketing campaign, the magazine achieved wide circulation, claiming a paid world-wide circulation of over 50,000 by the end of 2002,[37] although circulation seems to have peaked in recent years.

Since the departure of the more moderate members, little dissent or criticism of the Committee has been seen in the pages of *Skeptical Inquirer*. Engineer George Hansen has closely monitored the activities of CSICOP over the years, and notes that:

> The magazine nearly always presents only one side of a controversy in its articles. Although "SI" sometimes published letters of complaint, full papers from CSICOP's critics almost never appear. This is in remarkable contrast to refereed parapsychology journals, and even some of the pro-paranormal magazines. For instance, the popularly written magazine *Fate* has carried full articles by CSICOP members Susan Blackmore, L. Sprague de Camp, Kendrick Frazier, Martin Gardner, Philip Klass, Larry Kusche, Lawrence Jerome, David Marks, Joe Nickell, James Oberg, Dennis Rawlins, Robert Sheaffer, Gordon Stein, and Marcello Truzzi. In keeping with CSICOP'S one-sided approach, "SI" has given scant attention to papers in well-known, orthodox scientific journals that present evidence for psi.[38]

The writers whose work appears in *Skeptical Inquirer* also largely ignore the specialized scientific journals that deal exclusively with psi research, such as the *Journal of Parapsychology* and the *Journal of the American Society for Psychical Research*. The existence of these journals is rarely acknowledged in the magazine, and when they are mentioned it is usually only in passing, despite the fact that the former journal has been published for more than 60 years, and the latter for more than 90. In fact, the Committee has even claimed that "the Skeptical Inquirer is the only major periodical in the world that examines paranormal and occult claims from a scientific viewpoint."[39]

Under the editorship of Kendrick Frazier, the *Skeptical Inquirer* has become CSICOP's organ of propaganda, the means by which the Committee almost always presents only one side of controversies. Although Frazier has written that "the Committee founded a quarterly journal, the *Skeptical Inquirer*, to disseminate accurate information about the results of ...inquiries to the scientific community and the public,"[40] the real purpose of the magazine is hardly the impartial, objective evaluation of anomalous claims. Henry Bauer has written that a publication such as *Skeptical Inquirer* "serves only the purpose of speaking to the already converted: These writings are better understood as rituals of self-motivation and self-assurance than as attempts to make a case that might persuade opponents or the general public, let alone as attempts to clarify the substantive issue."[41] But Bauer's penetrating analysis implies that the magazine's purpose is also propaganda, a systematic attempt to persuade the uncommitted that the study of these anomalous phenomena has nothing to offer science.*

Even some skeptics have expressed dismay over the nature of the writing in *Skeptical Inquirer*. For instance, skeptical psychologist Elizabeth Mayer describes how she began investigating psi phenomena:

> I had high hopes for what CSICOP's journal might provide. At the very least it would, I thought, offer useful balance to journals with a clear bent toward belief in the paranormal. I was particularly enthused about the *Skeptical Inquirer's* policy of reviewing research on anomalous mental capacities published elsewhere. I figured that CSICOP would help me come up with useful challenges to articles written from the more credulous side.
>
> But it didn't work that way. Reading the *Skeptical Inquirer* was like reading a fundamentalist religious tract. I found the journal dismayingly snide, regularly punctuated by sarcasm, self-congratulation, and nastiness, all parading as reverence for true science.[42] **

NATURE OF CSICOP MEMBERSHIP

The major features of CSICOP's membership that affect its goals and spheres of influence would seem to be: the high educational level of its membership; the disproportionate number of magicians among its members; and the influence of religious convictions.

Educational level

The academic status of many of the Committee's members gives the organization its legitimacy in the eyes of important segments of society. CSICOP has sought support (and thus prestige) by actively recruiting people such as Murray Gell-Mann (Nobel laureate in physics), Francis Crick (Nobel laureate for physiology), and (now-deceased) members Carl Sagan, Stephan Jay Gould, and B.F. Skinner. When such

---

* In a 1989 issue of the *Journal of Scientific Exploration* Bauer reported an exchange of letters with Frazier in which the *Skeptical Inquirer's* editor argued that "the magazines purpose is not to consider what the best evidence for anomalous claims might be but to argue against them." (Bauer's words)

** Contrast this with what she wrote about the literature on psi research: "I began discovering mountains of research and a vast relevant literature I hadn't known existed. As astonished as I was by the sheer quantity, I was equally astonished by the high caliber. Much of the research not only met but far exceeded ordinary standards of rigorous mainstream science."

prestigious people lend their names to an anti-paranormal crusade, readers may assume that such individuals are experts on anomalies research and that scientists speak with one voice on the matters CSICOP "investigates."

According to George Hansen:

> The prominence of the membership gives the Committee a number of benefits. It allows CSICOP's voice to be heard in academic debates on the paranormal. The National Research Council report on parapsychology is an example. Non-member academics are likely to consider CSICOP's views when refereeing papers, evaluating grant proposals, and counseling students. CSICOP's views are likely to be influential when it comes to deciding how, and to what extent, the paranormal will be scientifically investigated within academia.[43]

Magicians

The proportion of magicians in CSICOP is much higher than in the general population, and the number of prominent magicians who are or have been members of CSICOP would include Henry Gordon, Milbourne Christopher, Robert Steiner and Persi Diaconis. Martin Gardner has contributed to magic magazines, Randi has been a professional magician since the age of 18, and Ray Hyman, although primarily a psychologist, has been featured on the cover of "Linking Ring," one of the most popular magic magazines in the world. All three of these have served on the Executive Council of the Committee. Even co-founder Marcello Truzzi (who as mentioned above, has long since resigned) has served as vice-president of the Psychic Entertainers Association.

The large and important role conjurors have played within CSICOP may give one the impression that most professional magicians are skeptical regarding the existence of psi. Surprisingly, various polls have shown that conjurors seem to believe in the reality of psi even more frequently than members of the general public. Birdsell polled a group of magicians in California and found that 82% of her sample expressed a belief in ESP;[44] Muller polled conjurors in Germany and found that 72% thought psi was probably real;[45] Truzzi polled members of the Psychic Entertainers Association and discovered that 87% thought that ESP "truly exists," and that 25% believed that "science has demonstrated the existence of extrasensory perception."[46] And many prominent magicians, such as Howard Thurston and Joseph Dunninger, have endorsed reports of psychic phenomena.[47] As Hansen concludes, "It is simply a myth that magicians have been predominantly skeptical about the existence of psi."[48]

Religious views

Many members of CSICOP hold religious views that are antagonistic toward the paranormal. The influence of religion on the anti-paranormal views of the Committee is apparent in the writing of many of its leading spokespersons, such as Paul Kurtz, James Alcock, and Martin Gardner, all of whom are, or have been, members of the Executive Council.

CSICOP Chairman and founder Paul Kurtz has been active in promoting atheism, both in his former role as editor of *The Humanist* and in his current role as president of Prometheus Books, which has published such titles as *The Atheist Debater's Handbook*, and *Atheism: the Case Against God*. Prometheus has also published books written by Kurtz himself, such as *The Transcendental Temptation: a Critique of Religion and the Paranormal*, the title of which speaks for itself.*

James Alcock has made several attempts to associate parapsychology with religion in order to discredit its status as a branch of science, even at one point referring to parapsychology as "the spiritual science."[49] Elsewhere, in a book titled *Parapsychology: Science or Magic?* Alcock writes:

> In the name of religion human beings have committed genocide,
> toppled thrones, built gargantuan shrines, practiced ritual murder,
> forced others to conform to their way of life, eschewed the pleasures
> of the flesh, flagellated themselves, or given away all their possessions
> and become martyrs... An examination of the origins and functions of
> religion...is a useful starting point for the study of modern parapsy-
> chology.[50]

But not all CSICOP members have anti-religious views. One can only guess what Kurtz and Alcock think of the opinions of fellow member Martin Gardner, who frankly acknowledged the influence his religious beliefs have had on his opposition to parapsychology when he wrote:

> It is possible that paranormal forces not yet established may allow
> prayers to influence the material world, and I certainly am not saying
> that this possibility should be ruled out... As for empirical tests of the

---

* Kurtz is widely regarded as the driving force behind CSICOP. Although he once taught philosophy, Kurtz has been more accurately described as a "business-person-missionary." He is the founder of Prometheus Books, the primary purveyor of anti-paranormal books in the U.S. But some of Kurtz's reviewers are not very impressed with the quality of his own writing. Stokes (1987a) has pointed out several examples of dogmatism and sheer misrepresentation in his review of *The Transcendental Temptation*. And Hansen wrote in 1992:

"Although Kurtz has shown exceptional dynamism and success as a businessperson and as a missionary for secular humanism, his position as a philosopher seems a bit less impressive. His *Exuberance: An Affirmative Philosophy of Life* is something of a 'positive thinking' book for humanists, and a recent review compared the level of his writing with that of Shirley MacLaine."

power of God to answer prayer, I am among those theists who, in the spirit of Jesus' remark that only the faithless look for signs, consider such tests both futile and blasphemous…let us not tempt God.[51]

However, his theistic beliefs appear to make Gardner a rare exception among Committee members. As mentioned, the roots of CSICOP are in the American Humanist Association, and several leading members have publicly identified themselves as holding atheistic or non-theistic views, including George Abell, Francis Crick, Paul Edwards, Antony Flew, Stephen Jay Gould, James Randi, Gordon Stein, and many others.[52]

To Kurtz and several other prominent Committee members, belief in the paranormal is based in part upon the same foundations as religious belief, and because religion is delusionary and harmful, paranormal beliefs are also a danger to society. There can be no doubt that some of the psychological needs that promote belief in religion (such as the desire to influence nature and for life after death) are in part responsible for the widespread interest in parapsychology. Modern science has discredited naïve and literal interpretations of many religions, and so some people have looked to parapsychology for empirical evidence of a mental and perhaps spiritual realm over and above the material world. Indeed, a desire to challenge what they regarded as the depressing mechanistic worldview proposed by nineteenth century science, combined with an intense curiosity about the evidence for life after death, formed an explicit and openly acknowledged part of the motivation of many of those who founded the Society for Psychical Research in 1882.

The revolutionary new science that began in the 17th century, with its mechanistic and materialistic assumptions, gave intellectuals the tools to effectively challenge the authority of Church and scripture, and to replace it with an appeal to human reason and secular values. In the new worldview, given birth by this new science, there was little if any room for the intervention of a deity, the action of an immaterial mind, and by corollary, for telepathy, second-sight, and other "supernatural" phenomena, which were now dismissed as vulgar superstition. It is this worldview that is defended by modern secular humanists, which they rightly see as threatened by the claims of parapsychology. For many humanists, the widespread acceptance of these claims would be the first step in a return to religious fanaticism, superstition, and irrationality.[53]

However, although CSICOP was ostensibly formed to defend society from "antiscientific and pseudoscientific irrationalism," there seems to be little if any evidence that the scientific adventure is threatened by unorthodox claims. Belief in the reality of psi phenomena is widespread among the general public, but polls have also shown that over 90 percent of the public regard scientists as having "considerable" or even "very great" prestige.[54] Furthermore, as we will see later, polls have shown that a majority of mainstream scientists consider ESP to be at least "a likely possibility", and many leading scientists have lent their support to parapsychological research. As Jerome Clark has written, "Some observers view CSICOP's claims about 'anti-science' components of paranormal interest not only as a rhetorical strategy, but also as an equation (explicitly stated in the literature) of the Humanist vision with the scientific vision."[55]

Most modern parapsychologists consider themselves committed to a *scientific* examination of so-called paranormal phenomena; furthermore, many believe there is persuasive scientific evidence for the existence of these phenomena, and do not consider this belief a danger to society or to science. This book will consider whether or not there is convincing scientific evidence for the existence of these phenomena; whether or not the existence of these phenomena would be in conflict with modern science; and whether or not parapsychology is a science.

CONCLUSIONS

Parapsychology is the only scientific discipline for which there is an organization of skeptics trying to discredit its work. As this organization no longer performs any research of its own, the true nature of CSICOP is clearly that of a scientific vigilante organization defending a narrow brand of scientific fundamentalism, whose major goal has been to influence the media, and through it, public opinion. Many writers have pointed out that true skepticism involves the practice of *doubt*, not of simple *denial*, and so, according to this criterion, CSICOP does not truly qualify as an organization of skeptics. As CSICOP's major moderate figure Ray Hyman has observed, "Many well-intentioned critics have jumped into the fray without carefully thinking through the various implications of their statements. They have sometimes displayed more emotion than logic, made sweeping charges beyond what they reasonably support, failed to adequately document their assertions, and, in general, have failed to do the homework necessary to make their challenges credible."[56]

Surveys have shown that over half of the adult population claim to have had psychic experiences and believe in the reality of the phenomena: For instance, the University of Chicago's National Opinion Research Center surveyed 1473 adults, of which 67% claimed that they had experienced ESP.[57] When these individuals encounter the debunking and dismissive attitudes of those claiming to be "scientific authorities" many are likely to conclude that scientists are dogmatic and closed-minded. Ironically, one of the major effects of CSICOP's relentless campaign may be an increased rejection of science by the public, as many individuals conclude that science itself is a dogma, with little relevance for important aspects of their lives.

As we will see in a later chapter, twentieth century models of science show that science has a marvelously self-correcting mechanism built into it, and so there is no need for self-appointed vigilantes to guard the gates. The debate over the reality of psi will be ultimately settled not at press conferences, but by the quality of the data gathered by those who conduct serious research. Indeed, the quality of the data has resulted in changing views among the skeptics in recent years, and several prominent skeptics have been forced to make some notable concessions which, for the most part, they are not eager to advertise.

But one prominent member of CSICOP, the late Carl Sagan, who on several occasions urged his fellow Committee members to resist dogmatic thinking and be open to new discoveries, made a candid admission in a 1995 book otherwise loaded with skepticism over various New Age and "psychic" claims:

> At the time of writing there are three claims in the ESP field which, in my opinion, deserve serious study: (1) that by thought alone humans can (barely) affect random number generators in computers; (2) that people under mild sensory deprivation can receive thoughts or images "projected" at them; and (3) that young children sometimes report the details of a previous life, which upon checking turn out to be accurate and which they could not have known about in any other way than reincarnation.[58]

Over the last ten years or so there have been signs that psi research is being taken much more seriously by mainstream scientific organizations. Parapsychologist Dean Radin pointed out that:

> In the 1990s alone, seminars on psi research were part of the regular programs at the annual conferences of the American Association for the Advancement of Science, the American Psychological Association, and the American Statistical Association. Invited lectures on the status of psi research were presented for diplomats at the United Nations, for academics at Harvard University, and for scientists at Bell Laboratories.
>
> The pentagon has not overlooked these activities.
>
> From 1981 to 1995, five different U.S. government-sponsored scientific review committees were given the task of examining the evidence for psi effects. The reviews were prompted by concerns that if psi was genuine, it might be important for national security reasons....all five reviews concluded that the experimental evidence for certain forms of psychic phenomena merited serious scientific study.[59]

The metaphor invoked at the beginning of this section was that of war, but a better comparison may be that of revolution. Radical new ideas in fields as diverse as physics and cognitive science have transformed our understanding of nature, and as a result a new scientific worldview is emerging, one that is consistent with the reality of psi. Parapsychologists have developed new and more rigorous experimental techniques, physicists and psychologists have developed testable theories about how psi may work, and the skeptics have been forced to make some notable concessions. As always, the defenders of the old order are not giving up without a fight. But as will be seen in the pages that follow, the old regime may be on the verge of collapse.

Many of the ideas presented in the pages that follow may seem strange, and many of them *are* strange. But I can do no better at this point than to quote the late biologist J.B. Haldane: "The fact about science is that everyone who has made a serious contribution to it is aware, or very strongly suspects, that the world is not only queerer than anyone has imagined, but queerer than anyone *can* imagine."

3

The Historical Evidence

It has always seemed to me most strange and most deplorable that the vast majority of philosophers and psychologists should utterly ignore the strong prima facie case that exists for the occurrence of many supernormal phenomena which, if genuine, must profoundly affect our theories of the human mind, its cognitive powers, and its relation to the human body.

C.D. Broad

One needs to remember that skepticism is not necessarily a badge of toughmindedness: it may equally be a sign of intellectual cowardice.

John Beloff

Herodotus tells us that back in 550 BC Croesus, King of Lydia, was becoming increasingly alarmed by the growing strength of the Persian Empire. He thus considered launching a pre-emptive strike against his enemies. Croesus wanted advice, but was unsure about which of the half-dozen oracles doing business in and around Greece he should consult. So he devised a test. He sent a message to each of the oracles, asking for a written description of his activities at a specified day and time.

The answers given to the messengers were to be taken down in writing and brought back to Lydia. None of the replies remain on record except that from the Oracle at Delphi. Herodotus tells us that the moment the Lydians entered the sanctuary, the Pythoness answered them in hexameter verse:

> *I can count the sands, and I can measure the ocean;*
> *I have ears for the silent, and know what the dumb man means;*

Lo! on my sense there strikes the smell of a shell-covered tortoise,
Boiling now on a fire, with the flesh of a lamb, in a cauldron—
Brass is the vessel below, and brass the cover above it.

On that day Croesus had cut a lamb and a tortoise into pieces and boiled the flesh in a brass cauldron. Impressed only with this answer, Croesus consulted the Oracle at Delphi a second time. Should he attack the Persians? The Pythoness answered that if Croesus attacked the Persians, he would destroy a mighty empire. So Croesus attacked, and lost both the war and his empire. Herodotus thus described the world's first recorded psi experiment.

Another ancient story concerns the Greek traveler and philosopher Apollonius of Tyana. While in Ephesus he suddenly began to describe an attack on the cruel Roman emperor Domitian in Rome, to the astonishment of bystanders. Later, they were still more astonished to learn that Domitian had in fact been assassinated at the time of the vision.[60]

The famous scientist and mystic Emanuel Swedenborg, while at a reception in Gothenburg in 1759 suddenly went into a trance and described in detail a disastrous fire that was sweeping Stockholm 300 miles away. He described where and when it had started, where it was burning, and was relieved when he informed the company that its progress had been halted not far from his own house. When a courier later arrived from Stockholm, it was found that the course of the fire exactly matched Swedenborg's description. The reception was attended by several local nobles who testified to the accuracy of Swedenborg's vision.[61]

Reports from tribal societies

The Zulus were studied by Bishop Henry Callaway, and his results published in his 1869 book *The Religious System of the Amazulu*. Callaway's work is of special interest, because he had studied the tribes before contact with European civilization had made much impression on them. In his book, he described how the Zulus assumed anyone could practice a form of distant vision:

> When anything valuable is lost, they look for it at once; when they cannot find it, each one begins to practice this inner divination, trying to feel where the thing is; for, not being able to see it, he feels internally a pointing which tells him, if he will go down to such a place, it is there, and he will find it. At length he sees it, and himself approaching it; before he begins to move from where he is he sees it very clearly indeed, and there is an end of doubt. The sight is so clear that it is as though it were not an inner sight, but as if he saw the very thing itself and the place where it is.[62]

The Zulus had a poetic name for this faculty: "Opening the gates of distance." Many similar reports have come from Africa. In *The Sixth Sense*, Joseph Sinel told of his son who lived among the tribesmen of the southern Sudan, and how he had found that "telepathy is constant." They always seemed to know where he was and what he was doing, even when far away. Once when he was lost, a group of them came out to collect him, as if they had sensed his plight. Laurens Van Der Post found that villagers in the Kalahari could tell in advance which of the bush pilots would be flying in to use their landing strip—"Red Nose", "Shining Face", or "Hippo-belly"—although there was no radio communication. The historian Brian Inglis wrote that

> When a Kalahari bushman killed an eland—regarded as a notable achievement—the camp immediately knew of it "by wire", as one bushman described it, evidently under the impression that the white man's telegraph also worked by telepathy. Before they reached the camp with the eland, Van Der Post would hear the sounds of the song which was used to celebrate on such occasions.[63]

On the other side of the world, it seems that telepathic communication was very much a part of the Australian aborigine way of life. In 1914 David Unaipon—described in the Melbourne journal that covered the story as "a Christianised and highly-educated brainy Australian native"—delivered a lecture in which he told how the aborigines used smoke signals not, as travelers had reported, as a kind of code, but to attract attention, so that communication could then be made by telepathy.

> He might want to give his brother, who might be twenty miles away, a message; so he would set to and make a smoke signal, and then sit down and concentrate his mind on his brother. The column of smoke would be seen by all the blacks for miles around, and they would all concentrate their minds, and put their brains into a state of receptivity. Only his brother, however, would get into touch with him, and he could then suggest to his brother the message which he wished to convey.[64]

SEEING THE FUTURE

In all parts of the world, in all eras, it has been assumed that certain individuals could glimpse the future. This has been one of the main functions of the tribal shaman. Unfortunately, most of the early explorers took little interest in testing the shamans they encountered; and at any rate, those missionaries who accepted the shaman's powers as genuine almost invariably considered them diabolical.

However, the French missionary Friar P. Boilat published the results of his investigation into the psychic powers of African witch doctors in his 1853 *Esquisses Senegalaises*. Boilat described how, hoping to prove that a witch doctor's powers were not genuine, put to him an unspoken question. The witch doctor not only guessed the question correctly, but also gave Boilat the accurate prediction that the documents he was waiting for would arrive in fifteen days.[65]

Dreaming of the future

In 1865 Abraham Lincoln told his wife and his friend Ward Lamon of a rather disturbing dream:

> About ten days ago, I retired very late. I had been up waiting for important dispatches from the front. I could not have been long in bed when I fell into a slumber, for I was weary. I soon began to dream. There seemed to be a death-like stillness about me. Then I heard subdued sobs, as if a number of people were weeping. I thought I left my bed and wandered downstairs. There the silence was broken by the same pitiful sobbing, but the mourners were invisible. I went from room to room; no living person was in sight, but the same mournful sounds of distress met me as I passed along. I saw light in all the rooms; every object was familiar to me; but where were all the people who were grieving as if their hearts would break? I was puzzled and alarmed. What could be the meaning of all this? Determined to find the cause of a state of things so mysterious and so shocking, I kept on until I arrived at the East Room, which I entered. There I met with a sickening surprise. Before me was a catafalque, on which rested a corpse wrapped in funeral vestments. Around it were stationed soldiers who were acting as guards; and there was a throng of people, gazing mournfully upon the corpse, whose face was covered, others weeping pitifully. 'Who is dead in the White House?' I demanded of one of the soldiers, 'The President,' was his answer; 'he was killed by an assassin.' Then came a loud burst of grief from the crowd, which woke me from my dream. I slept no more that night; and although it was only a dream, I have been strangely annoyed by it ever since.[66]

Three days later the president was dead, and shortly after his body lay in state in the East Room.

Less well known is the fact that General Ulysses Grant and his wife Julia were scheduled to accompany Lincoln to Ford's theater that fateful night, to sit with the President in his balcony box. The honor was due to Grant's acceptance a few days earlier of the unconditional surrender of Confederate General Robert E. Lee.

On the morning of the day of the assassination, Mrs. Grant felt a great sense of urgency that she, her husband, and her child should leave Washington and return to their home in New Jersey. The General had appointments throughout the day and could not leave, but as Mrs. Grant's sense of urgency increased she kept sending him messages begging him to leave. Her insistence was so great that he finally agreed to leave with her, even though they were scheduled to accompany the President to the theater that night. When they reached Philadelphia, they not only heard that the president had been assassinated, but that they were also on the assassin's list of intended victims.[67]

The sinking of Titanic

A startling case of precognition emerged in a work of fiction, *Futility*, published in 1898. It told the story of a new monster ocean liner, the largest ever built, designed to be unsinkable and so, despite a capacity of 3,000 passengers, carried only 24 lifeboats, the minimum number required by regulation. It was described as being 800 feet long, and built with 19 watertight compartments, separated by bulkheads that would close automatically upon impact.

However, a starboard impact with an iceberg near midnight on her Atlantic crossing sank the liner, with heavy loss of life. Fourteen years later *Titanic*, 882 feet long, with 16 watertight compartments, and despite a capacity of 3,000 passengers equipped with only 20 lifeboats, collided with an iceberg on her starboard side at 11:40 pm, and sank shortly afterward with heavy loss of life. What made the resemblance between the novel and the actual sinking even more uncanny was the name Morgan Robertson had given his fictional liner: *Titan*.

Churchill's close call

In her autobiography, Lady Churchill recalled that after a tour of inspection he made during the Blitz of London, Winston Churchill was about to get into a staff car on the nearside, as he always did, when for no apparent reason he stopped and got into the other side of the car instead, something Lady Churchill had never known him to do before. While being driven back a bomb fell near the car, lifting it up on its two nearside wheels. Had Churchill been sitting on that side as usual, the car would have turned over: "Only Winston's extra weight had prevented disaster." Later, when asked by his wife why he had changed his mind getting into the car, Churchill said that something made him stop, in a way that told him he was meant to sit on the other side. "I sometimes have a feeling—in fact I have had it very strongly—a feeling of interference," he told a gathering of miners later in the war. "I have a feeling sometimes that some guiding hand has interfered."[68]

David Booth and Flight 191

On May 15, 1979 David Booth of Cincinnati woke up from a nightmare. In his dream he had been watching a jet liner coming in for a landing, but "not making the sound

that it should—being so close to home it should have been louder than it was."
Booth described his dream to his wife Pam, in which the plane suddenly banked
right, turned upside down, and went down nose first.

The dream was repeated every night from then on, until on May 24 Booth
called Paul Williams of the Federal Aviation Administration at the Cincinnati airport.
Booth told Williams of his dream and was described as being "very distraught."

The next day American Airlines Flight 191 approached O'Hare airport in
Chicago, and was given permission to land. When the DC10 was 300 feet off the
ground it suddenly banked right, turned upside down and crashed nose first, with
273 lives lost. Paul Williams later described the pre-crash maneuver as "very
unusual—as a matter of fact the only one I've heard of for a plane that size." When
asked if he believes Booth foresaw the crash, he replied "All I can say is, I don't
know," but quickly added "If David told me that a certain plane was going to crash,
I certainly wouldn't get on that plane."[69]

Is the future fixed?

A burning question that arises from reports like these is: Are these glimpses of what
will happen, or only of what *might* happen if steps are not taken to avoid it? Louisa
Rhine examined this question in great detail. She examined 433 cases in which the
foreseen event was so unpleasant that anyone would want to prevent it. In about
two-thirds of the cases, no attempt was made to prevent the event, because the person simply forgot, feared ridicule, or for some other reason. In the end she was left
with 191 cases in which people had attempted to prevent a foreseen event from taking place.

In 31 percent of the cases, the attempted intervention was unsuccessful, most
often because the psychic experience had not provided enough information to
allow the experient to prevent the occurrence. However, in the remaining cases (69
percent) the people were able to take adequate steps to prevent the event, or at
least to avoid some of the undesirable consequences. Here is an example, in Louisa
Rhine's own words:

> It concerns a mother who dreamed that two hours later a violent
> storm would loosen a heavy chandelier to fall directly on her baby's
> head lying in a crib below it; in the dream she saw her baby killed
> dead. She awoke her husband who said it was a silly dream and that
> she should go back to sleep… The weather was so calm the dream did
> appear ridiculous and she could have gone back to sleep. But she did
> not. She went and brought the baby back to her own bed. Two hours
> later just at the time she specified, a storm caused the heavy light
> fixture to fall right on where the baby's head had been—but the baby
> was not there to be killed by it.[70]

Cases such as this suggest that the individual precognizes not the *actual* future event but rather the *potential* event that may occur. These cases suggest that the future exists not deterministically but only as a range of probabilities, and that human intervention may affect those events of varying probability that actually do occur.

Louisa Rhine advised a pragmatic approach to what appear to be glimpses into the future. If it appears to be a warning, then it should be treated as such, and steps should be taken to avoid the problem. But with the present state of our ignorance, and because of the number of cranks in our midst, she advised against issuing public warnings. And since we know so little about the nature of these experiences, and because efforts to prevent disasters often fail for reasons entirely beyond the control of the person who had the experience, she also counseled that there is absolutely no reason to feel any guilt over failures to prevent these mishaps.

Psychic Spies

From 1978 to 1995 the U.S. government ran its controversial *Stargate* program, studying, among other things, remote viewing, which has been defined as the "ability of human participants to acquire information about spatially and temporally remote geographical targets, otherwise inaccessible by any known sensory means."

When Army Brig. Gen. James Dozier was kidnapped by the Red Brigade in northern Italy in 1981, the remote viewers in the program were assigned the task of locating Dozier, with the idea that any information provided would be used as an adjunct to more conventional sources. Six hours after Dozier was kidnapped, the remote viewers, including Joe McMoneagle, were given a photograph of the General and his name, and asked to describe his location. Enough time had elapsed to have moved Dozier out of Italy, so no one was sure if he was still in the country. McMoneagle provided the name of the town where Dozier was being hidden—Padua—and another remote viewer gave the name of the building.

Meanwhile, the Italian authorities received a tip from a relative of one of the kidnappers, and Dozier was rescued by the Italian paramilitary police shortly before information from the remote viewers arrived. However, it was later reported that the information provided by the remote viewers regarding Dozier's location was accurate, right down to the bed where he had been chained.

Remote sensing

The following case was related to a prominent parapsychologist by a manager at a high-technology firm:

> In the middle of the night, out of a deep sleep, Fred suddenly jerked upright into a sitting position. He clutched his chest, gasping for breath.

His wife, abruptly awakened by her husband's sudden movement, anxiously asked, "What's wrong?" A few moments later, when Fred was able to breathe normally again, he told his wife that he was all right, but he had a feeling that something terrible had happened. They glanced at the clock: 2:05 A.M.

Fifteen minutes later, as they settled back to sleep, the phone rang. Fred's father was on the line. "I have bad news," he said. "Your mother just had a heart attack. We were sleeping, when she suddenly sat bolt upright, clutched her chest, and...she passed away." Fred was shocked. "When did this happen?" he asked. "About fifteen minutes ago, just after 2:00 A.M.," replied his father.[71]

Animals and ESP

Biologist Rupert Sheldrake has collected and analyzed hundreds of cases of what appear to be ESP in animals. Here is one reported by Stephen Hyde of Acton, London:

> My brother Michael was a copilot in a Wellington bomber during the war. He went on many raids over Germany in 1940. At that time we had a dog, Milo, who was half spaniel, half Collie, and was particularly fond of Michael. One night in June, Michael was on his way home from a raid when he radioed to base to say that he was just off the coast of Belgium and would soon be back. That same night Milo, who slept in a stable at the back of the house, howled so much that my mother had to get up and bring him into the house. Michael never returned from his mission, that night. He was reported missing, believed killed, June 10, 1940.[72]

Of course dogs are social animals that form bonds not only with people but also with each other. So if there is evidence of telepathic contact between dogs and humans, there should also be evidence of telepathy between dogs. Here is one of seven collected by Sheldrake in which the death of one dog occurred unexpectedly and at a distance; this one was reported by Dr. Max Rallon of Chateauneuf le Rouge, France:

> I have a Beance Sheepdog, Yssa, two years old, who came with me to France at the age of three months from the island of Reunion in the Indian Ocean, 10,000 kilometers away. There I left her mother, Zoubida, aged ten. On February 13 this year, Yssa was sleeping in my son's room. About 3:00 A.M. she came scratching at my door, whining,

crying, and excited. She didn't want to go outside. At 9:00 A.M. my brother-in-law called from Reunion. The guard of our house had found Zoubida dead. She had been poisoned.[73]

From his studies with our animal cousins, Sheldrake has concluded that "telepathy usually occurs between animals that are bonded with each other", and that "in schools, flocks, herds, packs, and other social groups telepathic communication may play an important role in the coordination of the activity of the group." Also, "at least in birds and mammals, telepathy has to do with emotions, needs, and intentions. Feelings communicated telepathically include fear, alarm, excitement, calls for help, calls to go to a particular place, anticipation or arrivals or departures, and distress and dying."[74]

He has also concluded that most of the psi abilities he has discussed in his work "are better developed in animals than in people. Normally dogs seem to be the most sensitive, followed by cats, horses, and parrots, with humans trailing far behind."[75]

ANECDOTAL VERSUS EXPERIMENTAL EVIDENCE

The cases discussed above are only a tiny sample of the total reported in the literature, but the skeptics dismiss all such reports as "anecdotal"—that is, based on spontaneous experience and not controlled observation. Anecdotal evidence is of course still evidence, but often it can only be considered merely suggestive, not conclusive. This is especially so when we are dealing with a complex phenomenon involving many variables. So, for instance, if a number of formerly depressed patients tell their physicians that they feel better after taking some herbal supplement, most of the physicians will not simply accept the reports at face value. After all, the positive effects in a patient may be due to any number of factors—a healthier diet, more exercise, nicer weather, the placebo effect, or any combination of such factors. With the accumulation of enough anecdotal reports, double-blind experiments might be performed, with the purpose of controlling as many causal variables as possible in order to determine if there really is an effect, and if so, of what magnitude.

Most of us may have no problem with accepting anecdotal reports on some subjects, such as, say, the amusing behavior of house cats, because most of us have seen domestic cats in action. But reports of psi phenomena are comparatively rare, and for this and other reasons their existence is highly controversial. So the conventional theorists have attempted to explain away the anecdotal reports as being due to coincidence, misperception, faulty memory, embellishment, hallucination, fraud, and so forth. The skeptics have demanded—quite reasonably—*experimental* evidence for the existence of psi. Has reliable experimental evidence been provided?

Part I

Is there Conclusive Experimental Evidence for Psi?

Psychic phenomena have failed to be verified after 150 years of attempts involving thousands of independent experiments. After all this time, we can safely assume they do not exist.
Victor Stenger
The Unconscious Quantum
1995

Using the standards applied to any other area of science, it is concluded that psychic functioning has been well established. The statistical results of the studies examined are far beyond what is expected by chance.
Jessica Utts
An Assessment of the Evidence for Psychic Functioning
1995

4

The Early Years

The year 1882 marks a milestone in psi research: in February of this year the Society for Psychical Research was founded in London. The early membership included many distinguished scholars and scientists of the late Victorian era, including the Cambridge philosopher Henry Sidgwick, distinguished physicists William Barrett and William Crookes, and Nobel laureates Lord Rayleigh and J.J. Thomson, the latter being the discoverer of the electron. Other prominent members included scholars Frederic Myers, Edmund Gurney and Richard Hodgson, and the Balfour family, into which Henry Sidgwick had married. His wife, Eleanor, was a woman of outstanding intellectual ability and a pioneer of women's education. Her brother Arthur Balfour was a philosopher, politician, and from 1902-5, Prime Minister of England. His younger brother Gerald was a classical scholar and politician, and all three Balfours took their turns serving as Presidents of the Society. In 1885 the distinguished philosopher-psychologist William James helped found the American Society for Psychical Research in Boston, and both organizations exist to this day.

The main work of the Society during the early years was carried out by officers appointed by its Council, in particular by Myers, Gurney, Hodgson, and Eleanor Balfour. Much of the early work involved investigation of spontaneous cases, and of hauntings and apparitions. But there was also experimental work, primarily involving the reproduction of drawings at a distance, and it was Myers who coined the term "telepathy"—Greek for "distant feeling." However, the work of the Society drew criticism from many scientists of the time, as it was seen as incompatible with the materialist doctrine that was then becoming prevalent. A particularly dogmatic response to the Society's work came from physiologist Hermann von Helmholtz, who remarked that "Neither the testimony of all the Fellows of the Royal Society, nor even the evidence of my own senses, would lead me to believe in the transmission of thought from one person to another independently of the recognized channels of sense. It is clearly impossible."[76]

But the work continued at a vigorous pace, and soon the SPR was publishing a scholarly journal. The SPR was also notoriously tough in its investigations, and exposed several fraudulent mediums. As mentioned, most of the early work focused on case studies, but a few of the early researchers were already conducting experiments involving card guessing and the remote viewing of drawings. Nobel Laureate Charles Richet is generally credited with being the first to recognize that probability theory could be applied to card-guessing experiments, and in 1884 he published a paper on the application of statistics to experiments testing clairvoyance. However, despite Richet's innovations, the statistical apparatus necessary to properly evaluate psi experiments was not fully in place until the 1920's, due to the work of R.A. Fisher and other pioneer statisticians. By this time, J.B. Rhine was setting up the first university laboratory to be devoted exclusively to parapsychological research.

STATISTICAL ISSUES

Replication and comparison with chance

First of all, few human capabilities are perfectly replicable on demand. Even the best hitters in baseball cannot produce home runs on demand, nor can we predict with certainty when home runs will occur. But this does not mean home runs don't exist.

Statistics are used whenever there is difficulty separating signal from noise. The frequency of home runs obviously depends on the player, but for any individual batter in a single game it will also depend upon the skill of the pitcher, his state of mind, the angle of the sun, the wind, and probably a host of other factors. Yet, *over the long run*, a good baseball player should hit the ball a fairly consistent proportion of times, and we should expect fairly consistent differences between players.

The same should be true of psi. If it exists, it may not be replicable on demand, but over the long run in well-controlled laboratory experiments we should expect to see a consistent level of results, above that expected by chance.

Evidence based on statistics comes from comparing what actually happened with what would have been expected to happen if chance alone were operating. Jessica Utts, professor of statistics at the University of California at Davis, illustrates this point by noting that about 51 percent of births in the United States result in boys. If someone claimed to have a method that enabled a couple to increase the chances of having a baby of the desired sex, then we could examine the validity of their claim by comparing the percentage of boys born with the percentage expected when chance alone is operating. If the actual percentage is higher than the chance percentage of 51 percent *over the long run*, then we may conclude that the claim is supported by statistical evidence.

However, simply showing that the results were greater than that expected by chance is not enough, because in smaller samples departures from chance are more likely. No one is likely to be impressed by finding two boys in a sample of only three births. But where do we draw the line? Is seven boys in a sample of ten births sufficient evidence to establish the claim? Or do we require at least 70 boys in 100 births? In order to answer questions such as these, statisticians have developed numerical methods for comparing actual results to those expected by chance. In assessing the results of an experiment, it is common to use the "p-value" to answer the following question: If chance alone were responsible for these results, how likely would we be to observe results this strong or stronger? If the p-value is very small, then we would be unlikely to have obtained these results by chance alone. Suppose, for example, someone performed an experiment with ten couples who desire boys, and out of ten births, seven were boys. If chance alone were responsible—that is, if the method of sex selection was in fact useless—then the probability of seven boys in ten births would be .19, or 19 percent. Thus, the result of the experiment would have a *p-value* of 0.19.

The standard convention is to use a p-value of .05 as a criterion of significance; if we observe a p-value of less than .05, we say the results are statistically significant at the 5 percent level of significance. Obviously, the smaller the p-value the more convincingly chance can be ruled out as an explanation for the observed results. According to the standard convention, in the example above, seven boys out of ten births would not qualify as a statistically significant departure from chance (since .19 > .05).

Note that a p-value can also be expressed in terms of odds against chance, with a p-value of .05 corresponding to results to odds against chance of about 20 to 1. So, we may expect about 1 in 20 experiments to provide results significant at the 5 percent level even if nothing but chance is responsible.

Replication and effect size

In the past few decades scientists have begun to realize that replication efforts need to take into account not only p-values but also the *magnitude* of the effect, or the effect size. This is because the p-value is heavily dependant on the size of the study. The smaller the effect size, the larger the study required to attain statistical significance. Very powerful effects only require small studies to convincingly rule out chance, whereas very small effects require large studies.

Jessica Utts illustrates this relationship with her example mentioned above:

> In our hypothetical sex-determination experiment, suppose 70 out of 100 births designed to be boys actually resulted in boys, for a rate of 70 percent instead of the 51 percent expected by chance. The experiment would have a *p-value* of 0.0001, quite convincingly ruling out chance. Now suppose someone attempted to replicate the experiment with only ten births and found 7 boys, i.e. also 70 percent. The smaller experiment would have a *p-value* of 0.19, and would not be statistically significant. If we were simply to focus on that issue, the result would appear to be a failure to replicate the original result, even though it achieved exactly the same 70 percent boys! In only ten births it would require 90 percent of them to be boys before chance could be ruled out. Yet the 70 percent rate is a more exact replication of the result than the 90 percent.[77]

Statisticians distinguish two types of errors when evaluating the results of an experiment: The Type I error and the Type II error. A Type I error occurs when we mistakenly conclude that there is an effect when there really is none: That is, it occurs when the experimental result occurred purely by chance. The level of significance is therefore a measure of the probability of a Type I error. In the example above, there is a probability of .0001 that 70 boys out of 100 births occurred purely by chance, and so the probability of a Type I error is of course .0001 (or .01 percent). A Type II error occurs when we mistakenly conclude that there is no effect when there really is one. This typically occurs when our sample size is too small to detect an effect as statistically significant, as in the example above using only ten births.[78]

Realizing that small samples may lack the necessary *statistical power* to detect a weak effect sizes, and that individual researchers often operate with limited time and resources, statisticians have developed a technique called *meta-analysis*. This is essentially a set of procedures for combining the results of many small studies into one large study in order to see if there is an overall effect, and if there is, to determine how big it is and whether it varies with variations in experimental procedure. Meta-analysis is widely used in medicine and the behavioral sciences.

The final statistic we need is the confidence interval. This is expressed as a range of values around the result of our experiment: For instance, the 95 percent confidence interval would be the range of values that we are 95 percent confident contains the actual underlying effect size. Another way of looking at it is to suppose we repeat the experiment 100 times in an identical manner: then about 95 percent of the results should include the "true" result within their confidence intervals.[79]

In the experiment above, the 95 percent confidence interval for the study with the sample of 100 would be 70 plus or minus 10, or (60—80); for the smaller study, it would be 7 plus or minus 3.57, or (3.43—10.57). Note that the first confidence interval does not include the chance value of 51, and so we can be fairly confident that the results were not simply due to chance. Our confidence should increase if we find additional studies with similar results.

THE REVOLUTION OF J.B. RHINE

Joseph Banks Rhine's first incursion into higher education, at Wooster College, Ohio, was seen as preparation for his becoming a Methodist minister. But his fervent fundamentalist faith did not survive the intellectual challenges it encountered there, and was soon abandoned. But like many others that had lost their religious faith, Rhine found the materialism of the then-prevailing scientific worldview distasteful. And so, like Sidgwick and Myers before him, he turned to the study of psychic phenomena as a possible means of finding an alternative to this bleak outlook without sacrificing an impeccable scientific approach.

After graduating with a PhD in plant physiology, Rhine joined Duke University in 1927, and shortly afterward asked Karl Zener, an authority on the psychology of perception, to design a set of cards with symbols that would be easy to visualize, but as distinctive from each other as possible. Zener came up with a set of 25 cards with five different symbols—circle, square, star, cross, and wavy lines—each repeated five times. These cards were then used in card guessing experiments; and so if chance alone were operating, over many trials each card should be chosen about 20 percent of the time. In the 800 preliminary trials Rhine and Zener carried out in 1930-31, 207 (nearly 26 percent) were guessed correctly when 160 would have been expected by chance. It was a modest start, but it launched Rhine on his long career as an experimental parapsychologist.

What really convinced Rhine that he was dealing with a genuine effect was the manner in which results varied according to various psychological and physiological conditions. For instance, Rhine found that a depressant drug such as sodium amytal decreased the level of scoring, whereas a stimulant such as caffeine increased scores. In later experiments, Rhine would find this relationship held true even when the subject was blind as to which drug he or she was taking.

The early tests focused on telepathy, with a subject in one room trying to identify the order of cards as they were read by a sender in another room. Rhine quickly realized the difficulty in distinguishing the effects of telepathy from clairvoyance, and devised an experiment to test pure telepathy, in which the sender would simply *think* of each successive symbol, using a coded numerical association unknown to the subject. Later experiments dispensed with an agent viewing the cards, and were therefore tests of clairvoyance. In these tests the subject usually tried to identify the order of the cards as they lay in an opaque envelope or in another room. Still later, Rhine introduced tests of precognition, in which the subject would try to guess the order of the cards *before* they were randomly shuffled.

Some of Rhine's most impressive results came from experiments with a student subject named Hubert Pearce. After attaining double the scores expected by chance in some preliminary experiments, Rhine was eager to devise a test for Pearce that would exclude every conceivable possibility of a normal explanation. Accordingly, he then asked a research assistant named Gaither Pratt to perform a long-distance experiment, in which the subject, Pearce, located in one building, would attempt to identify the order of the cards as they were handled, but not viewed, by Pratt, the experimenter, located in another building. In this way 1,850 trials were completed, resulting in 558 hits when only 370 would be expected by chance. The odds against these results occurring by chance were calculated to be astronomical, at 22 billion to one.

By 1934 Rhine was ready to publish his findings, and this he did in a book titled *Extra-Sensory Perception*, thereby introducing the acronym "ESP" to the English language. Rhine's book was greeted as the start of a new era, and laboratories at other universities readily adopted the card-guessing methodology. The scientific community was now faced with the largest body of evidence for psychic phenomena ever collected through conventional experimental methods.

But acceptance would not come easily. Critical articles began to appear, challenging almost every aspect of the evaluative techniques and experimental conditions. Between 1934 and 1940 approximately 60 critical articles by 40 authors appeared, primarily in the psychological literature. Since Rhine had based his conclusions entirely on statistical analysis of data, many of the earliest criticisms focused on the statistical methods Rhine had used. One of the most persistent critics was a psychologist from McGill University named Chester Kellogg, who questioned the fundamental underpinning of Rhine's statistical approach.[80] Rhine and his colleagues responded to these criticisms, and the debate went back and forth, until statistician Burton Camp, then president of the Institute of Mathematical Statistics, finally settled the issue. At a press conference in 1937 Camp released a statement to the press that read:

> Dr. Rhine's investigations have two aspects: experimental and statistical. On the experimental side mathematicians, of course, have nothing to say. On the statistical side, however, recent mathematical work has established the fact that, assuming that the experiments have been properly performed, the statistical analysis is essentially valid. If the Rhine investigation is to be fairly attacked, it must be on other than mathematical grounds.[81]

The criticisms also focused on the methodology of the experiments, with allegations that subjects could have produced the correct answers through the use of ordinary sensory cues. It is true that some of the early exploratory experiments did not provide adequate shielding against sensory cues. But while Rhine did not base major conclusions on such poorly controlled data, criticisms of these experiments distracted attention away from experiments whose results could not be explained by sensory cues, such as the Pearce-Pratt series.

With the popularity of Rhine's book, several companies had begun marketing commercial versions of the Zenar cards. Critics pointed out that under certain conditions the cards could be read from the back, because of the printing impression, and this explanation for the positive results began to circulate. The parapsychologists retorted that defective cards had not been used in any of the experiments reported in the literature, and in any case, this defect could not explain the results when the cards were shielded in opaque envelopes, behind a screen, or when, as in the Pearce-Pratt series, tester and subject were in different buildings. And there was no way sensory cues could explain the results of the precognition experiments, in which the target series did not even exist until the responses had been safely recorded.

In order to answer the criticisms that had been leveled at the experiments described in Rhine's earlier book, in 1940 Rhine and his colleagues published their book *Extra-Sensory Perception After Sixty Years*. The phrase "after sixty years" was a reference to 1882, the year the original SPR had been founded. In *ESP-60* (as it came to be known) statistical procedures used were explained in detail, criticisms were rebutted, and it was shown how results from the six best parapsychology experiments could not be explained away by any of these criticisms. The professional response to this book was far more positive, and parapsychology gained a measure of acceptance. Other laboratories began ESP research without fear of ridicule, and independent replications began to be reported.

Parapsychologist Charles Honorton performed a detailed statistical review of the early experiments, and this was his conclusion:

> By 1940 nearly one million experimental trials had been reported under conditions which precluded sensory leakage. These included five studies in which the target cards were enclosed in opaque sealed envelopes, 16 studies employing opaque screens, ten studies involving separation of subjects and targets in different buildings and two studies involving precognition tasks.... The results were independently significant in 27 of the 33 experiments. By the end of the 1930s there was general agreement that the better-controlled ESP experiments could not be accounted for on the basis of sensory leakage.[82]

There has been a widespread belief that most of the positive results came from Rhine's laboratory at Duke University, and that most of the experiments performed elsewhere failed to confirm Rhine's results.[83] Honorton investigated, and wrote:

> A survey of the published literature between 1934 and 1940 fails to support this claim. [The table below] shows all the published experimental reports during this period. Inspection of this table reveals that a majority (61 percent) of the outside replications report significant results (p < .01) and that the proportion of significant studies was not significantly greater for the Duke University group.[84]

Table 1: Breakdown of experimental ESP studies (1934-1939)			
	# studies*	# studies reported significant (p<.01)	% significant
Duke group	17	15	88
Non-Duke	33	20	61
Total	50	35	70

* includes all English-language studies involving assessment of statistical significance of data, 1934-1939 inclusive.

X^2 (Duke vs. non-Duke X significant vs. non-significant) = 1.70 (1df)

Source: Honorton, 1975.

Since 1940, most of the criticisms on the early results have focused on the possibility of fraud, on the part of the subject, the experimenter, or both. One of the
most prominent critics was the English psychologist C.E.M. Hansel, who wrote that,
"It is wise to adopt initially the assumption that ESP is impossible, since there is a
great weight of knowledge supporting this point of view."[85] Hansel provided no
documentation at all for this assumption, and went on to develop elaborate fraud
scenarios to explain how each experiment could have been accomplished by fraud
on the part of subject or experimenter.

For instance, in the case of the above-mentioned Pearce-Pratt experiments,
Hansel pointed out that Rhine and Pratt had failed to assign someone to watch
Pearce at all times during the experiment. So it was conceivable, Hansel argued, that
Pearce could have left his station, made his way to where Pratt was situated, peered
through a glass window or through a trap door in the ceiling and watched Pratt as
he turned over the cards while compiling the target-sheet, and only *then* completed
his own target sheet. Hansel never provided any direct evidence that fraud actually
did occur; he merely raised the possibility that fraud *could have* occurred, and
thereby argued that the experiments cannot be considered conclusive proof of ESP.
Almost 40 years after *ESP-60*, Hansel wrote:

> A possible explanation other than [ESP], provided it involves only well
> established processes, should not be rejected on the grounds of its
> complexity.... If the result could have arisen through a trick, the
> experiment must be considered unsatisfactory proof of ESP, whether
> or not it is finally decided that such a trick was, in fact, used.[86]

His comments show the lengths a skeptic must be prepared to go in order to
discount the early ESP experiments.

5

Psychokinesis: mind over matter

With ESP, we are dealing with a transfer of information; with psychokenesis (PK) we are dealing with a physical effect; but with both ESP and PK we are dealing with the automatic *realization of an intention*, conscious or unconscious. This realization of intention is the essential property of psi. With ESP it occurs without the use of the recognized sense organs; with PK it occurs without the use of our muscles.

When most people think of PK, they think of claims about metal bending, or of levitation of objects. Most modern PK research is of phenomena far less dramatic and impressive, but the evidence for these less-impressive phenomena is considered much sounder. Typically, skeptics dismiss dramatic reports of PK as due to the work of clever illusionists. However, reports concerning the activities of at least one individual cannot be so easily dismissed.

His name was Daniel Dunglas Home, born in Scotland in 1833, raised in Connecticut, and one of the most famous international figures of the 1870's. Reports of séances with Home would strain credibility, if it were not for the prominence and respectability of many of his investigators. A typical séance with Home, which might include a dozen sitters, might start off with the room itself shaking. Later, the table around which all were seated might tilt, with objects on the table staying in one place instead of sliding off. Musical instruments would be seen and heard playing recognizable tunes, apparently without anyone playing them. The climax of the séance would often be the levitation of a large, mahogany dining room table. Early in his career Home was investigated by William Cullen Bryant, journalist, and Dr. David Wells of Harvard, both of whom intended to expose him as a fraud. The men were allowed to inspect the room beforehand to their satisfaction, and the séance took place in a well-lit room. This was their report:

> Three gentlemen, Wells, Bryant, and Edwards, seated themselves
> simultaneously on top of the table, and while these men were so
> seated, the table started to move in various directions. After some time
> the table was seen to rise completely from the floor and floated about
> in the air during several seconds, as if something more solid than air

> was upholding it. ...*we have the certainty that we were not imposed upon and neither were we the victims of optical illusions.*[87]

Prominent scientists who investigated Home included Robert Hare, Professor of Chemistry at the Medical College of the University of Pennsylvania, and William Crookes, of the SPR. Both were originally skeptics; both were impressed with Home; and for their empiricism both were savagely attacked by many of their colleagues.[88]

Crookes had urged other scientists to witness Home's phenomena for themselves, but few were willing to risk upsetting their preconceptions. One of the few well-known scientists who did respond to Crookes' invitation was Francis Galton. After attending three séances with Home, he was so impressed that he wrote his cousin Charles Darwin and urged him to visit Home to see for himself. In his letter dated 19 April 1872, he mentions that the séance was conducted in "full gas-light", and describes how an accordion held by its base played by itself. He goes on to say:

> What surprises me is the perfect openness of Miss F. and Home. They let you do whatever you like within certain limits, their limits not interfering with adequate investigation. I really believe the truth of what they allege, the people who come as men of science are usually so disagreeable, opinionated and obstructive and have so little patience, that the séance rarely succeeds with them.... I am convinced that the affair is no matter of vulgar legerdemain and believe it is well worth going into, on the understanding that a first rate medium (and I hear there are only three such) puts himself at your disposal.[89]

Darwin was impressed, and Galton wrote to Home with a letter enclosed from Darwin. No reply came, as Home had gone to Russia, and so Crookes and Darwin decided to wait until he returned the following spring. But Home's health, which had never been very good, had deteriorated, and so he never returned to England. Unfortunately, we will never know what would have happened if there had been a historic encounter between Darwin and Home.

Was he a fraud? Home normally held his séances in good light, often in private houses, or occasionally in hotels. The use of machinery or of accomplices seems out of the question. Mass hallucination? Hundreds of individuals witnessed his phenomena, but we do not have even one instance of anyone failing to see what everyone else claimed to see. Home remains an enigma to this day.

Micro-PK

Although there have been some more recent investigations of large-scale PK phenomena, most notably with the Russian woman Nina Kulagina,[90] such investigations form only a very small part of modern PK research. Unfortunately, most of the research into large-scale PK effects consists only of anecdotal reports, rather than results from controlled experiments. Since the 1930's, most of the work has not been concerned with PK effects that are directly observable, but rather with smaller scale effects detectable only with statistical analysis: so-called "micro-PK."

Rhine and other researchers originally performed these experiments using ordinary dice, with subjects attempting to mentally influence which dice faces would land face up. It quickly became apparent that, compared to results obtained in the clairvoyance and telepathy experiments, the results with PK were very weak. As is typical in research involving weak effects, the results from the dice-PK experiments remained controversial for years, even among parapsychologists. But in 1990 meta-analysis was applied to the dice experiments. Parapsychologists Dean Radin and Diane Ferrari combed the English-language literature and found 148 studies performed between 1935 and 1987, involving over 2,500 subjects attempting to influence more than 2.5 million dice throws. For each study they calculated a 50 percent equivalent hit rate. The overall hit rate for the control studies (that is, no influence intended) was 50.02 percent; for the experimental studies, it was 51.2 percent. Obviously a very weak effect, but for a sample of this size, the odds against these results occurring by chance are more than a billion to one.[91]

Other conclusions from this study were that positive results were not negatively correlated with measures of study quality; results did not depend upon a handful of a few extreme studies or upon studies coming from only a handful of laboratories; and that the quality of the experiments significantly improved over time, indicating that parapsychologists were responding to constructive criticism throughout this period.

The age of electronics and PK

German physicist Helmut Schmidt is the world's leading exponent of modern PK research. After earning his doctorate from the University of Cologne, Schmidt settled in the United States, where from 1965 to 1969 he worked as senior research scientist at the Boeing research laboratory in Seattle. Since then, however, he has been fully committed to psi research.

It was Schmidt who first introduced automated electronic testing devices into PK research. A random number generator (RNG) developed by Schmidt employs an extremely rapid clock which is stopped at random intervals by the emission of electrons as radioactive strontium-90 decays. What is so unusual about Schmidt's RNGs is that the precise rate of radioactive decay is theoretically unpredictable, and so his experiments are essentially tests to see if human intention can influence random events at the quantum level.

In order to test PK, Schmidt employed a binary counter, one that rapidly flipped back and forth between two positions (recorded as "0" or "1"). This electronic coin flipper would be stopped in one of its two positions by the emission of an electron from the radioactive material. It is theoretically impossible to predict when an elec-tron will be emitted: The timing of the event appears completely random. So, in the absence of any psi effect, the behavior of the RNG should be completely random, and an approximately equal number of "0"s and "1"s should be recorded.

The 0's and 1's generated by the RNG were usually presented to the subject in one of two ways: Either as a series of clicks in the left or right earpiece of a set of headphones, or as a display of lights arranged in a circle. If the headphone device was employed, the goal of the subject was to produce more clicks in one earpiece than in the other. With the display of lights, the situation was a bit more complicated. If the oscillating device stopped in one position, the light moved one step clockwise; if it stopped in the other, it moved one step counter-clockwise. If only chance is oper-ating, the lights should then be expected to make a random walk around the circle, with about an equal number of clockwise and counter-clockwise moves. The goal of the subject was to "will" the lights in one direction around the circle.

The absolute deviation from chance with Schmidt's experiments was slight, but because the experimental design allows enormous numbers of trials to be collected in a short space of time, highly significant results can be obtained. Most modern RNG experiments are based on Schmidt's original design, and by 1987 an enormous database of results had accumulated. In that year, Dean Radin and Roger Nelson at Princeton University searched the literature and found 832 PK studies conducted by 68 different investigators between 1959 and 1987. These experiments all involved the use of truly random event generators (as described above) or else electronic pseudo-random number generators. Radin and Nelson subjected the database to meta-analysis, and their results, published in the prominent physics journal *Foundations of Physics*, showed an overall hit rate of about 51 percent, when 50 per-cent was expected by chance. Because of the size of the database, the odds against chance were beyond a trillion to one. They also assigned each study a quality score derived from many published criticisms of PK experiments, and concluded:

> This meta-analysis shows that effects are not a function of experimen-tal quality, and that the replication rate is as good as that found in exemplary experiments in psychology and physics. ...Skeptics often assert that only "believers" obtain positive results in such experiments. However, a thorough literature search finds not a single attempted replication of the RNG experiment by a publicly proclaimed skeptic.[92]

Of the 597 experimental studies (235 were control studies), 258 came from the Princeton Engineering Anomalies Research (PEAR) laboratory at Princeton Uni-versity, founded by Robert Jahn in 1979. Since then, the majority of RNG PK studies have come from the PEAR lab. Unlike Schmidt, who selected and trained his subjects carefully, Jahn and his colleagues have made a practice of accepting all comers. This has resulted in an effect magnitude not as large as that generally found in Schmidt's studies. Yet the PEAR lab has generated an enormous database of trials, and has corroborated Schmidt's results to a highly significant degree.[93] In about a fourth of the experiments, the distance between subject and the RNG was varied, with the distance varying from a few meters to several thousand miles. Distance did not affect the results.[94]

Implications for physics

The RNG devices pioneered by Schmidt are driven by purely random events at the quantum level. So the subjects in these experiments are not really shifting matter around, but rather shifting *probabilities of events* in desired directions. It is useful to remember that many of our modern "laws of nature" are statistical in nature rather than absolutely true at all times. For instance, laws dealing with the behavior of large numbers of particles, such as the gas laws, are true only in the statistical sense and do admit of violations, no matter how improbable those violations may be. The smaller the number of particles involved, the more likely such a violation is to occur. Similarly, the second law of thermodynamics (disorder tends to increase) is a statistical law: If we have two rooms of equal temperature joined by a door, it is possible (though not likely) that the highest energy particles will end up in one room and the lowest energy particles in the other. This decrease in entropy becomes more likely the fewer the number of particles in each room.

According to quantum mechanics—physic's most successful theory to date—even events concerning single particles can occur in a *truly* random fashion: That is, some individual events and properties would be unpredictable even if we had perfect information regarding the initial conditions. Such events and properties can be predicted only in the statistical sense. The experiments of Schmidt and others suggest that human consciousness can influence the timing of these events. As some readers will no doubt be aware, the role that consciousness plays in quantum mechanics is one of the burning issues in modern physics. As we will see in the next chapter, Schmidt's experiments may be able to settle this controversy.

Final points

Schmidt and the theoretical physicist Evan Harris Walker do not view micro-PK as a force, but rather as a type of information flow from the consciousness of the observer to the indeterminate quantum state. Rhine's tumbling dice experiments can be incorporated into a PK model involving quantum mechanics because the act of tumbling may introduce sufficient quantum mechanical uncertainty into the system to make the outcome truly random. Since it seems difficult to extend this explanation to *macro*-PK phenomena, it may be that micro-PK and macro-PK (assuming the latter is real) are two separate phenomena. But at this point, the relationship between the two, if any, is completely unknown.

Skeptics of psychokenesis are fond of pointing out that there are well-established laboratories for testing PK in Reno, Las Vegas, and Monte Carlo. So, could PK be used to beat the odds in the casinos? Not likely. The PK effects observed in the laboratories are simply far too weak. Physicist Nick Herbert has calculated that the odds in favor of the house on even the most favorable casino games are about 100 times larger than most of the deviations from chance observed in the PK experiments.[95] Even the most gifted micro-PK subjects do not even come close to displaying results that would allow them to consistently beat the house.

Can PK ability be increased with proper training? Does it have practical applications? Like so many other poorly funded areas of psi research, at this point there are more questions than answers regarding PK. But there is one thing we should have no doubt about: These highly significant results, coming from several laboratories, have made some skeptics very uncomfortable. Admitting the difficulty she experiences maintaining her well-publicized skeptical beliefs in the face of mounting experimental evidence, psychologist Susan Blackmore writes:

> Human beings are not built to have open minds. If they try to have open minds they experience *cognitive dissonance.* Leon Festinger first used this term. He argued that people strive to make their beliefs and actions consistent and when there is inconsistency they experience this unpleasant state of "cognitive dissonance," and they then use lots of ploys to reduce it. I have to admit I have become rather familiar with some of them.
>
> First, there is premature closure. You can just pick one theory and stick to it against all odds. ...Or the disbeliever can refuse to look at the positive results. You may think I wouldn't refuse, but I have to admit that when the *Journal of Parapsychology* arrives with reports of Helmut Schmidt's positive findings I begin to feel uncomfortable and am quite apt to put it away "to read tomorrow."[96]

6

Telepathy: silent communication

By the 1960's a number of researchers were becoming dissatisfied with the repetitive forced-choice card guessing experiments that had been pioneered by J.B. Rhine in the 1930's. Subjects simply became bored after guessing dozens of cards, and so researchers sought a more interesting experimental technique, one that also would more closely replicate the conditions that seemed to facilitate psi experiences in real life.

One such condition seems to be dreaming. History records many famous psychic dreams, and cross-cultural surveys indicate that about half of all real-life psi experiences occur during dreams.[97] These findings motivated psychiatrist Montague Ullman and clinical psychologist Stanley Krippner at the Maimonides Medical Center in Brooklyn, New York, to develop a laboratory technique to test telepathy in dreams. Encouraging results were reported, with odds against chance of millions to one.[98]

Unfortunately, there have been few attempted replications of these studies. Part of the problem is that dream laboratories are notoriously expensive to run; indeed, a lack of funds caused the Maimonides Dream Lab to close in 1978. As an alternative to the rather prosaic card guessing experiments of an earlier era, the dream experiments did show promising results. So, as the dream experiments began to wind down in the late 1970's, parapsychologists began searching for an alternative with less expensive overhead.

THE GANZFELD

One of these parapsychologists was Charles Honorton, who spent several summers as an assistant at J.B. Rhine's lab in Durham, North Carolina, then worked for several years as a researcher at the Maimonides Dream Lab. Honorton noted that historically, apparent psi effects have frequently been associated not only with dreaming but with other altered states of consciousness, such as meditation and hypnosis. Spontaneous cases are of course anecdotal, and Honorton thought that no conclusions should be based upon them, but he also rightly considered that such cases can be used to generate hypotheses that can then be tested experimentally. And his work at the Dream Lab convinced him that, in the case of dreaming at least, the anecdotal reports had been experimentally corroborated to an impressive degree.

These anecdotal reports and experimental findings led Honorton to postulate that psi may operate as a weak signal that is normally masked by the stronger signals constantly besieging us from our conventional sense organs. The altered states discussed above—dreaming, meditation, hypnosis—have something in common: physical relaxation combined with reduced sensory input and an alert, receptive mental state. Honorton speculated that the recreation of these conditions in the laboratory might be an excellent technique for investigating psi. The hypothesis formed was that, by reducing ordinary sensory noise while keeping the subject relaxed and alert, the subject's mind would become starved for stimuli and thus more receptive to any faint or weak signals that ordinarily would not reach consciousness. In order to test this "noise-reduction" model of psi, Honorton and other researchers turned to the ganzfeld technique.

Like the dream studies, the ganzfeld procedure has most often been used to test for telepathic communication between a sender and a receiver. Typically, the subject is led into an acoustically sealed room and onto a comfortable reclining chair. A table tennis ball is cut in half, and the halves are placed over the subject's eyes. A red lamp shines above, causing the subject to see only a warm reddish glow. Headphones are placed over the ears, and the subject is then led through a progressive series of relaxation exercises designed to clear the mind of the day's worries and distractions. After about fifteen minutes, the relaxation exercises end and a voice asks the subject to simply relax and describe whatever thoughts and images come to mind. For the next thirty minutes the subject hears only a steady, not-unpleasant white noise through the headphones, and sees only the reddish glow. This is the *Ganzfeld*, a German word meaning "total field" that refers to the homogeneous, undifferentiated perceptual field that the experimenter wishes to create.

About fifteen minutes after the receiver begins the relaxation exercises, a sender in another acoustically sealed room opens a sealed envelope and removes the target picture, or begins to watch a randomly chosen video clip. The target is chosen from a large pool of potential targets, and the sender's task is to concentrate on the target and attempt to send the visual image to the receiver. Often there is a one-way audio link from the receiver to the sender so that the sender may adjust his or her thoughts in response to the feedback coming from the receiver.

After thirty minutes the session ends and the receiver is shown a set of four pictures or video clips. Unlike the dream experiments, the subjects usually rank the pictures themselves, on the grounds that they should best know what has gone through their own minds during the session. Each of the possibly-used targets receives a ranking from 1 to 4, with "1" being considered a direct hit and all other rankings considered complete misses. So, if chance alone is operating, we would expect receivers to correctly guess which target was used about 25% of the time.

By 1982, Honorton was ready to present the results of a series of ganzfeld experiments. At the annual convention of the Parapsychological Association of that year, Charles Honorton summarized the results of all the forty-two ganzfeld studies that had been published between 1974 and 1981: An amazing 55 percent of the studies reported statistically significant results, whereas only 5 percent would have been expected to do so if chance alone had been operating. It appeared that parapsychologists had finally found their long-sought repeatable experiment.

Acceptance, however, would not come easy. One of parapsychology's most sophisticated critics was spoiling for a fight.

7

The Great Ganzfeld Debate

Psychologist Ray Hyman, a long time critic of psi research and a founding member of CSICOP, disagreed with Honorton's conclusions, and undertook his own meta-analysis of the ganzfeld data. This disagreement led to a debate, the opening rounds of which were carried in two full issues of the *Journal of Parapsychology* in 1985 and 1986.

Ray Hyman opened the debate by claiming that the estimate of 55 percent significant studies was far too high because of a number of problems with the forty-two studies. First of all, he pointed out that some investigators used more than one measure of a successful outcome (multiple-analysis); even worse, there was a possibility that some investigators had "shopped around", applying different criteria to the data until they found a measure that was "significant." He also raised the possibility of a bias in favor of reporting successful outcomes. This is the so-called "file-drawer" problem, which alleges that experiments with successful results tend to be reported, while the unsuccessful results simply languish in file drawers. Finally, Hyman presented the results of a statistical analysis that claimed to show a relationship between the number of flaws in each study and the reported success: He claimed that the most flawed studies tended to report the highest scores. Adjusting for all these factors, Hyman concluded that the actual success rate was close to what chance would predict.

Honorton agreed with the first of these criticisms, that multiple-analysis was indeed a problem. In response, he restricted his analysis to only those 28 studies that actually reported the hit rates obtained so that he could calculate the percentage of direct hits, defining a successful outcome only as one in which the subject ranked the target in first place. Using this uniform measure, 23 of the 28 studies had results greater than the chance expectation, and 43 percent of the 28 studies yielded significant results. The over-all hit rate was 35 percent (with 25 percent expected by chance) and the 95 percent confidence interval ranged from 28-43 percent. The odds against these results happening by chance alone were a billion to one.[99]

Honorton demonstrated that these positive results were not due to only one or two labs. These 28 studies came from 10 different labs: One lab, directed by British psychologist Carl Sargent, contributed nine of the studies, Honorton's own lab contributed five, two other labs contributed three each, two contributed two each, and the remaining four labs each contributed one study. Thus, half of the studies came from only two labs, one of them Honorton's. Accordingly, Honorton analyzed the results for each lab separately, and found that results were significant for six of the ten laboratories. Even if we excluded the results from the two most prolific labs, the odds against chance were still ten thousand to one.[100]

Thus, the positive results could not be explained by multiple-analysis, or as the effect of just one or two labs contributing the lion's share of the studies. Honorton then adressed Hyman's other criticisms.

Selective Reporting

It has long been believed that in all fields there may be a bias in favor of reporting and publishing studies with positive outcomes. Given the controversial nature of their subject, parapsychologists were among the first to become sensitive to this problem, and in 1975 the Parapsychological Association adopted a policy opposing the withholding of nonsignificant data, a policy unique among the sciences. In addition, in 1980 the skeptical British psychologist Susan Blackmore conducted a survey of parapsychologists to see if there was a bias in favor of reporting successful ganzfeld results, and concluded that there was none. She uncovered only nineteen completed but unreported ganzfeld studies. Seven of these had significantly positive results, a proportion (37%) very similar to the proportion of the studies in the meta-analysis that achieved independently significant outcomes (43%).[101]

Still, since it is impossible in principle to know how many unreported studies may be sitting in file drawers, Honorton used a technique of meta-analysis to calculate just how many unreported, nonsignificant ganzfeld studies would be needed to reduce the reported outcomes to chance levels. It turns out that for the 28 direct-hit ganzfeld studies, it would take 423 unreported, nonsignificant studies, for a ratio of unreported-to-reported studies of approximately fifteen to one. Given that a single ganzfeld session takes over an hour to conduct and considering the small number of laboratories in the world equipped to conduct ganzfeld experiments, it is not surprising that Hyman concurred with Honorton that selective reporting could not explain the significance of the results.[102]

Study Flaws

One of the most frequent criticisms of psi research is that many, if not most, psi experiments have methodological flaws. It is claimed that these poorly-designed and executed studies account for most of the positive outcomes. Furthermore, it is maintained that if these flawed studies were removed, the positive results would vanish.

Fortunately, meta-analysis provides a technique for determining the extent to which, if any, methodological flaws can account for positive results. Each study is rated according to the degree that a given flaw is present; these ratings are then correlated with study outcomes. Large positive correlations between the presence of flaws and successful outcomes would support the skeptics' contention that the successful outcomes are simply due to study flaws.

One of the most fatal flaws in psi research is that of sensory leakage, in which a subject is able to gain knowledge of the target through the use of ordinary senses, either inadvertently or through intentional cheating.

Sensory Leakage

With its use of sensory deprivation and acoustically sealed rooms, the design of the ganzfeld tends to minimize any opportunity for sensory leakage of the target. Nevertheless, critics have raised some possibilities: If the experimenter dealing with the subject knows the target, he or she may somehow bias the subject's choice. One study did contain this flaw, but there the subjects actually scored slightly *below* chance. Another possibility for leakage arises if the actual physical picture used by the sender is included in the set of pictures given to the receiver for judging: Perhaps the receiver may consciously or unconsciously notice that the target picture was handled. This is the so-called "greasy fingers" hypothesis, and although contemporary ganzfeld experiments use duplicate sets of targets, some of the early studies did not.

Hyman and Honorton both concluded that there was no systematic relationship between flaws possibly leading to sensory leakage and study outcome. Honorton also reported that, even if the studies that failed to use duplicate target sets were excluded, the results were still highly significant, with odds against chance of about 100,000 to 1.[103]

Inadequate Randomization

Hyman then concentrated his attack on what he claimed were flaws in randomization procedures. Randomization is important in ganzfeld experiments, in two respects: It is important that each potential target have an equal chance of being selected, and it is important that the target does not appear in a predictable position when the target pool of four pictures is presented to the subject at the end of the session.

Hyman claimed that there was a significant relationship between randomization flaws and successful outcomes; Honorton claimed that there was no such relationship. The source of the disagreement can be traced to conflicting definitions of flaws. Perhaps the differences over this part of the analysis could be due to differences in bias. After all, Hyman is a confirmed long-time skeptic, and Honorton had been conducting psi research for decades.

However, none of the ten contributors to the subsequent debate published in 1986 agreed with Hyman's conclusions, whereas four non-parapsychologists—two statisticians and two psychologists—explicitly agreed with Honorton's conclusion.[104] David Saunders, a psychological statistician, was one of the first to independently examine Hyman's flaw study, and he concluded that "the entire analysis is meaningless."[105]

Yet, it is worth pointing out that while many critics have historically argued that experimental flaws can explain positive results in psi experiments, Hyman's analysis was the first to attempt to actually quantify the relationship between flaws and significant results, and for this he should be congratulated. At any rate, Hyman continued to insist that there was a positive relationship between inadequate randomization and study outcome, but he also finally agreed that "the present database does not support any firm conclusion about the relationship between flaws and study outcome."[106]

As mentioned above, ten additional critics and supporters of parapsychology contributed commentary on the debate. For the most part, the critics remained unconvinced, but there was one notable exception: The British mathematician and well-known critic Christopher Scott described Honorton's reasoning as "the most convincing argument for the existence of ESP that I have yet encountered."[107]

The Joint Communiqué

Perhaps the biggest surprise of the second round of the debate was a joint communiqué, co-authored by Hyman and Honorton. Instead of continuing with the debate, the two decided to jointly write a paper, which started out listing their points of agreement and disagreement:

> We agree that there is an overall significant effect in this database that cannot reasonably be explained by selective reporting or multiple analysis. We continue to differ over the degree to which the effect constitutes evidence for psi, but we agree that the final verdict awaits the outcome of future experiments conducted by a broader range of investigators and according to more stringent standards.[108]

They then described the "more stringent standards" for the conditions under which future ganzfeld experiments should be conducted. These included strict security precautions against sensory leakage and possible fraud; required testing of randomization methods; and an insistence on the thorough documentation of the experimental procedures, randomization methods, and of the status of the experiment (whether it was meant to merely confirm previous findings or explore novel conditions). One of Honorton's parapsychology colleagues pointed out that "Honorton was especially interested in getting Hyman to agree publicly to these criteria, as skeptics are notorious for changing the rules of the game after all previous objections have been met and new experiments continue to provide significant results."[109]

It is worthwhile at this point to mention how very unusual this debate really was, as it marked a sharp departure from the usual rhetorical exchanges between parapsychologists and their critics. Shortly before the opening rounds, Hyman wrote "The level of the debate during the past 130 years has been an embarrassment for anyone who would like to believe that scholars and scientists adhere to standards of rationality and fair play."[110] After the joint communiqué, psychologist Robert Rosenthal wrote, "Parapsychologists in particular and scientists in general owe a great debt of gratitude to Ray Hyman and Charles Honorton for their careful and extensive analytic and meta-analytic work on the ganzfeld problem. Their debate has yielded an especially high light/heat ratio, and many of the important issues have now been brought into bold relief."[111]

The culmination of the second round in a joint communiqué was also remarkable, as it marked the first time a parapsychologist and a critic collaborated on a joint statement of this type. The stage was now set to see if future ganzfeld experiments, conducted according to these more stringent standards, would continue to provide significant results. But before the results of new ganzfeld experiments were revealed, a rather disturbing incident occurred.

The National Research Council Report

"Perhaps our strongest conclusions are in the area of parapsychology" continued the speaker, reading the prepared statement. The room was quiet as the speaker paused for slight dramatic effect and then went on. "The committee finds no scientific justification from research conducted over a period of one hundred thirty years for the existence of parapsychological phenomena."[112]

The paragraph above is an account of a statement read by John Swets to a roomful of journalists at a December 1987 press conference. Swets was the chairman of a committee created by the National Research Council to investigate various techniques of enhancing human performance in which the U.S. Army was interested. He called the press conference to announce the results of this two-year, nearly half-million dollar project.

Three years earlier, the U.S. Army Research Institute (ARI) asked the National Research Council (NRC), a branch of the National Academy of Sciences, to evaluate various techniques of enhancing human performance, such as sleep learning, guided imagery, meditation, telepathy and clairvoyance. To help ensure fairness, ARI normally appointed an unbiased observer to monitor research contracts. But in this case, they appointed Dr. George Lawrence, a civilian army psychologist with a history of opposition to psi research. For instance, along with Ray Hyman, he was instrumental in getting a Pentagon-funded parapsychology project at Stanford cancelled in 1972.[113]

And when the NRC began to form subcommittees to investigate the different areas, they appointed Ray Hyman to head the parapsychology subcommittee. At the time Hyman held this position, he was an active member of the executive council of CSICOP.

The only psi studies evaluated in the report were the ganzfeld experiments, and the NRC evaluation was based upon the meta-analysis conducted by Hyman. Although two years earlier he had agreed with Honorton that "there is an overall significant effect in this database that cannot reasonably be explained by selective reporting or multiple analysis" and that "significant outcomes have been produced by a number of different investigators",[114] neither of these points is mentioned in the report. At the press conference, Hyman announced that the "poor quality of psi research was a surprise to us all—we believed the work would be of much higher quality than it turned out to be."[115]

The NRC committee requested several reports from outside experts, but for parapsychology, no parapsychologist was consulted. Instead, they commissioned psychologist James Alcock to prepare a report. Like Hyman, Alcock is also a member of CSICOP, and is widely known for his books and articles attacking parapsychological research.

Psychologist Robert Rosenthal of Harvard University was also asked to prepare a report. Rosenthal is world-renowned as an expert in evaluating controversial research claims in the social sciences, and along with Monica Harris, he prepared a report on the quality of research in all five controversial areas studied by the committee. In direct contradiction to Hyman's remark at the press conference, Harris and Rosenthal wrote that, of the five areas "only the Ganzfeld ESP studies meet the basic requirements of sound experimental design."[116] Their report concluded:

> The situation for the ganzfeld domain seems reasonably clear. We feel it would be implausible to entertain the null [that is, conclude the results are due to chance] given the combined p [probability] from these 28 studies.... When the accuracy rate expected under the null is 1/4, we estimate the obtained accuracy rate to be about 1/3.[117]

In other words, Harris and Rosenthal concluded that the ganzfeld results were not simply due to chance, and that the accuracy rate was about 33 percent, when 25 percent would be expected if chance alone were responsible.

Incredibly, committee chairman John Swets phoned Rosenthal and asked him to withdraw the section of his report that was favorable to parapsychology. Rosenthal refused. In the final NRC report, the Harris-Rosenthal paper is cited only in the several sections dealing with the *non*-parapsychology topics. There is no mention of it in the section dealing with parapsychology.

An extended and detailed refutation of the committee's report was prepared by psychologist John Palmer, Charles Honorton, and Jessica Utts, professor of statistics at the University of California, Davis. This paper led U.S. Senator Claiborne Pell to request that the Congressional Office of Technology Assessment conduct an investigation with a more balanced group. His request led to a one-day workshop held on September 30, 1988, which brought together parapsychologists, critics and experts in related fields. The workshop's report concluded that parapsychology needs "a fairer hearing across a broader spectrum of the scientific community, so that emotionality does not impede objective assessment of experimental results".[118]

An article written the following year by Colonel John Alexander (U.S. Army, retired) was far more blunt. Alexander was involved with the army's investigation of many of the subjects the NRC committee was asked to examine, and it seems worthwhile here to quote at length from the article he wrote as a challenge to the NRC report:

> I was a briefer to the NRC committee members as they researched the EHP Report. I have served as chief of Advanced Human Technology for the Army Intelligence and Security Command (1982-84) and, during the preparation of the EHP Report, was director of the Advanced Systems Concepts Office at the U.S. Army Laboratory Command. I believe I am personally well qualified to review the committee's findings.

> Many organizations in the Army had already been experimenting with various techniques to enhance human performance and frequently they had reported some very exciting results.... It was felt by several in the top leadership of the Army that contracting such an august body as the NRC...would provide a credible report on which the stewardship of the public funds for Army research allocations in the field of enhancing human performance could be based.

> The task of administering the contract fell to ARI. It was they who proposed that Dr. George Lawrence, a civilian army psychologist with a background in biofeedback, be assigned as the Contracting Officers Technical Representative (COTR). A COTR is normally an unbiased observer who does not participate in the study and who is there to ensure that the study is technically sound.

> Unfortunately...Lawrence was far from unbiased. He had a prior history in the field of being firmly and publicly in opposition to several of the areas to be studied. In fact, in a previous assignment with the U.S.

Defense Advanced Research Projects Agency (DARPA), Lawrence had
been instrumental in the cancellation of funding for psychic ("psi")
research at Stanford Research Institute (SRI). ...To accomplish that end,
Lawrence had gone to SRI with a well-known critic of the psi-research
field, Dr. Ray Hyman...Lawrence and Hyman effectively killed DARPA's
funding for SRI, which was the only government sponsored research at
the time.

Prior to the formal organization of the EHP board, Lawrence told me
in personal conversation in 1984 that he was seeking to get Hyman on
the EHP committee, an effort at which he proved to be successful. The
issue to be raised concerning the credibility of the EHP Report here is
that the *only* person assigned to the committee who had had any
previous familiarity with the parapsychological research literature was
Ray Hyman—who was known from the outset to have his mind
already made up. Hyman is a founding member of the Committee for
the Scientific Investigation of Claims of the Paranormal (CSICOP)—
the self-appointed vigilante committee that opposes parapsychological
research....

Thus, I questioned from the beginning the issues of "bias" and "objec-
tivity" as they related to the committee's constitution. For it seems
clear that Lawrence, and then Hyman and James Alcock (another
charter CSICOP member and public critic of this research) proceeded
on an intentional path to discredit the work in parapsychology....
Throughout the parapsychology section of the EHP Report, the
committee referred only to those published articles that supported
its position and ignored material that did not....

What, then, are we to conclude about the EHP report? ...First, it is
significant that a determined group of psi debunkers could find no
"smoking gun" and no "plausible alternative" to the psi hypothesis....
Second, we should worry about the fact that the highest scientific
court in the land operated in such a biased and heavy-handed manner,
and that there seems to be no channel for appeal or review of their
work. *What, we may ask, are they afraid of? Is protecting scientific orthodoxy
so vital that they must deny evidence and suppress contrary opinion?*[119]

The Autoganzfeld

Shortly after the Congressional Office report, results were presented from new
ganzfeld experiments that fully adhered to the tough standards spelled out in the

joint communiqué. Since 1983, Honorton and his colleagues worked on a new series of ganzfeld experiments that were computer-controlled. Research with the new automated ganzfeld system—called the "autoganzfeld"—continued until 1989, when lack of funding forced Honorton's laboratory to close.

The major innovations of the autoganzfeld were the use of computers to control the experiment and the introduction of closed-circuit video cameras to present short film clips and still pictures as targets. During the session neither the experimenter nor the receiver could monitor events inside the sender's room, which was also acoustically sealed and electro-magnetically shielded.

The targets consisted of 80 still pictures (static targets) and 80 short video clips complete with soundtracks (dynamic targets), all recorded on videotape. Since meta-analysis of the earlier experiments revealed a positive relationship between hit rates and the use of dynamic targets, the autoganzfeld experimenters wished to test the hypothesis that the use of dynamic targets would result in greater success.

The automated controls and sealed rooms were of course meant to reduce any possibility of sensory leakage, due either to accident or intentional cheating. In addition, two "mentalists"—magicians that specialize in simulating psi—were brought in to inspect the autoganzfeld system to see if it was vulnerable to cheating, deception, or conjuring tricks. One of these was Ford Kross, a professional mentalist and officer of the Psychic Entertainer's Association. He provided the following written statement:

> In my professional capacity as a mentalist, I have reviewed Psychophysical Research Laboratories' automated ganzfeld system and found it to provide excellent security against deception by subjects.[120]

The other magician was Cornell University psychologist Daryl Bem, who fully concurred with Kross's assessment of the security procedures, and coauthored a paper on the 1994 ganzfeld experiments with Honorton.[121] Bem has performed as a mentalist for many years and is also a member of the Psychic Entertainers Association.

Results

During the six-year autoganzfeld program, 100 men and 140 women participated as receivers in 354 sessions. The participants ranged in age from 17 to 74 years, and eight different experimenters, including Honorton, conducted the studies.

Over the eleven experiments involving 354 sessions, 122 direct hits were obtained for an overall hit rate of 34 percent, when 25 percent is expected by chance. These results are almost identical to the 35 percent hit rate obtained in the 1985 meta-analysis. The new 95 percent confidence interval ranged from 30-39 percent, and the odds against these results occurring by chance are about forty-five thousand to one.

The 11 studies comprise all sessions conducted during the six years of the auto-ganzfeld program. In other words, there is no "file drawer" of unreported studies.

The hypothesis that dynamic targets would yield higher hit rates was strongly confirmed. Overall, sessions using dynamic targets yielded hit rates of 40 percent, versus 27 percent with static targets.[122]

Other results included corroboration of the relationship between psi perform-ance and various personal traits of the receivers, such as extraversion, previously reported psi experiences, and creativity or artistic ability. Successful performance was significantly predicted by all of these factors, but the relationship with artistic ability was particularly marked. In a session with 20 undergraduates from the Julliard School of Performing Arts, the students achieved a hit rate of 50 percent, one of the highest hit rates ever reported for a single sample. The musicians were particularly successful: 6 out of 8 (75%) successfully identified the targets, with odds against chance of about 250 to 1.[123]

Have the ganzfeld results been corroborated?

In their joint communiqué Honorton and Hyman wrote: "We agree that the final ver-dict awaits the outcome of future experiments conducted by a broader range of investigators and according to more stringent standards." The autoganzfeld exper-iments certainly met the "more stringent standards" requirement. The results were statistically significant and consistent with those in the earlier database. In addition, there were reliable relationships between conceptually relevant variables and psi performance, relationships that also replicated previous findings. Hyman com-mented on these studies:

> Honorton's experiments have produced intriguing results. If...
> independent laboratories can produce similar results with the same
> relationships and with the same attention to rigorous methodology,
> then parapsychology may indeed have finally captured its elusive
> quarry.[124]

As Hyman's remark implies, Honorton's autoganzfeld experiments did not sat-isfy the requirement that replications be conducted by "a broader range of investi-gators."

However, by 1995 the results of the autoganzfeld were replicated by three addi-tional laboratories, and the results are summarized below. The first line shows the results of the first autoganzfeld replications at Honorton's Psychophysical Research Laboratories (PRL) in Princeton, New Jersey. The next three lines show the results from three different laboratories in three different countries.

Table 2: Ganzfeld Replications as of 1995		
Laboratory	Sessions	Hit Rate
PRL, Princeton, NJ	354	34%
University of Amsterdam, Netherlands	124	37%
University of Edinburgh, Scotland	97	33%
Institute for Parapsychology, NC	100	33%
Totals	675	34%

Dick Bierman at the University of Amsterdam reported in 1995 results from a set of four experiments: The hit rates were 34 percent, 37.5 percent, 40 percent, and 36 percent, for a total of 124 sessions and a combined hit rate of 37 percent.[125] Morris, Dalton, Delanoy, and Watt also in 1995 reported results from 97 sessions at the University of Edinburgh.[126] Finally, Broughton and Alexander reported their results in the same year for 100 sessions at the Institute for Parapsychology in North Carolina.[127]

The 28 studies in the original meta-analysis produced a combined hit rate of 35 percent; Robert Rosenthal later estimated the true hit rate to be about 33 percent, when 25 percent is expected by chance alone. As can be seen in the final row in the table above, the overall combined hit rate for all of these studies, totaling 675 sessions, is 34 percent. It was these results that led statistician Jessica Utts at the University of California Davis to write:

> This is a robust effect that, were it not in such an unusual domain, would no longer be questioned by science as a real phenomenon. It is unlikely that methodological problems could account for the remarkable consistency of results.[128]

A New Challenge

The year 1999 was marked by a challenge to Honorton's claims of replication with the autoganzfeld. The challenge appeared in the form of a short article by psychologists Julie Milton and Richard Wiseman, in which they presented the results of thirty ganzfeld studies completed since 1987, the starting date chosen so that "the studies' designers would have had access to Hyman and Honorton's (1986) guidelines for ganzfeld research."[129] These thirty studies were retrieved from 14 papers written by 10 different principle authors from 7 laboratories, comprising altogether 1,198 sessions. No criteria were used to select the studies: The authors simply followed a policy "of including in our database all psi studies that used the ganzfeld technique."[130]

The combined hit rate for these thirty studies is 27.5%, just below the 95 per-

cent confidence intervals of the first two major studies. At the end of their brief article Milton and Wiseman concluded:

> The new ganzfeld studies show a near-zero effect size and a statis-
> tically nonsignificant overall cummulation…. This failure to replicate
> could indicate that the autoganzfeld's results were spurious…
> Alternatively, the differences in outcome between the autoganzfeld
> studies and the new database could have been due to the latter not
> being carried out under psi-conducive conditions.
>
> Whatever the reason, the autoganzfeld results have not been repli-
> cated by a "broader range of researchers." The ganzfeld paradigm
> cannot at present be seen as constituting strong evidence for psychic
> functioning.[131]

About one year later, Milton and Wiseman's meta-analysis was independently
repeated, but with the addition of 10 new ganzfeld studies that had since been performed. These ten new studies yielded an overall hit rate of 36.7%; when added to
the thirty ganzfeld experiments analyzed by Milton and Wiseman, the combined hit
rate for all forty studies was 30.1 percent. The results were again statistically significant, as Milton conceded, but somewhat below the 35 percent result in the original meta-analysis and the 34 percent result from the replications reported in 1995.

It later turned out that Milton and Wiseman had botched their statistical analysis of the ganzfeld experiments, by failing to consider sample size. Dean Radin simply added up the total number of hits and trials conducted in those thirty studies
(the standard method of doing meta-analysis)* and found a statistically significant
result with odds against chance of about 20 to 1.[132]

Not only that, but Milton and Wiseman did not include a large and highly successful study by Kathy Dalton[133] due to an arbitrary cut-off date, even though it was
published almost two years before Milton and Wiseman's paper; had been widely
discussed among parapsychologists; was part of a doctoral dissertation at Julie
Milton's university; and was presented at a conference *chaired by Wiseman* two years

---

* Skeptics sometimes point out that different meta-analyses of the Ganzfeld data produce different results,
  but this is incorrect. All Ganzfeld meta-analyses published to date that use the simple, correct method
  described above have reached the same conclusions.

The 30 studies that Milton and Wiseman considered ranged in size from 4 trials to 100, but they used a
statistical method that simply ignored sample size (N). For instance, say we have 3 studies, two with N
= 8, 2 hits (25%), and a third with $N = 60$, 21 hits (35%). If we ignore sample size, then the unweighted
average percentage of hits is only 28%; but the *combined* average of all the hits is just under 33%. This, in
simplest terms, is the mistake they made. Had they simply added up the hits and misses and then performed a simple one-tailed t-test, they would have found results significant at the 5% level. Had they performed the even more accurate binomial test, the results would have been significant at less than the 4%
level, with odds against chance of 26 to 1.

before Milton and Wiseman published their paper (Richard Wiseman is a well-known British skeptic, frequently appearing in the British media to "debunk" psychic research).

And there is yet another simple explanation for Milton and Wiseman's curious results. In their joint communiqué, Hyman and Honorton asked future ganzfeld investigators, as part of their "more stringent standards," to clearly document the status of the experiment: that is, whether it was meant to merely *confirm* previous findings or to *explore* novel conditions.[134] The problem with the Milton and Wiseman study was that it simply lumped all studies together, regardless of whether the status of each study was confirmatory or exploratory. In other words, Milton and Wiseman made no attempt to determine the degree to which the individual studies complied with the standard ganzfeld protocol as spelled out in the joint communiqué.

Milton and Wiseman's paper led to a vigorous online debate, culminating in a paper published in *The Journal of Parapsychology*, jointly written by a psychologist and two parapsychologists. After a brief summary of the debate so far, Bem, Palmer, and Broughton wrote:

> One of the observations made during the online debate was that several studies contributing negative z scores to the analysis [results were *less* than expected by chance] had used procedures that deviated markedly from the standard ganzfeld protocol. Such a development is neither bad nor unexpected. Many psi researchers believe that the reliability of the basic procedure is sufficiently well established to warrant using it as a tool for the further exploration of psi. Thus, rather than continuing to conduct exact replications, they have been modifying the procedure and extending it into unknown territory. Not unexpectedly, such deviations from exact replication are at increased risk for failure. For example, rather than using visual stimuli, Willin modified the ganzfeld procedure to test whether senders could communicate musical targets to receivers. They could not. When such studies are thrown into an undifferentiated meta-analysis, the overall effect size is thereby reduced, and perversely, the ganzfeld procedure becomes a victim of its own success.[135]

Bem, Palmer and Broughton set out to test their hypothesis that the decline in average scoring was due to the studies that were meant to be exploratory rather than confirmatory. Accordingly, three independent raters unfamiliar with the recent ganzfeld studies, and unaware of each study outcome, were asked to rate the degree to which each of the recent studies deviated from the standard ganzfeld protocol. The database was then re-examined to test the hypothesis that hit rates were positively correlated with the degree to which the experimental procedures adhered to the standard protocol.

The raters assigned a rank to each of the forty studies, and the ranks were then averaged for each study. The ranking ranged from "1" to "7", with a rank of "7" indicating the highest degree of adherence to standard protocol as described in two articles written by Honorton in the early 1990's.

Results

As hypothesized, hit rates were significantly correlated with the degree to which the experimental procedures adhered to the standard protocol. If we define as "standard" those studies that ranked above the mid-point of the scale (4), then the standard replications obtained an overall hit rate of 31.2 percent; the non-standard studies obtained a hit rate of only 24 percent. The results are even more dramatic if we consider only those replication studies ranked "6" and above: These 21 studies (more than half the sample) achieved an overall hit rate of 33 percent, almost identical to that of the earlier studies.

There is little point in continuing with more replication studies: Some of those with a prior commitment to contrary views may never change their publicly stated opinions, no matter how many replication studies are performed. Real progress can only be made if investigators are willing to explore new frontiers.

Results from the ganzfeld are summarized below. Table 3 should be compared with Table 2. Table 4 summarizes all reported ganzfeld experiments performed over nearly three decades.

Table 3: Standard Ganzfeld Replications 1996 on		
Laboratory	Sessions	Hit Rate
University of Amsterdam, Netherlands	64	30%
University of Edinburgh, Scotland*	128	47%
Institute for Parapsychology, NC	259	28%
University of Gothenburg, Sweden	150	35%
Totals	**601**	**34%**

artistically gifted sample

Table 4: All Ganzfeld Studies 1974—1999		
Source	Years	Hit Rate
Original 28 ganzfeld	1974—1981	35%
95% confidence interval		28% - 43%
11 autoganzfeld	1983—1989	34%
95% confidence interval		30% - 39%

Table 4: All Ganzfeld Studies 1974—1999 (*continued*)		
Source	Years	Hit Rate
Standard replications (rated 6+)	1991—1999	33%
Standard replications (rated > 4)	1991—1999	31%
Non-standard studies (rated < 4)	1991—1999	24%
All forty studies:	1991—1999	30.1%

These figures should make the conclusion clear: The earlier results have been replicated by a variety of researchers in different laboratories in different cultures, with similar hit rates. A few years ago Hyman wrote: "The case for psychic functioning seems better than it has ever been.... I also have to admit that I do not have a ready explanation for these observed effects."[136] Hyman and the other skeptics have lost the ganzfeld debate.

Some notes on effect size and sample size

As we have seen, researchers have isolated a few variables, such as artistic ability and the use of dynamic targets, which seem to enhance psi performance beyond what we may typically expect. But the overall hit rate so far seems fairly consistent at around 33 percent, when 25 percent is expected by chance. This corresponds with a hit about every third session, when chance would predict one out of every four.

This may not seem very impressive, but it may be instructive to compare these results with that of a major medical study that sought to determine whether aspirin can reduce the risk of a heart attack. The study was discontinued after six years, because it was already clear that taking aspirin reduced the risk, and it was considered unethical to keep this treatment away from the control group taking a placebo. The results of this study were publicized as a major medical breakthrough, but the size of the aspirin effect is quite small: Taking aspirin reduces the probability of a heart attack by only .8 percent. This is about ten times as small as the effect observed in the ganzfeld experiments.[137]

The fact that the size of the effect observed in the ganzfeld is usually not large enough to be observed without the aid of statistics partly explains why the controversy has continued as long as it has. When effect sizes are small, large samples are required to provide the statistical power necessary to detect the effect. The aspirin study mentioned above was performed with over 22,000 participants. If it had been conducted with only 2,200 participants, the results would not have attained statistical significance.

If the true hit rate in the ganzfeld were only 33 percent when 25 percent was expected by chance, then an experiment with 30 sessions (the average for the 28 studies in the 1985 meta-analysis) has only about one chance in six of finding an effect significant at the 5 percent level. With 50 sessions, the chance rises to about one in three. One has to increase the sample size to 100 sessions in order to reach the break-even point, at which there is a 50-50 chance of finding a significant effect.[138]

Some skeptics seem to have difficulty grasping the importance of sample size, or perhaps they simply choose to ignore it. Statistician Jessica Utts emphasizes this point: "When dealing with a small to medium effect, it takes hundreds or sometimes thousands of trials to establish 'statistical significance.' ...Despite Professor Hyman's continued protests about parapsychology lacking repeatability, I have never seen a skeptic attempt to perform an experiment with enough trials to even come close to ensuring success."[139]

8

The Research of the Skeptics

Charles Honorton, in his classic article "Rhetoric Over Substance," noted an important difference between the psi controversy and more conventional scientific disputes. Controversies in science normally occur between groups of *researchers* who formulate hypotheses, design experiments, and then collect data in order to test their hypotheses. But as Honorton wrote, "In contrast, the psi controversy is largely characterized by disputes between a group of researchers, the parapsychologists, and a group of critics who do not do experimental research to test psi claims or the viability of their counterhypotheses."[140]

This lack of research may surprise anyone whose main source of information has been the skeptical literature. For instance, in 1983 the well-known skeptic Martin Gardner wrote:

> How can the public know that for fifty years skeptical psychologists
> have been trying their best to replicate classic psi experiments, and
> with notable unsuccess? It is this fact more than any other that has led
> to parapsychology's perpetual stagnation. Positive evidence keeps
> coming from a tiny group of enthusiasts, while negative evidence
> keeps coming from a much larger group of skeptics.[141]

But as Honorton pointed out, "Gardner does not attempt to document this assertion, nor could he. It is pure fiction. Look for the skeptics' experiments and see what you find."

For the most part, skeptics have simply criticized from the sidelines, and have produced no experimental research of their own.

The Research of Susan Blackmore
One notable exception to this rule has been British psychologist Susan Blackmore. She began working on a PhD in parapsychology in the 1970's, but has repeatedly claimed that she has failed to find any evidence for the existence of psi. For instance,

she wrote in 1996: "When I decided to become a parapsychologist I had no idea it would mean 20 years of failing to find the paranormal."[142] Blackmore has made a career for herself as one of the world's most well-known skeptics of psi, and in 1988 was elected a Fellow of CSICOP.[143]

In a number of publications, Blackmore claims to have become increasingly skeptical of the existence of psi phenomena after "ten years of intensive research in parapsychology."[144] These claims led parapsychologist Rick Berger to critically examine the Blackmore experiments in great detail, and he found that "The claim of 'ten years of psi research' actually represents a series of hastily constructed, executed, and reported studies that were primarily conducted during a 2-year period."[145] These consisted of a set of experiments conducted between October 1976 and December 1978 for her PhD dissertation.

Blackmore reported 29 experiments completed over this two-year period, of which 21 were eventually published as separate experiments in five parapsychology journal papers. Seven of these experiments produced statistically significant results. Although these experiments form the basis of Blackmore's claim of "failing to find the paranormal", the odds against 7 successes out of 21 attempts happening by chance are over 20,000 to one!

So, how does Blackmore reconcile the fact of 7 successful experiments out of 21 total experiments with her often-repeated claim that her own research led her to become a skeptic? Simple: As Berger pointed out, Blackmore applied a double-standard to her experiments. When her experiments seemed to show evidence of psi, the results were dismissed as due to flaws in the experiment. But when the results did not seem to show evidence of psi, she simply ignored the quality of the study.

There are many design flaws that can lead to false positive results, but there are also many that can lead to false negatives, such as inadequate sample size (low statistical power), inappropriate sampling and so forth. Berger writes "Blackmore's database is replete with examples of such flaws,"[146] and continues:

> Some skeptics, including Blackmore, argue that differing standards of experimental design can be held depending on study outcome: Significant positive outcomes must have tighter designs than the same study with a negative outcome. This post hoc determination of experimental criticism leads to the paradox exemplified by the Blackmore work: Had such work produced consistently positive outcomes, the results could all be dismissed as having arisen from design flaws… Negative conclusions based on flawed experiments must not be given *more* weight than positive conclusions based on the same flawed experiments.[147]

In other words, our decision to invoke study flaws to dismiss the results of an experiment should not be influenced by our preconceptions of what the result "should have been." But this seems to have been exactly what Blackmore has done in order to justify her beliefs, as evidenced in the following remark of hers:

> Well, if you don't find evidence of ESP, what can you say? Only that you have failed to find something which, according to science, shouldn't have been there in the first place![148]

As we shall see, this appeal to "science" as a monolithic body of conclusions that tell you in advance how experiments should turn out is a rhetorical tactic often used by Blackmore. Berger finally concluded:

> Blackmore's claims that her database shows no evidence of psi are unfounded, because the vast majority of her studies were carelessly designed, executed, and reported, and in Blackmore's own assessment, individually flawed. As such, no conclusions should be drawn from this database…. Blackmore is extremely vocal in decrying psi research in her writings, on television and radio, and before the skeptical advocacy group CSICOP (the Committee for Scientific Investigation of Claims of the Paranormal), citing her own work as the basis for her strong convictions.[149] …[She] has achieved a notable position in the skeptical community based on her conversion from believer to skeptic during her "ten years of negative research." Her insistence to the contrary notwithstanding, I believe that my review of her psi research has achieved a constructive end by showing that her conversion from parapsychologist to CSICOP Fellow had no scientific basis in her own experimental work.[150]

The same journal issue also includes a response by Blackmore to Berger's critique, in which Blackmore conceded, "I agree that one cannot draw conclusions about the reality of psi based on these experiments."[151] Near the end of his critique, Berger had written "During my aborted meta-analysis of Blackmore's published work, I was struck by patterns in the data suggestive of the operation of psi…. Without a serious meta-analysis of the original unpublished source material, complete with weighting for flaws,…the issue of whether the Blackmore experiments show evidence *for* psi cannot be resolved."[152] Presumably eager to nip this embarrassment in the bud, Blackmore hastened to add: "I am glad to be able to agree with his final conclusion—'that drawing *any* conclusion, positive or negative, about the reality of psi that are based on the Blackmore psi experiments must be considered unwarranted.'"[153]

It is interesting to examine Blackmore's writings before and after Berger's critique. Two years earlier, in an article for the *Skeptical Inquirer* entitled "The Elusive Open Mind: Ten Years of Negative Research in Parapsychology," she wrote:

How could I weigh my own results against the results of other people, bearing in mind that mine tended to be negative ones while everyone else's tended to be positive ones? I had to find some kind of balance here. At one extreme I could not just believe my own results and ignore everyone else's.... At the other extreme I could not believe everyone else's results and ignore my own. That would be even more pointless. There would have been no point in *all those years of experiments* if I didn't take my own results seriously." [154] [emphasis added]

In another article written at about the same time she wrote:

The other major challenge to the skeptic's position is, of course, the fact that opposing positive evidence exists in the parapsychological literature. I couldn't dismiss it all. This raises an interesting question: just how much weight can you or should you give the results of your own experiments over those of other people? On the one hand, your own should carry more weight, since you know exactly how they were done... On the other hand, science is necessarily a collective enterprise.... So I couldn't use my own failures as justifiable evidence that psi does not exist. I had to consider everyone else's success.

I asked myself a thousand times, as I ask the reader now: is there a right conclusion?

The only answer I can give, after ten years of intensive research in parapsychology, is that I don't know. [155]

After Berger's critique, Blackmore was willing to concede in an academic journal that "I agree that one cannot draw conclusions about the reality of psi based on these experiments." But her writings in the popular press have not reflected this admission. Commenting on the ganzfeld experiments in a newspaper article in 1996, she wrote:

My own conclusion is biased by my own personal experience. I tried my first *ganzfeld* experiment in 1978, when the procedure was new.... Of course the new autoganzfeld results are even better. Why should I doubt them because of events in the past? The problem is that my personal experience conflicts with the successes I read about in the literature and I cannot ignore either side. The only honest reaction is to say "I don't know". [156] *

---

* In her autobiography, in a chapter titled "I Don't Know", she writes "I don't know, I don't know, *I don't know!*"

Wouldn't a more honest reaction be for Blackmore to admit in the popular press that "one cannot draw conclusions about the reality of psi" based on her own experiments, and that a scientific opinion should be based only upon a critical evaluation of *other* peoples' published works?

But perhaps this is asking too much. After all, Blackmore pursued a PhD in parapsychology in order to become a "famous parapsychologist".[157] Having failed to produce research supporting the psi hypothesis, she evidently decided to try to make a name for herself by *attacking* the psi hypothesis, which must at the time have seemed to be an easy target. Apparently, though, in a recent article she claims to have given up. "At last, I've done it. I've thrown in the towel," she wrote.

> Come to think of it, I feel slightly sad. It was just over thirty years ago that I had the dramatic out-of-body experience that convinced me of the reality of psychic phenomena... *Just a few years of careful experiments changed all that.* I found no psychic phenomena... I became a sceptic. [emphasis added]
>
> So why didn't I give up then? There are lots of bad reasons. Admitting you are wrong is always hard, even though it's a skill every scientist needs to learn. And starting again as a baby in a new field is a daunting prospect. So is losing all the status and power of being an expert. I have to confess I enjoyed my hard-won knowledge.
>
> ...None of it ever gets anywhere. That's a good enough reason for leaving.
>
> But perhaps the real reason is that I am just too tired—and tired above all of working to maintain an open mind. I couldn't dismiss all those extraordinary claims out of hand. After all, they just might be true, and if they were then swathes of science would have to be rewritten.[158]

The Research of Richard Wiseman

Another British psychologist, Richard Wiseman, now carries on where Blackmore has left off. Wiseman is very well funded by a variety of skeptical organizations, including CSICOP, and frequently appears in the British media to criticize, condemn, and generally debunk psi research. Wiseman was briefly mentioned earlier, as one of the authors of the report that used botched statistics and flawed methodology in an attempt to refute the results from the Ganzfeld experiments.

Like Blackmore, Wiseman is unusual among skeptics in the sense that he sometimes actually does experiments, instead of merely criticizing from the sidelines. And like Blackmore, Wiseman has been very vocal with claims that he has never found any evidence of psi. Let us now examine some of Wiseman's research, which has frequently been reported in the British press.

One of Wiseman's most highly publicized experiments concerned a dog named Jaytee. His owner, Pamela Smart, claimed that the dog could anticipate her arrival home, even when she arrived home at unpredictable times. Pamela adopted Jaytee, a mixed-breed terrier, when he was only a few weeks old, and Jaytee became very attached to her. When Pam was working as a secretary in Manchester, England, she would leave Jaytee with her parents, who were retired and lived in a flat next door. Her parents noticed that, on most weekdays around 4:30 p.m., Jaytee would wait by the French window when Pam was on her way home. Since Pam worked routine hours, her parents assumed that the dog's behavior was based upon some sense of time.

Pam was laid off in 1993, and for a while no longer kept regular hours. However, her parents noticed that Jaytee still seemed to anticipate Pam's return, even when Pam returned at completely unpredictable times. It seemed as though Jaytee would begin waiting by the window at about the time she set off on her homeward journey.

In April 1994 Pam read an article in the *Sunday Telegraph* about research into animals that seem to know when their owners were coming home, being undertaken by biologist Rupert Sheldrake, whom we met earlier. She contacted Sheldrake and volunteered to take part in his research. The first stage of the research required Pam's parents to keep a log of the dog's behavior when Pam was out. Between May 1994 and February 1995, they made notes of Jaytee's reactions on 100 occasions that Pam was out, and Pam also recorded where she went, how long she was out, how far she traveled, how she returned, and when she set off to come home. On 85 of these 100 occasions, the log indicated that Jaytee began to wait at the French window before Pam returned, usually ten minutes or more in advance.

When Sheldrake analyzed the data statistically, he found that Jaytee's reactions were very significantly related to the time that Pam set off for home. It also did not seem to matter how far away Pam was, or what vehicle—her own car, bicycle, or taxi—she used to return.

However, on 15 out of 100 occasions Jaytee did *not* react. On some of these occasions the researchers could find an obvious explanation: Jaytee was ill, or there was a bitch in heat in a neighbor's flat. But on three of these occasions there was no obvious explanation. So, Jaytee did not always react as Pam set off home, and he could be distracted.

By this stage Sheldrake decided that it was important to start taping Jaytee's behavior, so that more precise and objective records could be kept. And just at this point, Sheldrake was approached by the Science Unit of the Austrian State Television (ORF), who expressed interest in filming an experiment with Jaytee. An experiment was designed in which one film crew would continuously film Jaytee in Pam's parent's flat, while the other would follow Pam as she went out and about.

The experiment took place in November, 1994. Pam was sent out on an excursion, and neither she nor her parents knew the randomly selected time she would be asked to return. Three hours and fifty minutes later, she was asked to return home. When the experiment was broadcast, the screen was split in two, showing Pam on one side and Jaytee on the other, in perfect time synchronization. Before Pam is asked to return, Jaytee spends most of his time lying at the feet of Mrs. Smart. Almost immediately after Pam is told it is time to go home, Jaytee shows signs of alertness, pricking up his ears. Eleven seconds after Pam is told to return, as she is walking to the taxi stand, Jaytee goes to the window and stays there until Pam returns, 10 minutes later.

There seems to be no way that Jaytee could have known by normal sensory means that Pam was returning. Since Jaytee responded before Pam actually climbed into the taxi, he seemed to have responded to Pam's intentions. In other words, Jaytee's response appears to be telepathic.

After receiving a grant from the Lifebridge Foundation of New York, Sheldrake began his own videotaped experiments with Jaytee in May 1995. Between May 1995 and July 1996, thirty videotapes were made of Jaytee's behavior under natural conditions while Pam was out and about. Pam's parents were not told when she would be returning, and Pam usually was not sure herself. The results showed that Jaytee waited at the window far more when Pam was on her way home than when she was not, and this difference was highly statistically significant ($p < .000001$).

The researchers discovered early that Jaytee responded even when Pam set off at randomly selected times. This was an important discovery, as it seemed to clearly rule out an explanation based upon routine, or expectations based upon the behavior of her parents. Consequently, twelve more experiments were videotaped in which Pam returned home at random times, determined by the throw of dice after she had left her home.

The chart below shows the results of these twelve videotaped experiments:

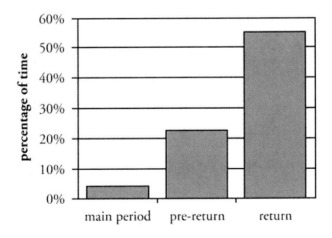

Figure 8.1: Sheldrake's results, random returns home

The chart clearly shows that Jaytee was at the window far more when Pam was on her way home than during the main period of her absence (55% versus 4%). The difference is highly statistically significant, with a p-value of .0001, implying odds against chance of over 10,000 to one.

The general pattern of Jaytee's response can be seen more clearly in the following three graphs, which summarize the average results from long, medium, and short absences. The horizontal axis shows the series of ten minute periods (p1, p2, etc.) from the time she went out until she was on her way home. The last period shows the first 10 minutes of Pam's return journey. The graphs clearly show that Jaytee spent more time at the window during Pam's return journey, and also that he usually started waiting at the window shortly before she set off, as she was thinking of returning.

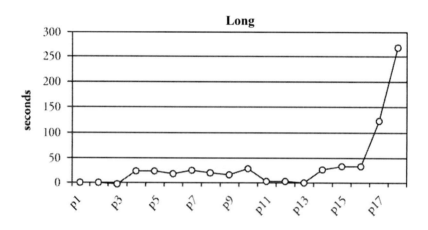

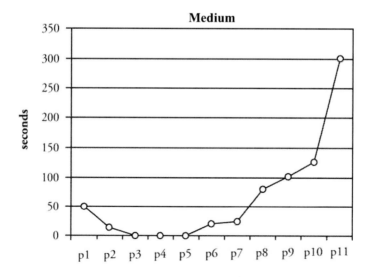

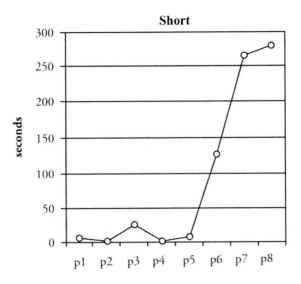

Figure 8.2:
Time courses of Jaytee's visit to the window during long, medium, and short absences.
The graphs represent the averages of eleven long, seven medium, and six short
experiments. Source: Sheldrake, 1999, p. 61.

Following the televised experiment carried out by ORF, a number of reports about this research appeared in British and European television and newspapers. Journalists sought out a skeptic to comment on the results, and the obvious choice for many was Richard Wiseman. He suggested a number of possible explanations, such as routine times of return and selective memory, that Sheldrake had already tested and eliminated. However, rather than debate the issue, Sheldrake simply invited Wiseman to perform some tests of his own. Pam and her family kindly agreed to help him.

In his four experiments, Wiseman himself videotaped Jaytee, while his assistant, Mathew Smith, went out with Pam and videotaped her. They went out to pubs or other places five to eleven miles away, and returned at times selected randomly by Smith once they were out. Smith himself knew in advance when they would be returning, but did not tell Pam until it was time to go. Wiseman, back in the apartment, did not know when they would be returning. Furthermore, Pam and Smith traveled by taxi or by Smith's car, in order to eliminate the possibility that Jaytee was listening for the sound of a familiar vehicle. Three of Wiseman's experiments with Jaytee were performed in the flat of Pam's parents, similar to the experiments Sheldrake had conducted. The fourth experiment was performed in the flat of Pam's sister, but Jaytee fell ill during the experiment.

The results from Wiseman's three experiments in Pam's parents' flat are shown below:

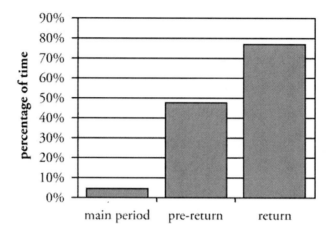

Figure 8.3: Wiseman's results

As in Sheldrake's experiments, Jaytee was at the window much more when Pam was on her way home than during the main period of her absence (78% versus 4%). With only three experiments, the sample size was small, but the results were still statistically significant, with a p-value of .03. In other words, Wiseman had replicated Sheldrake's results.

However, much to Sheldrake's astonishment, in the summer of 1996 Wiseman went to a series of conferences announcing that he had refuted the "psychic pet" phenomenon, and later appeared on a series of television shows claiming to have refuted Jaytee's abilities. How did he justify his conclusions?

Simple: Wiseman used an arbitrary criterion for success in the experiment, a criterion that enabled him to ignore most of the data he gathered. If Jaytee went to the window "for no apparent reason" at any time during the experiment, Wiseman simply ignored all the rest of the data and declared the experiment a failure. These "failures" occurred during the four percent of the time Jaytee was at the window when Pam was absent. After these "failures", the rest of the data was ignored, even though Jaytee was at the window 78% of the time when Pam was on her way home.

Sheldrake met with Wiseman in September 1996 and pointed out to Wiseman that his data showed the same pattern as the data Sheldrake had gathered. Sheldrake made it clear that far from refuting Sheldrake' results, Wiseman's own data replicated them. He even gave Wiseman copies of graphs showing Wiseman the data from his own experiments. Here, for instance, are the graphs from the three experiments that Wiseman did with Jaytee in Pam's parents' apartment.

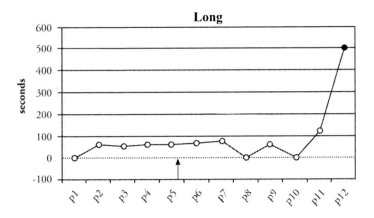

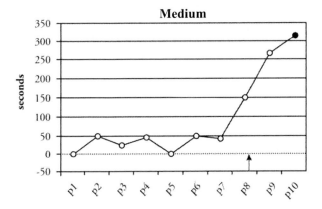

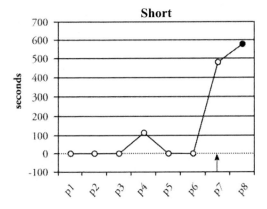

Figure 8.4:
Wiseman's results, 3 experiments in Pam's flat. The periods after which Wiseman
ignored the data are indicated by arrows. The final points on each graph represent the
first 10 minutes of Pam's return journey, indicated by a filled circle.

By Wiseman's standards, only the fourth experiment—the one performed in Pam's sister's apartment—was a partial success, because only in this trial did Jaytee go to the window "for no apparent reason" for the first time during the period Pam was on her way home. (The videotape record showed that his visit to the window coincided *exactly* with Pam setting off on her way home). However, Wiseman did not consider the fourth trial a success, because Jaytee did not stay there for at least two minutes, but instead left the window and vomited.

Over the next two years, Wiseman repeatedly announced through the media that he had discredited the dog's ability to anticipate his owner's return. For instance, on a British television program called *Strange But True*, he said of Jaytee: "In one out of four experiments he responded at the correct time—not a very impressive hit rate, and it could just be a coincidence."[159] The three "misses" are the experiments summarized in Figure 8.4.

Wiseman dismissed Sheldrake's graphical analysis of his data, calling it "post hoc" (Latin for "after this"), implying that it is somehow unscientific to graphically analyze data someone else has collected. However, it is important to remember that Sheldrake applied exactly the same graphical analysis to his own data two months *before* Wiseman arrived on the scene and for two years afterward.

As mentioned, Wiseman used an arbitrary criterion for success in the experiment, a criterion that enabled him to ignore most of the data he gathered. An analogy would be if Wiseman set out to test the claim that smokers have a greater risk of developing lung cancer; set the criterion that smokers must show a greater frequency of developing lung cancer within two years of starting to smoke; used this criterion to ignore all the rest of the data, and then announced to the press that his experiment shows that smokers do *not* have a greater risk of developing lung cancer.

During the controversy that followed, Susan Blackmore came to Wiseman's aid in a newspaper article, claiming that there was a fatal flaw in Sheldrake's experiment.

> Sheldrake did 12 experiments in which he beeped Pam at random times to tell her to return. Now surely Jaytee could not be using normal powers, could he? No. But there is another simple problem. When Pam first leaves, Jaytee settles down and does not bother to go to the window. The longer she is away, the more often he goes to look.[160]

Blackmore's point is simply that Jaytee spends more and more time by the window the longer Pam is out, and so of course he spends more time by the window as Pam is on her way home, but not because of any telepathic ability. But anyone who looks at the actual data can easily see that Blackmore's remark is simply not true. For instance, in Figure 3, we can see that, during the short absences, Jaytee spends the most time by the window when Pam is on her way home, but there is no comparable increase in time spent at the window in this same period during the medium and long absences. Likewise, the spike in time Jaytee spends by the window when Pam is on her way home during the medium absences does not show up in period 11 of the long absences.

Sheldrake also made a series of videotapes on evenings when Pam was not coming home until very late, or staying out all night. These tapes serve as controls, and they show that Jaytee did not go to the window more and more the longer Pam is away.

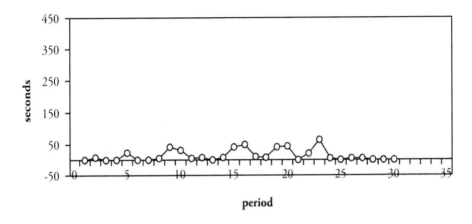

Figure 8.5:
Time spent by Jaytee at the window on evenings when Pam was not coming home during the experiment, in 10-minute periods. Averages from ten evenings.

Once again, a close examination of the evidence shows the need to treat the claims of the skeptics with skepticism.

In public lectures and on TV shows, Wiseman claimed over and over again that he had refuted Jaytee's abilities. As recently as April 2004, he was still making this claim on his website.[161] However, as Sheldrake notes, "His presentations are deliberately misleading."

> He makes no mention of the fact that Jaytee waits by the window far more when Pam is on her way home, nor does he refer to my own experiments. He gives the impression that my evidence is based on one experiment filmed by a TV company, rather than on more than two hundred experiments, and he implies that he has done the only rigorous scientific tests of this dog's abilities. I confess that I am amazed by his persistence in this deception.[162]

Despite the fact that his criticism of the ganzfeld has been shown to be clearly flawed, and despite the fact that his own experiments with Jaytee clearly replicated

Sheldrake's results, Wiseman still cheerfully tells the media that he has "never come across a paranormal experiment that can be replicated."[163]

James Randi

At least Blackmore is willing to admit that results from the best experiments leave her stumped. But another well-known critic simply ignores the ganzfeld; indeed, his work is so irrelevant to serious psi research that for the most part parapsychologists simply ignore it. In his classic article on skepticism, Honorton devotes only one paragraph to him:

> Randi's contribution is pure polemic and fails to deal in any substantive way with the scientific issues underlying the psi controversy. His disparaging comments about meta-analysis suggest that he does not understand meta-analysis and is unaware of its widespread use in medicine and the behavioral sciences. Randi's skill as a magician is well-known; but despite well-publicized claims to methodological expertise, his ability to design scientifically adequate psi experiments is not at all apparent from an examination of his public efforts. Serious methodological weaknesses and statistical errors occur, for example, in his book on testing ESP and in his televised tests of psychics.[164]

Here is Randi's opinion of academic freedom, taken from his book *Flim Flam! Psychics, ESP, Unicorns, and Other Delusions*.

> The public has been badly served by scientists who lean upon their considerable reputations in other fields to give weight to their declarations on the subject of parapsychology. I have noted that possession of a driver's license permits one to drive an automobile only if the privilege is not abused; perhaps Ph.D.s should similarly be withdrawable in science.[165]

Randi (a non-scientist) obviously thinks that any scientist that disagrees with CSICOP's narrow brand of scientific fundamentalism should be excommunicated for the crime of heresy. One such scientist would surely be Rupert Sheldrake, who earned his Ph.D. in biochemistry at Cambridge University. Here is Sheldrake's account of his experiences with Randi:

> The January 2000 issue of *Dog World* magazine included an article on a possible sixth sense in dogs, which discussed some of my research. In this article Randi was quoted as saying that in relation to canine ESP, 'We at the JREF [James Randi Educational Foundation] have tested these

claims. They fail.' No details were given of these tests. I emailed James Randi to ask for details of this JREF research. He did not reply. He ignored a second request for information too.

I then asked members of the JREF Scientific Advisory Board to help me find out more about this claim. They did indeed help by advising Randi to reply. In an email sent on February 6, 2000 he told me that the tests he referred to were not done at the JREF, but took place 'years ago' and were 'informal'. They involved two dogs belonging to a friend of his that he observed over a two-week period. All records had been lost. He wrote: 'I overstated my case for doubting the reality of dog ESP based on the small amount of data I obtained. It was rash and improper of me to do so.'

Randi also claimed to have debunked one of my experiments with the dog Jaytee, a part of which was shown on television. Jaytee went to the window to wait for his owner when she set off to come home, but did not do so before she set off. In *Dog World*, Randi stated: "Viewing the entire tape, we see that the dog responded to every car that drove by, and to every person who walked by." This is simply not true, and Randi now admits that he has never seen the tape.[166]

Randi often publicizes his "challenge" to psychics, in which he offers to pay $1 million for any convincing demonstration of psychic ability under controlled conditions. The problem with this test is that Randi himself acts as policeman, judge, and jury. Given his countless disparaging and insulting remarks concerning parapsychology, and his financial stake in the debunking movement, he can hardly be considered an unbiased observer. It is also Randi who decides who will be tested, and he has explicitly refused to test at least one challenger: Homeopath John Benneth. Randi also backed down from a challenge issued by Dr. Jule Eisenbud, who wagered $10,000 that Randi could not duplicate the "thought photography" of Ted Serios, even with the aid of a prop in which a gimmick could be housed.[167] More typically, Randi simply ignores challenges, such as the challenge to test English psychic Chris Robinson live on television.

Occasionally, Randi will appear to agree to a serious test. Dick Bierman, a psychologist at the University of Amsterdam with a PhD in experimental physics, has published extensively in the fields of experimental physics, psychology, and parapsychology for over a quarter of a century. Bierman took up Randi's challenge with an offer for an experiment testing a form of precognition known as presentiment, to which Randi responded:

Dr. Bierman:

I've received and read your response. Thank you. I've turned this over to my colleague, Andrew Harter, for first viewing, and it will eventually go to several other persons who will give me their learned opinions. That should not take very long. ...I will stay in touch with you as we consider your proposal.

Sincerely, James Randi

Bierman described what happened next:

Basically this was followed by a few other irrelevant mails between me and Randi and then I never heard anything on my proposal again.[168]

Randi also insists on a "preliminary test" before the real test, and has never let anyone past the preliminary stage. Randi's "challenge" is really nothing but a publicity gimmick.

With regard to his "challenge" Randi has been quoted as saying, "I *always* have an out."[169] However, because of his many outrageous remarks, Randi has been the target of several expensive lawsuits, and in May 1991 Randi resigned from CSICOP in order to prevent it being named as a defendant in subsequent suits.

This concludes our review of the experimental evidence. So where are we now? Former member of CSICOP Marcello Truzzi summed up the history of laboratory parapsychology:

As proponents of anomalies produce stronger evidence, critics have sometimes moved the goal posts further away.... To convince scientists of what had been merely been supported by widespread but weak anecdotal evidence, parapsychologists moved psychical research into the laboratory. When experimental results were presented, designs were criticized. When protocols were improved, a "fraud proof" or "critical experiment" was demanded. When those were put forward, replications were demanded. When those were produced, critics argued that new forms of error might be the cause (such as the "file drawer" error that could result from unpublished negative studies). When meta-analyses were presented to counter that issue, these were discounted as controversial, and ESP was reduced to being some present but unspecified "error some place" in the form of what Ray Hyman called the "dirty test tube argument" (claiming dirt was in the tube making the seeming psi result a mere artifact). And in one instance, when the scoffer found no counter-explanations, he described the result as a "mere anomaly" not to be taken seriously so just belonging on a puzzle page. The goal posts have now been moved into a zone where some critics hold unfalsifiable positions.[170]

Susan Blackmore seems to have retreated into this zone, at least as recently as 1995:

> I am skeptical because believing in psi does not get me anywhere....
> I am not waiting for even stronger evidence that psi exists. I am waiting for the psi hypothesis to reach the point at which it does more scientific work than rejecting it. I do not think that point has been reached, and accordingly I am happy to call myself a skeptic about psi.[171]

In other words, Blackmore can continue to call herself a skeptic regardless of what evidence the researchers present, because in response she can always claim that "believing in psi does not get me anywhere." This trivialization of the reality of psi is startling, coming as it is from someone who claims to have spent the last 30 years searching for hard evidence of psi. It will seem even more startling when we see later that the reality of psi has implications for everything from physics to philosophy.

CONCLUDING REMARKS

This is not the first time in history that psychic researchers finally seemed to have established a solid case for the reality of psi. Back in 1955 Dr. George Price, then a research associate at the Department of Medicine at the University of Minnesota, published an article in the prestigious journal *Science* that began:

> Believers in psychic phenomena...appear to have won a decisive victory and virtually silenced opposition.... This victory is the result of careful experimentation and intelligent argumentation. Dozens of experimenters have obtained positive results in ESP experiments, and the mathematical procedures have been approved by leading statisticians.... Against all this evidence, almost the only defense remaining to the skeptical scientist is ignorance.

But Price then argued "ESP is incompatible with current scientific theory" and asked:

> If, then, parapsychology and modern science are incompatible, why not reject parapsychology? ...The choice is between believing in something "truly revolutionary" and "radically contradictory to contemporary

thought" and believing in the occurrence of fraud and self-delusion. Which is more reasonable?

More than forty years later, arch-skeptic Ray Hyman has run out of plausible counter-explanations for the results of the latest sets of now-automated experiments, yet he remains undiscouraged. Commenting on the report "An Assessment of the Evidence" by statistician Jessica Utts, he writes:

> If Utts's conclusion is correct, then the fundamental principles that have so successfully guided the progress of science from the days of Galileo and Newton to the present must be drastically revised. Neither relativity theory nor quantum mechanics in their present versions can cope with a world that harbors the psychic phenomena so boldly proclaimed by Utts and her parapsychological colleagues.[172]

In the next section of the book we deal with this, the most fundamental of all the skeptical objections.

Part II
Would the Existence of Psi Contradict Established Science?

Say this about assertions that aliens have been, are or will soon be landing on Earth: at least a scenario like that of "Independence Day" would not violate any laws of nature. In contrast, claims in other fringe realms, such as telepathy and psychokinesis, are credible only if you ignore a couple or three centuries of established science.
Sharon Begely
"Science on the Fringe",
Newsweek, July 1996

Psychologists, much more than physicists and biologists, are apt to cherish the delusion that science has reached the point where it can perfectly delimit between the possible and the impossible, that its principles and final concepts have been perfectly and fully ascertained. Science has been in our own time a changing panorama, continually enlarging the circle to introduce facts formerly regarded impossible, tearing down old and erecting new theories and altering some of its very foundation principles.
Walter Franklin Prince
Is Psychic Research Worth While?,
1927

Scientism is a psychological process of taking the currently accepted scientific theories about how the universe functions and subtly starting to regard them as if they were the absolute truth, beyond any further serious questioning. A theory, always subject to further test and refinement, becomes a law. Thus the process of science becomes an "ism," becomes a psychological stopping point, becomes a dogmatic belief system, like many of our most dogmatic religions.
Charles Tart
Forward to *Mindsight*,
1999

9

The Roots of Disbelief

Remarks such as the one from Sharon Begely's article are common in the skeptical literature. Such remarks are based on the assumption that the existence of psi phenomena is somehow incompatible with fundamental, well-established scientific principles. So, no matter what evidence the parapsychologists produce, the skeptics stoically maintain their denial and doggedly search for *any* possible counter-explanation. As we have seen, Ray Hyman has simply run out of plausible counter-explanations, yet he refuses to accept the latest results from a long line of experiments as conclusive. He seemed to consider himself the spokesperson for mainstream scientists when he wrote recently in the *Skeptical Inquirer*: "What seems clear is that the scientific community is not going to abandon its fundamental ideas about causality, time and other principles on the basis of a handful of experiments* whose findings have yet to be shown to be replicable and lawful."[173] Although surveys consistently show that most people either accept the reality of ESP or have had psychic experiences themselves, remarks such as this in the skeptical literature can give one the impression that all such phenomena are "scientifically impossible."

But many mainstream scientists do not hold this opinion. Two surveys of over 500 scientists in one case and over 1,000 in another were made in the 1970's. Both surveys found that the majority of respondents considered ESP "an established fact" or "a likely possibility": 56% in one and 67% in the other.[174] Yet if most scientists are open to the possibility of psi, how can we account for the following story?

> Robert Jahn was dean of the School of Engineering and Applied Science
> at Princeton University and a noted authority on aerospace engineering
> with a long record of work for NASA and the Department of Defense
> when he decided that certain parapsychological problems were worth
> investigating. Did his colleagues applaud his pioneering spirit? Not

---

* At the time Hyman wrote this article (1996) the "handful of experiments" included 61 independent Ganzfeld experiments, 2,094 PK experiments using random event generators, and hundreds of other experiments involving tossing dice, dream research, and remote viewing.

exactly. They as much as said he was crazy and a disgrace to science and the university. The university even convened an ad hoc committee to oversee his research—something unheard of for a scientist of his stature.[175]

And yet not all scientists reacted this way, as Jahn pointed out in a 1983 address to the Parapsychological Association. Referring to his Princeton Engineering Anomalies Research program, he said, "We have had commentary on our program from no less than six Nobel laureates, two of whom categorically reject the topic, two of whom encouraged us to push on, and two of whom were categorically evasive. So much for unanimity of high scientific opinion." [176]

However, despite the willingness of many scientists to express favorable opinions toward psi research, parapsychology courses are *not* routinely taught at universities; there are only two labs conducting full-time psi research in the United States, and only a handful of such labs in the entire world. One explanation for this (and for Robert Jahn's experience) is that skeptical opinions of psi seem more common among the administrative elite than among ordinary working scientists. Sociologist Dr. James McClenon surveyed the council and selected section committees of the American Association for the Advancement of Science (AAAS) in 1981.[177] He found that these scientists were more skeptical of ESP than scientists in general, with just under 30 percent believing that ESP was "an established fact" or "a likely possibility." Surveyed members in the social sciences (where parapsychology courses would normally be categorized) were even more skeptical (20 percent believers) than those in the natural sciences (30 percent believers). Worried about the reputations of their schools and labs, administrators seem far more reluctant to express favorable opinions of psi research than ordinary working scientists.

The skepticism of those who run the scientific establishment is surely one reason why, throughout its history, the resources devoted to psi research have been extremely meager. Psychologist Sybo Schouten compared the funding directed toward parapsychology over the one hundred years spanning 1882 to 1982 and found that it was approximately equal to the expenditures of *two months* of conventional psychological research in the United States in 1983.[178] The other reason funding is difficult to come by is that many private and public funding agencies have no wish to be associated with what the skeptics call "pseudo-science." Is it any wonder they feel this way? Not when scientific journals continue to publish hostile attacks on the scientific validity of parapsychology. For instance, the prominent journal *Nature* published the following in a commentary by skeptical psychologist David Marks:

Parascience has all the qualities of a magical system while wearing the mantle of science. Until any significant discoveries are made, science can justifiably ignore it, but it is important to say why: parascience is a pseudo-scientific system of untested beliefs steeped in illusion, error, and fraud.[179]

Clearly then, many scientists find the claims of parapsychology disturbing. The existence of psi implies that the minds of people can sometimes communicate, perceive events, and influence objects without the use of the five ordinary senses or their limbs. Science in its present state cannot explain these phenomena. This in itself should not be a problem: There are plenty of other phenomena that science cannot currently explain, such as consciousness, the placebo effect, and the fact that the expansion of the universe appears to be accelerating. But is the existence of psi in *conflict* with well-established scientific principles?

EINSTEIN'S OPINION

In 1946 parapsychologist Dr. Jan Ehrenwald sent Albert Einstein a copy of a book he had recently written called *Telepathy and Medical Psychology*, asking Einstein if he would read it and perhaps write an introduction. This was his response:

8 July 1946

Dear Mr. Ehrenwald:

I have read your book with great interest. It doubtlessly represents a good way of placing your topic in a contemporary context, and I have no doubt that it will reach a wide circle of readers. I can judge it merely as a layman, and cannot say that I have arrived at either an affirmative or negative conclusion. It seems to me, at any rate, that we have no right, from a physical standpoint, to deny a priori the possibility of telepathy. For that sort of denial the foundations of our science are too unsure and too incomplete.

My impressions concerning the quantitative approach to experiments with cards, and so on, is the following. On the one hand, I have no objection to the method's reliability. But I find it suspicious that "clairvoyance" [tests] yield the same probabilities as "telepathy," and that the distance of the subject from the cards or from the "sender" has no influence on the result. This is, a priori, improbable to the highest degree, consequently the result is doubtful.

Most interesting, and actually of greater interest to me, are the experiments with the mentally retarded nine-year old girl and the tests by Gilbert Murray. The drawing results seem to me to have more weight than the large scale statistical experiments where the discovery of a small methodological error may upset everything.

I find important your observations that a patient's productivity in psychoanalytic treatment is clearly influenced by the analyst's "school." This portion of your book alone is worth careful attention. I cannot fail to note that some of the experiences you mention arouse the reader's suspicion that unconscious influences along sensory channels, rather than telepathic influences, may be at work.

At any rate, your book has been very stimulating for me, and it has somewhat softened my originally quite negative attitude toward the whole of this complex of questions. One should not walk through the world wearing blinders.

I cannot write an introduction, as I am quite incompetent to do so. It should be provided by an experienced psychologist. You may show this letter privately to others.

Respectfully yours,
(signed) A. Einstein[180]

Einstein's main problem with reports of telepathy was that the reported effect did not seem to decline with distance. All of the four known forces of nature—gravity, electromagnetism, the strong and the weak nuclear forces—diminish in strength as they radiate from a source. The famous parapsychologist J.B. Rhine considered this proof that psi phenomena operate entirely outside the bounds of known physical laws.

However, the laws of physics have been rewritten several times in just the last century. This continual modification of the scientific worldview is called progress. Einstein was profoundly uncomfortable with many of the claims of quantum physics that are now commonly accepted. However, a number of leading physicists such as Henry Margenau, David Bohm, and Olivier Costa de Beauregard have repeatedly claimed that nothing in quantum mechanics forbids psi phenomena. Costa de Beauregard even maintains that the theory of quantum physics virtually *demands* that psi phenomena exist.[181] Nobel laureate Brian Josephson has stated that some of the most convincing evidence he has seen for the existence of psi phenomena comes not from the experiments of parapsychologists but rather from experiments in quantum physics.[182]

10

Modern Science versus
Classical Science

A serious problem has arisen. Most of the fundamental assumptions underlying classical science have been severely challenged in recent years. As the old assumptions dissolve because of advancements in many disciplines, new assumptions are carrying us toward a conception of the world that is entirely compatible with psi. Few scientists have paid attention to this dramatic shift in scientific fundamentals, and the general public has heard almost nothing about it…. Thus, the persistent controversy over psi can be traced back to the founding assumptions of modern science.

Dean Radin
The Conscious Universe

Many of the skeptical arguments are based on the assumptions that current scientific theories are complete, and that they are in conflict with the existence of psi. The former is laughable to anyone familiar with the history of science. Until about one hundred years ago, Newtonian physics was assumed to be correct and complete, and was based upon the metaphysical assumptions of localism, determinism, the assumption that an observer did not affect a system being observed and on an absolute view of space and time. Then two new theories replaced Newtonian physics. Quantum mechanics did so by abandoning the first three assumptions while retaining the fourth, and Einstein's theory of relativity did so by abandoning the fourth while retaining the first three. Because relativity retained most of the assumptions of classical physics while introducing a new conception of space and time, it is considered to be the crowning achievement of *classical* physics.

The predictions of quantum mechanics differ from those of Newtonian physics primarily but not entirely at the level of the molecule and below. Relativity differs from Newtonian physics most noticeably on the scale of the very large and the very fast—it is a theory of space, time, and gravity, and so most of its predictions are corroborated by astronomical observations. Yet the theories are inconsistent: Relativity breaks down at the atomic level, and quantum mechanics cannot accommodate relativity's assumptions regarding space and time. Each theory is incomplete and limited.

It is thought that the reason the theories conflict is because each retained and abandoned different assumptions from Newtonian physics. Some or all of these assumptions must be either wrong or incomplete, and if a unified theory of physics is someday developed, then quantum mechanics and relativity will both be considered special cases of the unified theory.[183]

Let us now examine the assumptions of classical science, assumptions that seem to be in conflict with the existence of psi.

- *determinism*—the idea that the future states of isolated systems can be predicted precisely (at least in principle) from current states.

- *observer independence*—the assumption that the act of observing a system or particle does not alter the behavior or characteristics of the system or particle.

- *localism*—the assumption that everything interacts only with its closest neighbors, and that therefore there is no action at a distance.

- *reductionism*—the idea that complex systems can be explained as the sum of their parts.

- *upward causation exclusively*—related to the idea of reductionism, this idea asserts that causation only flows upward, from the simpler to the more complex.

- *materialism*—the idea that everything in the universe can ultimately be explained in terms of the fundamental particles and the four forces of physics.

DETERMINISM AND THE ROLE OF THE OBSERVER

Quantum mechanics replaces the deterministic universe described by classical physics with a probabilistic universe. This is the idea that the behavior and various properties of subatomic systems and particles cannot be predicted precisely, that only a range of probable values can be specified. If you roll a series of marbles at a hill, at velocities below a certain critical velocity, all the marbles will roll back down; at velocities above the critical level, all the marbles will make it over the hill. In our classical macroscopic world, either they all get over or they all fall back. Things are not so simple at the quantum level.*

For instance, if subatomic particles such as electrons are fired at a potential barrier at a given velocity, it may not be possible to say with certainty whether or not an individual electron will pass through the barrier. Fire the electrons at a low enough velocity and most will be reflected, although a minority will pass through; fire them at a high enough velocity and most will pass through; and at some intermediate velocity about half will pass through, and half will be reflected. But for any individual electron (out of a group of apparently identical electrons) all we can specify is the *probability* that the electron will pass through. And probability enters here for a different reason than it does in the tossing of a coin, the throw of a dice, or a horse race: In these cases probability enters because of our lack of precise knowledge of the original state of the system. But in quantum theory, even if we had complete knowledge of the original state, the outcome would still be uncertain and only expressible as a probability. (Philosophers refer to these two sources of uncertainty as *subjective* and *objective* probability. Quantum mechanics suggests that in some situations probability has an objective status).

Another surprising proposition is that subatomic particles do not have definite properties for certain attributes, such as position, momentum, or direction of spin, until they are measured. It is not simply that these properties are unknown until they are observed; they do not *exist* in any definite state until they are measured.

This conclusion is based, in part, on the famous "two-slit" experiment, in which electrons are fired one at a time at a barrier with two slits. Measuring devices on a screen behind the barrier indicate the electrons seem to behave as waves, going through both slits simultaneously, with patterns of interference typical of wave phenomena: Wave crests arriving simultaneously at the same place in time will reinforce each other; waves and troughs arriving simultaneously at the same place will cancel each other. These waves are only thought of as *probability* waves—or "wavefunctions"—as they do not carry any energy, and so cannot be directly detected. Only individual electrons are detected by the measuring device on the screen behind the barrier, but the distribution of numerous electrons shows the interference patterns typical of waves. It is as though each unobserved electron exists as a wave until it arrives at the screen to be detected, at which time its actual location (the place the particle is actually observed on the screen) can only be predicted statistically, according to the interference pattern of its wavefunction.

If, however, a measuring device is placed at the slits, then each electron is observed to pass through only one slit, and no interference pattern in the distribution of electrons is observed. In other words, electrons behave as waves when not

---

* Those encountering quantum theory here for the first time may wish to bear in mind the words of physicist Niels Bohr: *If a person does not feel shocked when he first encounters quantum theory, he has not understood a word of it.*

observed, but as particles in a definite location when observed.[184] All quantum entities—electrons, protons, photons, and so on—display this wave-particle duality,
behaving as wave or particle, depending on whether or not they are directly
observed.

A variation of this experiment, due to physicists Rosenblum and Kuttner,[185]
makes this bizarre point even more clearly. If a wave corresponding to a single atom
encounters a semi-transparent reflecting surface (such as a thin film), it can be split
into two equal parts, much as a light wave goes through *and* reflects from a window-
pane. One part then reflects from a fully reflecting surface, and the two parts of the
wave can finally be trapped in two boxes, as in Figure 10.1.

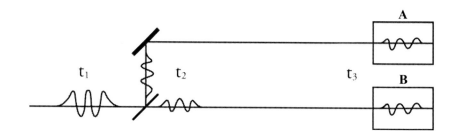

Figure 10.1: The wave function at three successive times: t_1, t_2, and t_3.

Since the wave was split equally, if you repeated this process many times, then
each time you looked into the boxes you would find a whole atom in Box A about
half the time and in Box B about half the time. But according to quantum theory,
before you looked, the atom was not in any particular box. The position of the atom
is thus an observer-created reality. Its position will also be the same for all subsequent observers, so it is an observer-*created* reality, not an observer-*dependent*
reality.

It may be tempting to think that the atom really was in one box or the other
before it was observed there, but in fact it can be demonstrated that, before observation, the atom as a wave was in a "superposition state", a state in which it was
simultaneously in *both* Box A *and* Box B. Take a pair of boxes that have not been
looked into and cut narrow slits at one end, allowing the waves to simultaneously
leak out and impinge on a photographic film, as shown in Figure 10.2 below. At
points where wave crests from Box A and Box B arrive together, they reinforce each
other to give a maximum in the amplitude of the wavefunction at that point—a
maximum of 'waviness.' At some points higher or lower, crests from Box A arrive
simultaneously with troughs from Box B. The two waves are of opposite signs at
these positions and therefore cancel to give zero amplitude for the wave function
at these points.

Since the amplitude of an atom's wavefunction at a particular place determines the probability for the atom to be found there when observed, the atom emerging from the box-pair is more likely to appear on the film at places where the amplitude of the wavefunction is large, but can never appear where it is zero. If we repeat this process with a large number of box-pairs and the same film, many atoms land, causing the film to darken near positions of wavefunction amplitude maxima, but none appear at wavefunction minima. The distribution of darker and lighter areas on the film forms the "interference pattern." *

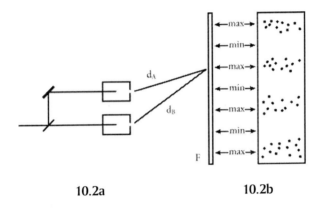

10.2a   10.2b

Figure 10.2:
(a) waves eminating from slits in the two boxes travel distances d_a and d_b and impinge upon a film at F; (b) the resulting pattern formed on the film by atoms from many box pairs.

The distribution of electrons on the film will show the interference patterns typical of two waves, which overlap to cancel each other at some places. To form the interference pattern, the wavefunction of *each* atom had to leak out of *both* boxes, since each and every atom avoids appearing in regions of the film where the waves from the two boxes cancel out each other. Each and every atom therefore had to obey a geometrical rule that depends on the relative position of both boxes. So, the argument goes, the atom had to equally be in *both* boxes, as an extended wave. But if instead of doing this interference experiment you looked into the pair of boxes, you would have found a whole atom in a particular box, as a particle. Before you look it is in both boxes; after you look it is only in one.

---

* Because this wave carries no energy and reveals itself only indirectly through its statistical influence on a large number of particle events, Einstein called it a *Gespensterfeld*, or ghost field. Since the wave carries not energy but probability—such as the probability that an electron will be found at a certain point—the French physicists have given the wavefunction the poetic name *densite de presence*—density of presence.

Rosenblum and Kuttner sum up the puzzle:

> Quantum mechanics is the most battle-tested theory in science. Not a single violation of its predictions has ever been demonstrated, no matter how preposterous the predictions might seem. However, anyone concerned with what the theory *means* faces a philosophical enigma: the so-called measurement problem, or the problem of observation. ... before you look we could have proven—with an interference experiment—that each atom was a wave equally in both boxes. After you look it was in a single box. It was thus your observation that created the reality of each atom's existence in a particular box. Before your observation, only probability existed. But it was not the probability that an actual object existed in a particular place (as in the classical shell game)—it was just the probability of a future *observation* of such an object, which does *not* include the assumption that the object existed there prior to its observation. This hard-to-accept observer-created reality is the measurement problem in quantum mechanics.[186]

Up until the moment of measurement, certain properties of quantum phenomena simply exist as a collection of probabilities, known as the state vector. Upon measurement, the state vector that contains all possible states "collapses" to a single value—the one that is observed. Measurements thus play a more positive role in quantum mechanics than in classical physics, because here they are not merely observations of something already present, but actually help produce it. According to one interpretation of quantum mechanics popular among many theorists, it is the existence of consciousness that introduces intrinsic probability into the quantum world.

This interpretation owes its origin to mathematician John von Neumann, one of the most important intellectual figures of the twentieth century. In addition to his contributions to pure mathematics, von Neumann invented game theory to model economic and social behavior as rational games, and made fundamental contributions to the development of the early computers. In the 1930's von Neumann turned his restless mind to the task of expressing the newly-developed theories of quantum mechanics in rigorous mathematical form, and the result was his classic book, *The Mathematical Foundations of Quantum Mechanics*. In it he tackled the "measurement problem" head on and rejected the so-called *Copenhagen interpretation* of quantum theory that was becoming the orthodox position among physicists (and arguably, still is). Although somewhat vague, the central tenets of the Copenhagen interpretation seem to be: 1) that all we have access to are the results of observations, and so it is simply pointless to ask questions about the quantum reality behind those observations, and 2) that although observation is necessary for establishing the reality of quantum phenomena, no form of consciousness, human or otherwise, is necessary for making an observation. Rather, an observer is anything that makes a record of an event, and so it is at the level of macroscopic measuring instruments (such as Geiger counters) that the actual values of quantum phenomena are randomly set from a range of statistical possibilities.[187]

Von Neumann objected to the Copenhagen practice of dividing the world into two parts: indefinite quantum entities on the one side, and measuring instruments that obey the laws of classical mechanics on the other. He argued that the entire physical world is quantum mechanical, and so the process that collapses the state vectors into actual facts cannot be a physical process: the intervention of something from outside of physics is required. Something non-physical, not subject to the laws of quantum mechanics, must account for the collapse of the state vector: the only non-physical entity in the observation process that von Neumann could think of was the consciousness of the observer. Von Neumann reluctantly concluded that this outside entity had to be consciousness, and that prior to observation, *even measuring instruments interacting with a quantum system must exist in an indefinite state.* Physicist Nick Herbert writes:

> Ironically this conclusion comes not from some otherworldly mystic examining the depths of his mind in private meditation, but from one of the world's most practical mathematicians deducing the logical consequences of a highly successful and purely materialistic model of the world—the theoretical basis for the billion-dollar computer industry.[188]

Von Neumann extended the Copenhagen interpretation by requiring the measurement process to take place in a mind.[189] His arguments were developed more completely by his illustrious followers, most notably Fritz London, Edmond Bauer, and Eugene Wigner. Wigner, who went on to win the Nobel Prize in Physics, wrote:

> When the province of physical theory was extended to encompass microscopic phenomena, through the creation of quantum mechanics, the concept of consciousness came to the fore again; it was not possible to formulate the laws of quantum mechanics in a fully consistent way without reference to the consciousness. ...it will remain remarkable, in whatever way our future concepts may develop, that the very study of the external world led to the conclusion that the content of consciousness is an ultimate reality.[190]

At this point, it should be stressed that this is only one interpretation of the facts of quantum mechanics: In addition to the Copenhagen interpretation, there are two other speculations about what is really happening when quantum possibilities settle down into one actuality.

Hidden-variable theory holds that the indeterminacy of quantum physics is an illusion due to our ignorance: If we knew more about the system in question—that is, if we knew the value of some "hidden variables"—then the indeterminacy would vanish. However, there are several reasons why the general community of quantum physicists never held the hidden variable theory in high regard.

One reason, according to quantum physicist Euan Squires, is that the hidden-variable theory is "extremely complicated and messy. We *know* the answers from quantum theory and then we construct a hidden-variable, deterministic theory specifically to give these answers. The resulting theory appears contrived and unnatural." Squires points out that the hidden variable theory never gained wide-spread acceptance, because "the elegance, simplicity and economy of quantum theory contrasted sharply with the contrived nature of a hidden-variable theory which gave no new predictions in return for its increased complexity; the whole hidden-variable enterprise was easily dismissed as arising from a desire, in the minds of those too conservative to accept change, to return to the determinism of classical physics."[191] Another reason the general community of quantum physicists consider the hidden-variable theory highly implausible, is that it explains away indeterminacy by postulating the existence of an *ad hoc* "quantum force" that, unlike any of the other four forces in nature, behaves in a manner completely unaffected by distance.

The many-worlds hypothesis is perhaps the strangest of all. When a measurement is made, we are told that the universe we are in splits into multiple universes, with one of the possible results in each of them. For instance, if a measurement may yield two possible results, then at the point of measurement the entire universe splits in two, with each possible result realized in each universe. If a measurement may yield a continuum of possible states –such as the position of an electron—then the instant such a measurement occurs, it is proposed that the universe splits into an *infinity* of universes. Since it is further assumed that these parallel universes cannot interact with each other, this hypothesis is completely untestable. Entities are being multiplied with incredible profusion. William of Occam must be spinning in his grave.

In the opinion of many physicists, the last two interpretations are simply desperate, last-ditch attempts to rescue the classical assumptions of determinism and observer-independence that have been abandoned by quantum mechanics. For instance, one interpretation salvages determinism from classical physics by postulating hidden-variables, and the other by speculating that everything that can happen *does* in fact happen in an infinity of constantly-splitting parallel universes—regardless of the way things may appear to any particular version of our constantly-splitting selves.

At any rate, these four interpretations are all consistent with the observed facts. They are attempts to describe what reality is really like between observations, to account for the seemingly bizarre behavior of matter predicted so accurately by the theory of quantum physics. They are not actually scientific theories about the nature of reality, but *metaphysical* theories, as within quantum mechanics there does not currently seem to be any obvious experiment that one could perform in order to choose between them.[192]

Physicist J.C. Polkinghorne summed up the metaphysical confusion many quantum theorists feel when he wrote:

> It is a curious tale. All over the world measurements are continually being made on quantum mechanical systems. The theory triumphantly predicts, within its probabilistic limits, what their outcomes will be. It is all a great success. Yet we do not understand what is going on. Does the fixity on a particular occasion set in as a purely mental act of knowledge? At a transition from small to large physical systems? At the interface of matter and mind that we call consciousness? In one of the many subsequent worlds into which the universe has divided itself?[193]

Perhaps one interpretation is simpler, or more logically consistent; or perhaps one of the interpretations is more aesthetically pleasing than the others. These considerations may provide philosophical reasons for preferring one over the others, but can hardly be considered decisive. However, recall that in the last chapter we described how the experiments of physicist Helmut Schmidt appeared to show that conscious intent can affect the behavior of otherwise purely random quantum phenomena. Could a parapsychology experiment be designed to test the von Neumann interpretation?

Consciousness is central to the von Neumann interpretation of quantum mechanics. According to this interpretation, some properties of quantum phenomena do not exist in any definite state except through the intervention of a conscious mind, at which point the state vector of possibilities collapses into a single state. The usual form of this interpretation allows the observer to collapse the state vector to a unique outcome, but not to have any effect on *what outcome* actually occurs. But the PK experiments of Schmidt and other physicists discussed earlier indicate that the observer may not only collapse the state vector to a single outcome but may also help specify what outcome occurs by shifting the odds in a desired direction. If the observer can affect the outcome of the collapse, it should be possible to design an experiment to test at which point the state vector collapses.

As mentioned earlier, physicist Helmut Schmidt has pioneered the use of PK experiments using random number generators (RNGs) that operate on the basis of truly random events at the quantum level. His standard experiments indicate that individuals can shift the probability of a binary event from a chance rate of 50 percent to between 51 and 52 percent, with a few gifted subjects achieving hit rates of a about 54 percent. But one variation of Schmidt's standard experiment is directly relevant to the choice between the von Neumann and Copenhagen interpretations.

First of all, Schmidt recorded signals (0's and 1's) from a binary random event generator simultaneously on two cassette tapes, without anyone listening to the signals or otherwise knowing the output of the RNG. One tape was kept in a secure location, the other was given to a subject with instructions to produce more 0's or

1's, usually distinguished as clicks in the left or right speaker of stereophonic head-phones. Results from these time-displaced PK experiments indicated that PK still operated, and that the two records still agreed after the PK effort.

Some theorists have speculated that the PK effort reached back in time to when the random events were generated. But of course there is another possibility, one more consistent with the von Neumann/Wigner interpretation of quantum physics. As Schmidt, Morris and Rudolph point out:

> Perhaps events are not physically real until there has been an obser-vation. From this viewpoint, the PK effort would not have to reach into the past because nature had not yet decided on the outcome before the PK subject, the first observer, saw the result. Then, the PK effort should no longer succeed if we have some other observer look at the pre-recorded data previous to the PK subject's attempt. [An] experiment to study this situation...has, indeed, reported a blocking of the PK effect by a previous observation.[194]

It appears that von Neumann, Wigner and the others were right: Prior to obser-vation, even measuring instruments interacting with a quantum system must exist in an indefinite state.

Could Schmidt's results be due to fraud? Well, Schmidt has even used this time-independence of PK to design a fraud-proof experiment involving skeptics. Essen-tially, it works like this: one of the unobserved tapes is sent to an outside observer, and the other is sent to a subject. The outside observer decides whether he/she wants to see more 0's or 1's, and this decision is communicated to the subject, who then listens to the tape and attempts to exert an influence in the desired direction. The observer then examines their copy of the tape and counts the number of 0's and 1's to see if the experiment was a success. Obviously, there can be no possibil-ity of fraud on the part of subject or experimenter—unless of course the skeptics are also in on the trick. Schmidt, Morris and Rudolph performed this experiment: Morris is an active parapsychology researcher and Rudolph is a communications engineer, and both were skeptical with regard to PK on pre-recorded events. But the experiment was a success, with odds against chance of one hundred to one.[195]

The von Neumann/Wigner interpretation of quantum physics, supported now by the experiments of Schmidt and others, may bring to mind the idealism of Bishop Berkeley, who thought that ordinary objects such as trees and furniture did not exist unless observed. But this interpretation does *not* deny that an external reality exists independently of anyone observing it. Properties of quantum phenomena are divided into *static* and *dynamic* properties, with the former, such as mass and charge, having definite and constant values for any observation. It is the dynamic proper-ties, those which do not have constant values—such as position, momentum, and direction of spin—that are thought to exist as potentialities that become actualities only when observed. But as quantum theorist Euan Squires points out, this raises a very strange question:

> The assumption we are considering appears even more weird when we realize that throughout much of the universe, and indeed through-out all of it in early times, there were presumably no conscious observers... Even worse are the problems we meet if we accept the modern ideas on the early universe in which quantum decays (of the 'vacuum', but this need not trouble us here) were necessary in order to obtain the conditions in which conscious observers could exist. Who, or what, did the observations necessary to create the observers?[196]

Squires enters the realm of theology with great trepidation, and considers what seems to be the only possibility under this interpretation: that conscious observa-tions can be made by minds outside of the physical universe. This of course is one of the traditional roles of God, or of the gods.

> Whether expressed in theological terms or not, the suggestion that con-scious minds are in some way connected and that they might even be connected to a form of universal, collective consciousness appears to be a possible solution to the problem of quantum theory. It is not easy to see what it might mean, as we understand so little about consciousness. That there are 'connections' of some sort between conscious minds and physical matter is surely implied by the fact that conscious decisions have effects on matter. Thus there are links between conscious minds that go through the medium of physical systems. Whether there are others, that exploit the non-physical and presumably non-localised nature of con-sciousness, it is not possible to say. Some people might wish to mention here the 'evidence' for telepathy and similar extra-sensory effects.[197]

Professor Squires concludes his discussion on the role of consciousness in physics with this remark:

> It is remarkable that such ideas should arise from a study of the behavior of the most elementary of systems. That such systems point to a world beyond themselves is a fact that will be loved by all who believe that there are truths of which we know little, that there are mysteries seen only by mystics, and that there are phenomena inexplicable within our normal view of what is possible. There is no harm in this—physics in-deed points to the unknown. The emphasis, however, must be on the unknown, on the mystery, on the truths dimly glimpsed, on things inex-pressible except in the language of poetry, or religion, or metaphor.[198]

LOCALISM

All interactions in classical physics are explicitly local. Interactions between a body at location A and another body at location B must be mediated by a force field that traverses the distance between A and B, at a speed not exceeding that of light. Body A causes a change in the force field, and this change in the field is propagated at or below light speed to Body B. So for instance, the gravitational field of the sun exerts an influence on the earth: if the sun were to be suddenly destroyed, the earth would drift out of its orbit about eight minutes later.

Localism implies that any information exchange must be mediated by a signal, and relativity implies that no such signal can travel faster than the speed of light. But experiments in quantum mechanics strongly suggest that we can in fact have action at a distance, with no signal required to transmit information.

This is one such experiment. Suppose a pair of electrons is split off from an atom. Quantum physics tells us that when the spin of the electrons is measured along a chosen axis they will be found to spin in *opposite* directions. Let the electrons travel light years apart and measure the spin of one. If it is found to be clockwise, then according to quantum theory the spin of the other is *instantaneously* determined to be in the opposite direction, despite no apparent force or signal linking them. Einstein called this "spooky action at a distance" and rejected this on the grounds that there could be no harmony without some signal passing between the distant particles, a signal that in this case would have to travel faster than the speed of light, which his theory of relativity did not allow.

For years David Bohm and other physicists tried to determine whether the adjustment was truly instantaneous. These experiments are difficult to do with sufficient accuracy, but a series of early experiments, with two exceptions in the early 1970's, supported non-locality. With progress in technology, more sophisticated experiments have become possible, usually using photons instead of electrons, and measuring polarization (direction of vibration of the electric field—*totally* polarized when its electric field vibrates in only one direction) instead of spin. In the 1980's a French team headed by Alain Aspect of the Institut d' Optique Theorique et Appliqué added to Bohm's experiment an ultra-fast switch to eliminate the possibility of any light-speed signal between the paired photons, and found the non-local prediction of quantum mechanics to hold.[199] David Bohm has commented:

> "All we can do is to look at several possible interpretations… It may mean that everything in the universe is in a kind of total rapport, so that whatever happens is related to everything else. Or it may mean that there is some kind of information that can travel faster than the speed of light. Or it may mean that our concepts of space and time have to be modified in some way that we don't now understand."[200]

As Bohm remarks, there are several possible interpretations, but non-locality appears to be an experimentally demonstrated fact.[201] It is these sorts of experiments that has provided Nobel laureate Brian Josephson with some of the most convincing evidence he has seen for the reality of psi. And it overcomes Einstein's objection that since the observed effects of telepathy do not seem to decline with distance, the phenomenon is therefore "a priori, improbable to the highest degree."

Several points about non-locality are worth noting. First of all, non-locality does not seem to violate special relativity's prohibition of faster-than-light signals, as no signals are sent. The four known forces of nature are thought to operate with the exchange of particles, all of which obey the cosmic speed limit. But in the case above, a change in the state at A (due to measurement) *instantaneously* causes a change at B, regardless of distance or barriers. Since no signal is sent through space, the quantum connection is immediate, and unaffected by barriers and distance. Another important point is that non-locality appears to have been established by arithmetic and experiment, and is thus a fact about the universe, independent of quantum mechanical theory.[202] So, any theory that eventually supersedes quantum mechanics will have to incorporate non-locality. Finally, it is worth noting that the quantum connection differs from ordinary forces in that it is very discriminating. Ordinary forces reach out and affect every particle of a certain kind in the immediate vicinity; for instance, gravity affects all particles, electromagnetism all charged particles. In contrast, the quantum connection only affects those systems that have interacted with each other since they were last measured. (Such systems are called "phase-entangled"). This brings to mind the discriminating nature of telepathy found in anecdotal reports and observed in the lab: Images are not sent at or received by everyone, but seem targeted at specific individuals.

So, could telepathy be an example of quantum non-locality? The answer would seem to depend upon whether or not the brain operates according to quantum mechanical principles. Scientists and philosophers intent on clinging to classical concepts usually argue at this point that quantum effects are normally observed only under certain strictly controlled conditions, that quantum effects will be wiped out in warm wet brains, and hence, classical physics is completely adequate for dealing with the relationship between thoughts and brain activity.

According to Berkeley physicist Henry Stapp, "That argument is incorrect." Quantum effects at the large scale are often difficult to observe *in practice*. This fact allows certain computations to be simplified in practice by treating a quantum system *as if* it were a classical one. But according to Stapp, if no true classical reality emerges at any macroscopic scale, "then the investigation of an issue as basic as the nature of the mind-brain connection ought *in principle* to be pursued within an exact framework, rather than crippling the investigation from the outset by replacing correct principles by concepts known to be fundamentally and grossly false, just because they allow certain *practical* computations to be simplified."[203]

So, theoretical rigor requires us to investigate the theoretical problem of the mind-brain relationship within the much more accurate framework of quantum physics. But there is also some empirical evidence that sheds light on the relationship between quantum principles and consciousness. Anesthesiologist Stuart Hameroff claims to have found evidence that anesthesia arrests consciousness by hindering the motion of electrons in microtubules, minute tunnels of protein that serve as a kind of skeleton for cells. Hameroff speculates that microtubules could be a possible site for quantum effects in the brain,[204] and his speculations have led mathematical physicist Roger Penrose to endorse the hypothesis.[205] Attempts to develop models of consciousness based on quantum mechanics have also been made by neuroscientist John Eccles, and physicists Henry Stapp and Evan Harris Walker.[206] Walker and the experimental physicist Helmut Schmidt (the latter responsible for many of the micro-PK experiments described earlier) have also proposed mathematical theories of psi based on quantum mechanics.[207] These theories rest upon two propositions that are now supported by experimental evidence: that mind can influence random quantum events, and that influence can occur instantaneously at a distance.

If consciousness exploits quantum mechanical principles, and if, as experiments indicate, reality is truly non-local, then our experience of psi may be our experience of the connectedness of nature that non-locality suggests: non-locality at the macroscopic level. This is highly speculative, of course, but both the anecdotal and experimental evidence for psi is consistent with the non-local effects of quantum physics.[208]

REDUCTIONISM

Science generally—and in particular all of classical physics—is highly reductionist, in that it seeks to explain objects and systems in terms of their parts. Scientists seek to take entities apart and to explain them in terms of smaller, simpler, localized entities. So, for instance, organisms are understood as composed of tissues and organs, which are in turn understood as collections of cells, cells are composed of molecules, which are composed of atoms composed of sub-atomic particles, and so forth. This method of reduction is a powerful form of analysis, and has led to many very successful explanations. Molecular biology has proved to be an extraordinarily powerful approach to understanding evolution, heredity, and other aspects of life. Quantum mechanics, the study of the smallest scale of reality, has provided insights into the life and death of stars, and the origin of the universe.

However, the successes of reductionist methods have sometimes led to claims that biology is really nothing but applied cell biology, cell biology is really nothing but applied molecular biology, which in turn is just chemistry, that chemistry is really just applied many-body physics, and that ultimately, everything can be explained by the laws of quantum mechanics. So, for instance, in his book *Of Molecules and Men* we have molecular biologist and *uber-reductionist* Francis Crick writing, "The ultimate aim of the modern movement in biology is to explain *all* biology in terms of physics and chemistry."

It was irritation with claims like this that led Phillip Anderson, a condensed-matter physicist, to write the essay "More is Different", published in *Science* in 1972.[209] Anderson, who went on to win the Nobel Prize in 1977, acknowledged the many successes of reductionism, but then argued that "the main fallacy with this kind of thinking is that the reductionist hypothesis does not by any means imply a 'constructionist' one: the ability to reduce everything to simple fundamental laws does not imply the ability to start with those laws and reconstruct the universe." Reality has a hierarchal structure, Anderson contended, ordered in terms of increasing complexity. And at each level of complexity entirely new properties unpredictably appear, so that "at each stage entirely new laws, concepts, and generalizations are necessary, requiring inspiration and creativity to just as great a degree as in the previous one." Or, in other words, "Psychology is not just applied biology, nor is biology applied chemistry."

As we go up the hierarchy of the sciences complexity increases, and new properties emerge at each new level. And it is the existence of these "emergent"—that is, unpredictable, irreducible, and holistic—properties that do not allow us to explain the social sciences in terms of psychology, psychology in terms of biology, and everything ultimately in terms of quantum mechanics. A simple example of an emergent property is the fluidity of water, which is nothing like any property of hydrogen and oxygen. Another example: Crystals have all sorts of properties, both geometrical and optical, that the molecules that compose them do not possess.

Indeed, it seems as though the entire history of the universe as we know it could be understood as the emergence of new entities and properties, with increasing levels of complexity. Heavy atomic nuclei emerged in the center of large stars, and later on organic molecules emerged on earth. When organic molecules were combined in special ways, single-celled life emerged, with all of the new properties of molecular and cell biology. The combination of individual cells into multi-cellular organisms also resulted in something new: the behavior of complex animals. When sufficient complexity was attained, something utterly new and completely different entered the universe: the emergence of conscious states. Conscious minds interacted with other minds, and in turn emerged the products of human minds, such as culture, works of art, and of course the scientific studies of all the preceding levels of reality, from quantum mechanics to chemistry to biology to psychology, and to the social sciences that study the products of human culture itself. As the celebrated philosopher of science Karl Popper often pointed out, the universe is creative.

Claims such as "psychology is just applied biology" or "organisms are nothing but collections of cells" are given the pejorative label of *reductionism* because they are considered to be *unwarranted* reductions. It is perfectly acceptable and often very useful to consider an organism as a collection of cells in the same sense that a building can be considered a collection of materials: The properties of any complex entity are determined largely (but not entirely) by the properties of its parts. The dispute is with the assertion that these complex entities are *nothing but* their component parts.

The "nothing but" reductions ignore the new properties that emerge when components are combined in special ways. Of course a complex entity like a building can be reduced to rubble, but this reduction destroys the space-time relationships of the building components. Emergent properties result from the parts and from the spacing and timing of the parts with reference to one another, but the laws of the components do not include these space-time factors. In other words, it is the spatio-temporal relationships between the components that make the whole greater than the simple sum of its parts.

And it is important to realize that the properties that emerge at new levels of complexity do not replace the more fundamental properties of the more basic levels: They are additions, not replacements or even amendments. This has an important implication for the hierarchy of sciences. For although a less basic science—for example, chemistry in relation to physics, biology in relation to chemistry—is still an independent science with its own principles, the less basic science should not usually make claims that are incompatible with well-established claims of a science that is more basic relative to it. Should claims be made that appear to be in conflict with the principles of a more basic science, they must be abandoned, modified, shown to be in conformity with the claims of the more basic science or—if there is sufficient evidence for the claims—considered as potential falsifications of the general yet more basic principle.

Anyway, from what we have seen so far, it would appear that the charge that the claims of parapsychology are incompatible with those of the more basic sciences is groundless, as they are not incompatible with quantum mechanics, at this time the most basic science of all. Given the existence of emergent properties, the operation of psi in our macroscopic world is *consistent with but not necessarily explained by* quantum mechanical principles.

> **Quantum systems exhibit an unexpected degree of togetherness.**
> **Mere spatial separation does not divide them from each other.**
> **It is a particularly surprising conclusion for so**
> **reductionist a subject as physics. After all, elementary particle physics**
> **is always trying to split things up into smaller and smaller**
> **constituents with a view to treating them independently of each other.**
> **I do not think we have yet succeeded in taking in**
> **fully what quantum mechanical non-locality implies about**
> **the nature of the world.**
>
> **J.C. Polkinghorne**

UPWARD AND DOWNWARD CAUSATION

From a purely reductionist standpoint, all causation must flow strictly in an upward direction, from the simpler to the more complex. For if we assume that psychology is nothing but applied biology, biology nothing but applied chemistry, and chemistry nothing but applied physics, then the more complex structures are nothing more than functions of their substructures, and so causation only flows upward. In this traditional view, the cosmos is physically driven from below by the elemental forces of chemistry and physics, and ultimately by quantum mechanics.

If however, with increasing complexity new phenomena emerge that are to some extent independent of the smaller-scale processes that created them, then they may be able to exert top-down control over their substructures. This is the concept of *downward causation*, which may be said to occur whenever a higher structure operates upon its substructure. According to this view, due mostly to neuroscientist Roger Sperry and biologist Donald Campbell, causation flows downward as well as upward. No one disputes that causation flows upward; the question is whether things are determined *exclusively* from below, or whether downward causation is also operating.

The concept of downward causation may be illustrated within the structural hierarchy of nature. A simple example is the downward control exerted by a molecule of water over its hydrogen and oxygen atoms. The laws defining the behavior of the atoms, particularly their course through space and time, become quite different after they are joined together in a molecule. Although the atomic properties are preserved, the atoms are now obliged to follow a new course through space and time, determined by the newly emerged properties of the water molecule. If the molecule is itself part of a single-celled organism such as a paramecium, then it in turn is obliged to follow a new course through space and time, determined by the forces driving the cell. If the cell is part of a multi-celled organism such as a cat, then the behavior of the cell is determined by its purpose in terms of cat physiology, and its fate is determined by the behavior of the cat, as may be described in terms of feline zoology and psychology. At all times the simpler lower-level forces and laws are all operating: They have not been replaced, but *superseded* by the properties of the higher-level organizational structures.[210]

A reductionist may agree with this account, but may then argue that the higher-level properties, as for instance those of a water molecule, may be predicted from the atomic properties. But predictability is not the issue here. Being able to predict the emergence of new properties does not make those properties any less real, important, or powerful as causal determinants. Perhaps evolution is *in principle* entirely predictable, starting with sub-atomic particles and forces (although this is extremely doubtful, given the *pure randomness* of many quantum phenomena); but this does not change the argument that evolution *does* occur, that new properties *do* emerge, and that these new properties in turn exert downward causal influence over their constituents, which are thereafter governed by new scientific laws.

Extending this discussion of emergent properties and their causal influence up the hierarchy of nature leads to the suggestion that minds may be able to have causal influence upon lower-level structures, and ultimately, that human culture may be able to influence human minds. This brings us to the final assumption of classical science, one that is of special relevance to the existence of psi phenomena.

MATERIALISM

The final assumption of classical science considered here is materialism. Often known today as physicalism, it asserts that everything in the universe can ultimately be explained entirely in terms of the fundamental particles and forces of physics. The cruder forms of materialism simply deny the existence of mental states, or hold that mental states are identical to brain states.[211] The more sophisticated forms of materialism consider mental states and consciousness as mere *epiphenomena* of brain activity—that is, as phenomena that accompany brain activity, are caused by brain activity, but are of no real use and carry no explanatory power.

This metaphysical hypothesis is the most drastic of the proposed solutions to the so-called mind/body problem—that is, what is the nature of the relationship between mind and body? After thousands of years of debate, three top contenders for a solution remain:

- *Materialism*—Mental events have no causal influence, they are simply by-products of physical events in the brain. The mind is a mere *epiphenomenon*, dependent upon and controlled by a physical brain, and therefore incapable of existing apart from a physical brain. All that matters is matter.

- *Mentalism*—Matter exerts causal influence on mind, but mind also exerts causal influence on matter, and has causal primacy. However, mind is an emergent property of physical brains, and so the existence of mind ultimately depends on matter.

- *Dualism*—Not only do mind and matter exert causal influence on each other, but both are entirely irreducible phenomena that can exist independently of each other.

The most ancient of these beliefs is dualism, found as it is in the old shamanistic religions around the world. Although the first formal statement of dualism was by Descartes, one of the earliest written references to dualist thinking may be found in Plato's description of the last hours of Socrates, in which Socrates ridicules the notion that purposeful behavior can be explained in physical terms. Plato made a sharp distinction between mind and body, holding that the mind could exist both before and after its residence in the body and could rule the body during that residence. An even earlier reference to a form of dualism may be found in a lecture given by Hippocrates on epilepsia (epilepsy), in which the brain is described as "the messenger to consciousness" and as "the interpreter for consciousness." Modern dualists can count among their ranks several distinguished modern philosophers and brain scientists.[212]

Materialism in all its varieties also has an ancient history, going back at least as far as Democritus, who back in the fifth century B.C. wrote that "nothing exists, but atoms and the void." It had a powerful and influential advocate in the 19th century in the form of Darwin's close friend Thomas Huxley, who proposed the thesis that animals and men are automata. Huxley did not deny the existence of mental events, but maintained that the relationship between mind and body was strictly one-sided, with the mental having no effect on the physical. Huxley described mental events as mere *epiphenomena*, or just useless by-products of brain activity. So men and animals for him were just automata, even if conscious ones. This is still the position of many philosophers, biologists, and neuroscientists.

Materialism was popular in psychology in the 1950's, as part of a movement known as "behaviorism," and the doctrine of behaviorism is still adhered to by some neuroscientists and psychologists. But in the 1960's, the concept of mentalism began to spread in acceptance among cognitive scientists, mostly due to the writings of neurobiologist Roger Sperry. Sperry, who won the 1981 Nobel Prize in Medicine for his work on the functions of the two hemispheres of the brain, rightly recognized that the profound mystery of consciousness makes a choice between the alternatives difficult:

> Once we have materialism squared off against mentalism in this way,
> I think we must all agree that neither is going to win the match on
> the basis of direct, factual evidence. The facts do not simply go far
> enough. Those centermost processes of the brain with which
> consciousness is presumably associated are simply not understood.
> They are so far beyond our comprehension at present that no one I
> know of has been able even to imagine their nature.[213]

Apart from the dwindling number of pure materialists that still deny the existence of consciousness, and the dwindling number of researchers in the field of artificial intelligence still trying to raise money for the construction of "thinking machines",[214] this position is reflected in the writings of most serious scientists. Nobel laureate Eugene Wigner writes, "We have at present not even the vaguest idea how to connect the physio-chemical processes with the state of the mind."[215] Physicist Nick Herbert concurs:

> Science's biggest mystery is the nature of consciousness. It is not simply
> that we possess bad or imperfect theories of human awareness; we

simply have no such theories at all. About all we know about consciousness is that it has something to do with the head, rather than
the foot.[216]

Materialists sometimes claim to represent the scientific viewpoint. But materialism is in no sense a more "scientific" hypothesis than the alternatives, as it does
not draw stronger support from current scientific thinking. Materialism is a legacy
of classical physics, which actually had two ways of dealing with the problem of consciousness and free will. The first, followed by Descartes and Newton, was to place
mind outside of the scope of physics, and consider it the sole exception in an otherwise deterministic, mechanistic universe. The other approach, followed by popu-
larizers of Newton's work such as Diderot and Voltaire, was to assume that the
physics of the time was a complete description of the world, and to argue that consciousness must then be epiphenomenal. But we now know that classical physics is
fundamentally incorrect, and so any world-view based upon it must also be flawed.
Sperry writes:

> To conclude that conscious, mental, or psychic, forces have no place in
> filling this gap in our explanatory picture is at least to go well beyond
> the facts into the realm of intuition and speculation. The doctrine of
> materialism in behavioral science, which tends to be identified with a
> rigorous scientific approach, is thus seen to rest, in fact, on an
> insupportable mental inference that goes far beyond the objective
> evidence and hence is founded on the cardinal sin of science.[217]

Our common sense would certainly seem to indicate that mental events such
as thoughts, beliefs, intentions and so forth all have causal effects. We normally
speak and think as if our thoughts, feelings and values *do* determine our course of
action. And of course our moral judgments also presuppose that these things have
real impact on human behavior. But common sense arguments, however seemingly
compelling, are not sufficient by themselves to draw strong conclusions, as on many
occasions science has shown common sense to have been dead wrong.

What then is the argument in favor of the causal efficacy of mental events? It is
simple and straightforward. First, it contends that mind and consciousness are
emergent properties of living brains, and then it goes a critical step further and
asserts that these emergent properties have causal potency, just as they do elsewhere in the universe. In other words, it applies the concepts of emergent properties and downward causation to mind and consciousness, and to everything they
seem to affect.

It is important to stress that the lower level forces and properties, of atoms,
molecules, and cells all continue to operate, and all continue to exert upward (and
in most cases downward) causal influence. None of these causal forces have been

cancelled or replaced, but they have been superseded by the properties of a higher organizational structure. According to this new view, mind and consciousness exert just as much (or even more) causal effect on the lower level structures than the lower level structures exert on them. Mental events interact with other mental events at their own level according to their own rules, and in the process exert downward control over the lower level structures. Sperry's model puts mind back into the driver's seat, and accordingly, thoughts, beliefs, judgment and so forth are recognized as having a real, not just imaginary, impact on the world.

> **The ultimate paradox of materialism is that the one feature of the universe which alone gives meaning to all the rest is the one feature which has to be declared redundant! Nothing can account for its emergence; nothing follows from its existence.**
>
> **John Beloff**

Shortly after Sperry first proposed these ideas in the mid 1960's, the philosopher Karl Popper seems to have come to an almost identical conclusion, although from a somewhat different perspective. Popper points out that no Darwinist should accept the one-sided action of body on mind proposed by the materialists. In his books *Origin of Species* and *Natural Selection*, Darwin discussed the mental powers of animals and men, and argued that these are products of natural selection.

Now if that is so, then mental powers must assist organisms in their struggle for survival. And it follows from this that mental powers must exert causal influence on the behavior of animals and men. If conscious states exist, then, according to Darwinism, we should look for their uses. If they are useful for living, then they must have real effects on the physical world.

As mentioned earlier, Darwin's close friend Thomas Huxley was a thoroughgoing materialist. While he did not deny the existence of mental events, he wrote that the relationship between mind and body was strictly one-sided, with the mental having no effect on the physical. Since mental events for Huxley were just useless byproducts of brain activity, he thought men and animals were just automata, with useless consciousness along for the ride.

Although Darwin liked and admired Huxley, he would have none of this. Supporting Huxley's opinion would have contradicted his life's work, as Popper rightly points out:

> The theory of natural selection constitutes a strong argument against Huxley's theory of the one-sided action of body on mind and for the mutual interaction of mind and body. Not only does the body act on the mind—for example, in perception, or in sickness—but our thoughts, our expectations, and our feelings may lead to useful actions in the

physical world. If Huxley had been right, mind would be useless. But then it could not have evolved…by natural selection.[218]

So, from a strictly Darwinian approach, the mental powers of animals and men should be expected to lead to useful actions, and should therefore be a causal influence in nature. According to this account, perceptions, emotions, judgments, and thoughts all have a real effect. And the more highly developed the mental powers, the more causal impact they should be expected to have. We should conclude from this that the mental powers of humans exert more causal potency than that of any other living creatures on earth, as arguably, we are the only creatures on earth with ideas and ideals. Sperry writes:

> In the brain model proposed here the causal potency of an idea, or an ideal, becomes just as real as that of a molecule, a cell, or a nerve impulse. Ideas cause ideas and help evolve new ideas. They interact with each other and with other mental forces in the same brain, in neighboring brains, and thanks to global communication, in far distant, foreign brains. And they also interact with the external surroundings to produce in toto a burstwise advance in evolution that is far beyond anything to hit the evolutionary scene yet.[219]

Mind-body interaction

Critics of mentalism and dualism often question how two fundamentally different properties such as mind and matter could possibly interact. How can something non-spatial, with no mass, location, or physical dimensions possibly influence spatially-bound matter? As K.R. Rao writes:

> The main problem with such dualism is the problem of interaction. How does unextended mind interact with the extended body? Any kind of causal interaction between them, which is presumed by most dualist theories, comes into conflict with the physical theory that the universe is a closed system and that every physical event is linked with an antecedent physical event. This assumption preempts any possibility that a mental act can cause a physical event.[220]

The implicit assumption here is that phenomena that exist as cause and effect *must* have something in common in order to exist as cause and effect. So, is this a logical necessity? Or, is it rather an empirical truth, a fact about nature? As David Hume pointed out long ago, anything in principle could be the cause of anything else, and only observation can establish what causes what. Parapsychologist John Beloff considers the issue logically:

If an event A never occurred without being preceded by some other event B, we would surely want to say that the second event was a necessary condition or cause of the first event, *whether or not* the two had anything else in common. As for such a principle being an empirical truth, how could it be since there are here only two known independent substances, i.e. mind and matter, as candidates on which to base a generalization? To argue that they cannot interact *because* they are independent is to beg the question.[221]

Popper also rejects completely the idea that only like can act upon like, describing this as resting on obsolete notions of physics. For an example of unlikes acting on one another we have light and matter: Light can be reflected, slowed, and split by matter. And then there is the example of interaction between forces and physical bodies. What do magnetic fields and iron filings have in common? It should be clear that the idea that only like can act upon like rests upon an obsolete, billiard-ball notion of causation in physics.[222]

So are we free?

And what does all this imply about free will? Sperry writes that "the proposed brain model provides in large measure the mental forces and abilities to determine one's own actions. It provides a high degree of freedom from outside forces as well as mastery over the inner molecular and atomic forces of the body. In other words, it provides plenty of free will as long as we think of free will as self-determination."[223] So, accordingly, a person does indeed determine with his own mind what he is going to do from a range of alternatives, but the ultimate choice is restricted by a variety of factors, including of course available information and mental acuity. Perhaps the ultimate form of free will would not be complete freedom from all causal factors, but rather unlimited causal contact with all relevant information, scenarios, choices, and possible results.

And of course, our choices are in large part determined by our personal preferences, experiences, and cultural and inherited factors. It could be argued that this is a form of determinism, but do we really wish to be free from ourselves? As Schopenhauer wondered, "We may be free to do as we please, but are we free to please as we please?"

With this conception of free will it could be argued that the more we learn, the wider the experience we gain, the more logical we become, the greater our knowledge of ourselves and of history, the more our sciences advance, the greater then the extent of true human freedom. However, an interesting experiment was performed by a psychologist in the late 1980's that seems to have bearing on the subject of free will, and may imply a different conclusion.

Benjamin Libet, at the University of California at San Francisco, asked subjects to push a button at a moment of their choosing while they noted the moment of their decision as displayed on a clock. He found that subjects on average took about a fifth of a second to flex their fingers after they had decided to do so. But data from an electroencephalograph monitoring their brain waves showed a spike in electrical activity about a third of a second *before* they consciously decided to push to button. Some have interpreted this result as implying that our decisions may be unconsciously determined for us before we are aware of the decision, and thus, free will is only an illusion.

Before we jump to this conclusion, however, we immediately recognize that we do not typically make our decisions the way these subjects arbitrarily decided to flex their fingers. Decisions on anything important are usually made by gathering information and mulling over the different possibilities and their implications. The decision to push a button at the moment of our choosing, by contrast, seems to involve waiting for the trivial urge to strike us, a rather random, indeterminate process. There seems to be no reason why low-level decisions should not be delegated to unconscious processes, such as the decision to push a button, or to activate a car's turn signal while engrossed in conversation.

Libet himself believes that one implication of his work is an altered view of how we exercise free will:

> The role of conscious free will would be, then, not to initiate a voluntary act, but rather to *control* whether the act takes place. We may view the unconscious initiatives for voluntary actions as 'bubbling up' in the brain. The conscious-will then selects which of these initiatives may go forward to an action or which ones to veto or abort, with no act appearing....
> The existence of a veto possibility is not in doubt. The subjects in our experiments at times reported that a conscious wish or urge to act appeared but that they suppressed or vetoed that.... All of us, not just experimental subjects, have experienced our vetoing a spontaneous urge to perform some act. This often occurs when the urge to act involves some socially unacceptable consequence, like an urge to shout some obscenity at the professor. [224]

He also considers and rejects the possibility that the conscious veto itself may have its origin in preceding unconscious processes, writing that:

> The conscious veto is a *control* function, different from simply becoming aware of the wish to act. There is no logical imperative in any mind-brain theory, even identity theory, that requires specific neural activity to precede and determine the nature of a conscious control function. And, there is no experimental evidence against the possibility that the control process may appear without development by prior unconscious processes.

Popper would take this as another example of downward causation, as non-random selection from a choice of random alternatives: "The selection of a kind of behavior out of a randomly offered repertoire may be an act of choice, even an act of free will."[225] If quantum phenomena have any real effect in the brain, then perhaps their random influences are accepted when they fit into the higher-level structure; otherwise they are rejected.

But there is another interpretation, due to another of Libet's experiments. In 1973 Libet found that electrical stimulation of the sensory cortex—that part of the brain's surface primarily responsible for processing tactile information from the skin—did not result in conscious sensation unless the stimulation was prolonged for at least 500 milliseconds (.5 second). The necessity of 500 milliseconds of cortical stimulation before the signal was felt also held for stimulation of the skin: In both cases, if the signal as recorded in the cortex was less than half a second long, it was not consciously experienced. This does not mean that the signal at the skin must last half a second, but rather that the secondary signals at the surface of the brain must last at least half a second before they can be consciously experienced.

However, Libet found that patients experienced their finger shocks *almost immediately*, between 10 and 20 milliseconds after the shock was applied. Typical reaction time—the time it takes to perceive a shock and push a button—is about 100 milliseconds (.1 second). So how can Libet's observation that 500 milliseconds of neural activity is required before a shock can be felt be reconciled with the fact that we can perceive and respond to such shocks in about one-fifth the time they apparently require to become part of conscious experience?

In a series of ingenious experiments involving electrical stimulation of both skin and cortex, Libet resolved this paradox. What appears to happen is that the tactile signal reaches the cortex in about 10 milliseconds but is not consciously perceived. However, the arrival time is unconsciously marked in some manner. Then, if the cortical activity due to the skin response is not interrupted but allowed to continue for at least 500 milliseconds, the shock is felt. But it is not felt half a second late: rather, it is "back dated" to the original arrival time of the signal.[226]

These surprising results seem to refute the idea that every mental experience is directly correlated with a physical process in the brain. Or, as neuroscientist John Eccles put it, "there can be a temporal discrepancy between neural events and the experiences of the self conscious mind."[227]

Dean Radin takes this idea a step further: He notes that the equations of both classical and quantum physics are neutral with respect to the direction of time, and so do not rule out the *possibility* of future events causing events in the past. In addition, he has presented some experimental evidence that individuals can subconsciously react to *future* events.

At the University of Nevada people were shown a series of pictures on a computer screen. Most of the images were of an emotionally calming nature, such as images of landscapes and various nature scenes, but some were meant to be arousing or disturbing, including pornographic photos and pictures of corpses. At the beginning of each trial, the screen was blank. The participant would start the trial by pressing a mouse button. After five seconds, one of these images, calm or emotional, was shown for three seconds, and then the screen would go blank again. Ten seconds later, a message informed the participant that he/she could press the mouse button again whenever he/she felt ready for the next trial. Five seconds after pressing the mouse button, another picture would be displayed, and the session would continue until forty pictures had been shown. The order the pictures were displayed in was chosen randomly by the computer. Throughout the session the participants' heart rate, skin resistance and blood volume in the fingertips were monitored.

Not surprisingly, dramatic changes in all three physiological measures were recorded when the emotional pictures were shown. But what was remarkable was that the arousal began *before* the emotional picture was displayed, even though the participants could not have known by any normal means what sort of picture was going to be displayed next. This effect, of unconsciously preparing for a reaction to an impending event, has been labeled "presentiment" and has been replicated independently by a laboratory in Holland.[228]

As Radin notes, if we allow "for the possibility of signals traveling backward in time, then what Libet saw [in the experiment involving deciding when to push a button] may be the brain's presponse to its own decision taking place a third of a second *in the future.*"[229] In other words, given the apparent temporal discrepancy between neural events and the experiences of the self-conscious mind, the sub-conscious mind may generate neural activity in order to prepare the brain for the execution of an impending decision. The second experiment described may be an example of the reverse: The mind may experience and respond to a sensation because of a signal from the future state of the brain.

The Consciousness Revolution

Since the early 1970's the idea that consciousness exerts causal effects has gained wide support in the cognitive sciences, especially in psychology, where it has become the majority position. This movement has been referred to variously as the "consciousness revolution", the "cognitive" or "mentalist" revolution, and has led to the overthrow of behaviorism as the dominant paradigm in psychology. Harvard psychologist Howard Gardner writes that "today the theoretical claims of behaviorism are largely of historical interest. The cognitive revolution…has carried the day."[230] And Sperry himself commented on the paradigm shift, writing that "The accepted role of conscious experience in brain function and behavior changed from that of a noncausal, epiphenomenal, parallel or identical status (and something best ignored or excluded from scientific explanation) to that of an ineliminable causal, or interactional role."[231] The appearance in neuroscience of a plausible, logical explanation for the causal effects of consciousness has also influenced other neuroscientists,[232] and has been accepted by some philosophers concerned with the ancient mind-brain problem.[233]

It is curious how quantum physicists in the tradition of von Neumann, studying the most fundamental level of reality, and cognitive scientists working at the other end of the spectrum of science, should come to almost identical conclusions regarding the causal role of consciousness. Wigner, in his essay "Remarks on the Mind-Body Question", first notes the effects that physical properties have on mental sensations, and asks "Does conversely, the consciousness influence the physico-chemical conditions?" He notes that the traditional answer among biochemists has been "no": The body influences the mind but the mind does not influence the body. Wigner then presents two reasons why physicists should not support this view. The first reason he gives is the causal role of the observer in quantum mechanics, as discussed above. The other is more classical: "The second argument to support the existence of an influence of the consciousness on the physical world is based on the observation that we do not know of any phenomenon in which one subject is influenced by another without exerting an influence thereupon."

Harold Morowitz, professor of molecular biophysics and biochemistry at Yale, noted in his article "Rediscovering the Mind" a strange phenomenon occurring in the dominant paradigms of psychologists, biologists, and physicists. He notes that while biologists have been relentlessly moving toward the hard-core materialism that characterized 19th century physics, "at the same time, physicists, faced with compelling experimental evidence, have been moving away from strictly mechanical models of the universe to a view that sees the mind as playing an integral role in all physical events. It is as if the two disciplines were on fast-moving trains, going in opposite directions and not noticing what is happening across the tracks."[234] Biologists of a materialist bent, such as Francis Crick, seek to explain mind and consciousness by activities of the central nervous system, which can be reduced to a biological substructure. They then seek to understand biological phenomena in terms of chemistry, biophysics, and ultimately in terms of quantum mechanics, which quantum theorists in the von Neumann tradition believe must be formulated with mind as a primary component of the system. As Morowitz writes, "We have thus, in separate steps, gone around an epistemological circle—from the mind, back to the mind."[235]

**At the logical core of our
most materialistic science we meet not dead matter
but our own lively selves.**

Nick Herbert

If Sperry's work is to be criticized, then it should be on the grounds that it is incomplete because it ignores the similar conclusions of the quantum physicists.

Sperry based his conclusions regarding consciousness on a rejection of classical *reductionism*; the physicists who follow von Neumann base their conclusions regarding the causal role of consciousness on a rejection of the classical assumptions of *determinism* and *observer independence*. The positions are similar, but not exactly the same. The main difference seems to be that Sperry's position is still rooted in the materialist hypothesis that mind ultimately depends upon matter for its existence, whereas the von Neumann interpretation of reality leaves open the possibility that the mind is not an emergent but rather an *elemental* property—that is, a basic constituent of the universe, as elemental as matter and energy. This is obviously a more radical position, but in its favor we should note that it would resolve the paradox mentioned earlier that is raised by the von Neumann interpretation: If consciousness depends on the physical world, and the value of many quantum physical properties depend on consciousness, then how did the physical world ever bring about consciousness in the first place?

These are fascinating and important issues, and will be discussed in more detail later. But for now, it is sufficient to note how the quantum theorists have come to almost the same conclusions as Popper and Sperry, but by rejecting different aspects of classical metaphysics. Quantum physicist Henry Stapp has described how for centuries philosophy has been hamstrung by its dependence upon the metaphysical implications of classical physics:

> Philosophers have tried for three centuries to understand the role of mind in the workings of a brain conceived to function according to principles of classical physics. We now know that no such brain actually exists…. Hence it is hardly surprising that those endeavors of philosophers have been beset by enormous difficulties, which have led to such positions as that of the 'eliminative materialists', who hold that our conscious thoughts do not exist; or of the 'epiphenomenalists', who admit that human experiences do exist but claim that they play absolutely no role in how we behave; or of the 'identity theorists', who claim that each conscious feeling is exactly the same thing as a motion of the particles that nineteenth century science thought brains and everything else in the universe to be made of. The difficulties in reconciling mental realities with pre-quantum physics is dramatized by the fact that for many years the mere mention of "consciousness" was considered evidence of backwardness and bad taste in most of academia, including, incredibly, even the philosophy of mind.[236]

So, what does all of this imply for the scientific acceptance of psi phenomena? In a nutshell, the refutation of materialism removes the last barrier skeptics can raise about the scientific legitimacy of psi. Psi phenomena such as telepathy are tightly bound up with notions such as "intent" and "values," and their operation seems to

indicate a causal role for consciousness. If consciousness were a mere epiphenomenon, how could it be that one mind influences another according to the desires,
values, and interests of both parties? Psi phenomena, if real, represent the opera-
tions of minds upon minds, and minds upon matter. And as they do not appear to
operate in a random manner, the desires and values of these minds appear to play
crucial causal roles. The new view of mind as causal that has gained widespread scientific acceptance since the early 1970's is consistent with the theoretical possibility of psi.[237] It can no longer be cogently argued that materialism is a pillar of the
modern scientific view, and that parapsychology is in serious conflict with modern
science because the acceptance of psi would undermine materialism.

Perhaps not surprisingly, Susan Blackmore disagrees. In a recent essay, she
notes that telepathy and psychokinesis are commonly seen as evidence for the
causal effect of consciousness, and then accuses parapsychologists of trying to
prove the power of consciousness. She writes, "It is a desire for this 'power of consciousness' that fuels much enthusiasm for the paranormal."[238] Then, in what
seems like a reversion to 1950's behaviorism, she adds:

> As our understanding of conscious experience progresses, this desire
> to find "the power of consciousness" sets parapsychology ever more
> against the rest of science (which of course is part of its appeal). The
> more we look into the workings of the brain the less it looks like a
> machine run by a conscious self. ...Indeed, the brain seems to be a
> machine that runs itself very well and produces an illusion that there is
> someone in charge. This illusion is just what meditators and spiritual
> practitioners have been saying for millennia; that our ordinary view of
> ourselves, as conscious, active agents experiencing a real world, is
> wrong—an illusion. Now science seems to be coming to the same
> conclusion.
>
> Parapsychology is going the other way. It is trying to prove that
> consciousness really does have power; that our minds really can reach
> out and "do" things.

Well, if a belief in the "power of consciousness" sets parapsychology "ever more
against the rest of science," then I suppose that neuroscientists Roger Sperry, Sir
John Eccles, and D.M. MacKay, brain surgeons Charles Sherrington and Wilder Penfield, philosopher of science Karl Popper, physicists Eugene Wigner and Henry
Stapp, and Charles Darwin are all set against the rest of science, not to mention the
majority of contemporary psychologists. It may be more plausible to say that her
dogmatic opposition to the power of consciousness sets Susan Blackmore ever
more against the rest of science.

Benjamin Libet, whose experimental work is sometimes offered as scientific

evidence that free will is an illusion, has expressed strong opposition to this interpretation.

> The intuitive feelings about the phenomenon of free will form a
> fundamental basis for views of our human nature, and great care should
> be taken not to believe allegedly scientific conclusions about them
> which actually depend upon hidden *ad hoc* assumptions. A theory that
> simply interprets the phenomenon of free will as illusory and denies
> the validity of this phenomenal fact is less attractive than a theory that
> accepts or accommodates the phenomenal fact.
>
> In an issue so fundamentally important to our view of who we are, a
> claim for illusory nature should be based on fairly direct evidence.
> Such evidence is not available; nor do determinists propose even a
> potential experimental design to test the theory.
>
> My conclusion about free will, one genuinely free in the non-deter-
> mined sense, is then that its existence is at least as good, if not a
> better, scientific option than is its denial by a determinist theory.[239]

In the same journal, Henry Stapp expresses the same opinion as Libet, writing
that epiphenomenalism is a mistake arising from outmoded classical physics:

> There is no compulsion from the basic principles of physics that
> requires any rejection of the sensible idea that mental effort can
> actually do what it seems to do. ...*It is therefore simply wrong to proclaim
> that the findings of science entail that our intuitions about the nature of our
> thoughts are necessarily illusory or false.* Rather, it is completely in line
> with contemporary science to hold our thoughts to be causally
> efficacious.[240]

Rather than being in conflict with the rest of science, evidence of psi phenomena provides *further* reason to think that materialism is fatally flawed. Indeed, it
would seem that the acceptance of psi would clinch the argument: In the absence
of psi, epiphenomenalism may be a strained and threadbare option, but still remains
a theoretical possibility. However, unlike ordinary communication, perception, or
action, psi phenomena seem to involve the *direct* action of mind-on-mind or
between mind and matter, bypassing the normal biological channels. For a dualist,
this poses no problem: It has been conjectured that when a person exercises psi his
mind is being influenced by or is influencing objects or brains outside of his body
in the same way his mind normally interacts with his own brain.[241] After all, each
type of interaction is no more mysterious than the other, even though one is com-

monplace and the other relatively rare. But as the arguments above have shown, and as Popper has written, "radical physicalism can be regarded as refuted, quite independently of the paranormal."[242]

Materialism may have been useful as a source of inspiration for classical science, but in hindsight it can be viewed as an error of determinism, observer-independence, and reductionism.

Why are we conscious?

With the emergence of consciousness something new and utterly different has entered the universe—something with no mass or physical dimensions, yet possessing enormous power. And while mental activity seems to exert causal influence, much of our mental activity is unconscious. Consciousness seems to be employed when dealing with novel situations and when learning new skills. Learning to drive a vehicle requires conscious attention to detail, but once we have mastered the skills required, we can operate the vehicle unconsciously, on automatic pilot, all the while carrying on a detailed conversation. But as soon as something out-of-the-ordinary happens, such as an animal darting into our path, conscious control returns to deal with the unexpected.

Renowned neurosurgeon Wilder Penfield thought that the relationship of mind to brain was that of programmer to computer: The mind programs the brain to handle routine tasks, freeing itself to do other things. From his work with epileptic patients, Penfield noted that an epileptic discharge may confine itself to one functional area within the brain. If, for instance, the speech area of the cerebral cortex were the only part affected, then the epileptic discharge would produce nothing more than paralytic silence. If however, the discharge occurred in the higher brain stem, which Penfield identified as the "seat of consciousness", then he described how the individual was converted into *a mindless automaton*: "He may wander about, confused and aimless. Or he may continue to carry out whatever purpose his mind was in the act of handing on to his automatic sensory-motor mechanism when the highest brain-mechanism went out of action. Or he follows a stereotyped, habitual pattern of behavior. In every case, however, the automaton can make few, if any, decisions for which there has been no precedent."[243]

Penfield provides several examples of patients that suffered attacks in the higher brain stem while playing piano, walking home through busy streets, or driving a car. In these cases the individuals continued on with what they were doing, although retained no memory of doing so. He describes what happens when the "seat of consciousness" is temporarily incapacitated:

> The human automaton, which replaces the man when the highest brain-mechanism is inactivated, is a thing without the capacity to make completely new decisions. It is a thing without the capacity to form new

memory records and a thing without that indefinable attribute, a sense of humor. The automaton is incapable of thrilling to the beauty of a sunset or of experiencing contentment, happiness, love, compassion. These, like all awareness, are functions of the mind. The automaton is a thing that makes use of the reflexes and the skills, inborn and acquired, that are housed in the computer. At times it may have a plan that will serve it in place of a purpose for a few minutes. This automatic coordinator that is ever active within each of us, seems to be the most amazing of biological computers.[244]

Consciousness seems to resemble a search light beam that illuminates the parts of our mental activity accessible to it, on demand, as determined by our drives and desires. But it remains a mystery why conscious mental activity is required at all, even for dealing with novel situations. Perhaps the reason has to do with emotion. It is possible to be conscious without emotion, but is it possible to feel emotion without being conscious? Perhaps our animal ancestors that were motivated by primitive emotion simply enjoyed a decisive advantage over their less-sentient competitors.

Consciousness, or at least aspects of it, may very well enhance an organism's ability to survive and propagate, but some conscious activity seems to have little if anything to do with biological survival, even among our cousins in the animal kingdom. Birds have been known to tumble in the wind, dolphins have been spotted body surfing, and wild eagles have been seen playing catch. It's difficult to explain these activities in terms of contributing to survival, as difficult as it is to explain the survival value of listening to music, playing chess, or drinking wine.

And it must be stressed how little we are actually saying when we describe consciousness as an emergent property. We certainly have no idea *how* consciousness could possibly emerge from the configurational properties of the brain. At any rate, saying consciousness emerges does not, to my mind, necessarily imply that consciousness depends for its existence on a material brain—that is, did not exist before the full development of brains, and cannot exist without material brains. It seems coherent to speculate that consciousness may have emerged into the material world when conditions finally allowed—that is, when primitive brains finally achieved the required level of complexity.

So, the brain may be necessary for consciousness to emerge into and interface with the material world. As mentioned, some writers, such as physicist Nick Herbert, would then describe consciousness as an *elemental* property, rather than an emergent one. Herbert and other physicists in the von Neumann tradition seriously entertain the idea that consciousness is a property of the universe as elemental as matter and energy, and that mind interacts with matter at the level of the emergence into actuality of individual quantum events. As mentioned earlier, this would resolve the paradox of existence that is raised by the von Neumann interpretation.

At any rate, it could be argued that the distinction between elemental and emergent is largely semantic. When we say a rabbit emerges from a hole, are we implying that the rabbit depends on the hole for its existence? Yet it must be admitted that when we describe a property as "emergent" we are usually referring to its creation as a result of the special arrangement in space and time of its constituent parts; and so perhaps a dependency *is* implied. Perhaps a respect for conventional usage requires a dualist to describe consciousness as an elemental rather than an emergent property.

However, without presenting any empirical evidence to support the existence of post-mortem consciousness, dualism is pure speculation. Nothing discussed so far has provided solid support for dualism as opposed to mere mentalism. Support for dualism depends upon the evidence for disembodied consciousness that will be discussed in the second book of this series.

11

The "Extraordinary Claims" of Parapsychology

Skeptics often quote Carl Sagan's remark that "extraordinary claims require extraordinary evidence", and certainly this rule of thumb is useful as a guide. But we must remember that we have no objective guidelines as to what constitutes an "extraordinary claim," or what counts as "extraordinary evidence." And as our theories change, what was once considered extraordinary can become quite ordinary—as, for instance, has happened with the acceptance of meteorites, continental drift, and quantum mechanics. What makes the claims of the psi researchers so extraordinary to the skeptics is the supposed inconsistency of psi with all of modern science. This misconception, probably more than any other factor, explains the continuing refusal of the skeptics to accept the best of the latest evidence as conclusive, even when they have run out of counter-explanations.

It also explains why the controversy has continued for as long as it has. In any other field, the debate would have ended long ago. Back in 1951, the psychologist Donald Hebb wrote:

> Why do we not accept ESP as a psychological fact? Rhine has offered enough evidence to have convinced us on almost any other issue… Personally, I do not accept ESP for a moment, because it does not make sense. My external criteria, both of physics and of physiology, say that ESP is not a fact despite the behavioral evidence that has been reported. I cannot see what other basis my colleagues have for rejecting it… Rhine may still turn out to be right, improbable as I think that is, and my own rejection of his view is—in the literal sense—prejudice.[245]

As mentioned earlier, in 1955 George Price wrote that "Dozens of experimenters have obtained positive results in ESP experiments, and the mathematical procedures have been approved by leading statisticians." Yet later in the same article, after writing that "ESP is incompatible with current scientific theory", he offers his conclusion:

My opinion concerning the findings of the parapsychologists is that
many of them are dependent on clerical and statistical errors and
unintentional use of sensory cues, and that all extrachance results
not so explicable are dependent on deliberate fraud or mildly
abnormal mental conditions.

As we have seen, similar views are still held by many in the skeptical community.
Parapsychologist Charles Honorton has shown how the skeptical criticisms fall
into three categories, and in each major phase of the controversy, have followed this
pattern:

- *Statistical criticisms seeking to demonstrate that the claimed effects are not really significant.* This type of criticism has usually been championed by psychologists,
  and refuted by statisticians. If critics could sustain their case at this point, the
  controversy would end here.

- *Methodological criticisms asserting that the effects are caused by procedural flaws.*
  ...advocates of flaw hypotheses have seldom subjected their flaw hypotheses to empirical test, but have tended instead to argue for their plausibility.
  In response, parapsychologists have conducted new experiments that eliminate the suspected flaws.

- *Speculative criticisms based on* a priori *and* ad hominem *arguments.* This form of
  criticism has usually been founded on the assumption that the existence of
  psi phenomena is incompatible with fundamental scientific principles, but
  the proponents of *a priori* arguments have never successfully demonstrated
  the nature of such incompatibilities.[246]

There is a relationship between these three categories of criticisms. At each
stage of the debate, the statistical criticisms have been advanced first and have been
easily refuted, as of the three they are the most straightforward and easily dealt
with. Then the other two types have followed, with the methodological criticisms
consisting of allegations that the results *could have been due to* such flaws as sensory
leakage, hidden cues, recording errors, and so forth. In response, parapsychologists
have conducted new experiments that have eliminated the suspected flaws, but the
critics have (until now in the case of the autoganzfeld) always returned with new
counter-explanations, sometimes alleging complex and elaborate fraud scenarios.[247] But the driving force behind the first two types of criticisms has always been
the belief behind the third, that the existence of psi phenomena is incompatible
with fundamental scientific principles. This is evident in the following remark from
Paul Kurtz, one of the founding fathers of CSICOP:

A high degree of replicability is essential to the further development of parapsychology. Some sciences may be exempt from the replicability criterion, but this is only the case if their findings do not contradict the general conceptual framework of scientific knowledge, which parapsychology seems to do. According to the parapsychologists, for example, ESP seems to be independent of space and does not weaken with distance; precognition presupposes backward causation; psychokinesis violates the conservation-of-energy law.[248]

The first alleged contradiction ("ESP seems to be independent of space and does not weaken with distance") has already been dealt with in our discussion of non-locality. What about the other two?

12

Psi and Physics

Although as we have seen, there is every reason to think that the current laws of physics are incomplete and will eventually be rewritten as they have been several times before, the acceptance of psi would not *by itself* require that they be rewritten, as the current laws of physics are not violated by paranormal phenomena. Despite psychologist Ray Hyman's insistence that our acceptance of the existence of psi would require that "we abandon relativity and quantum mechanics in their current formulations,"[249] it appears that many physicists do not share this opinion. Consider this remark by quantum theorist Euan Squires that seems to bear directly on what is probably the most intuitively distressing of all psi phenomena—precognition:

> Bearing in mind the issue of causality, we might ask…why we believe that the past causes the present. Indeed, we could wonder why there is such a difference between the past, which we remember, and the future, which we don't! In case we are tempted to think these things are just obvious, we should note that *the fundamental laws of physics are completely neutral with regard to the direction of time*, i.e. they are unchanged if we change the direction of the time variable. Concepts like 'past' and 'present', separated by 'now' do not have a natural place in the laws of physics. Presumably this is why Einstein was able to write to a friend that the distinction between past and present was only a 'stubbornly persistent illusion'. …What effect does quantum theory have on such discussions? Like classical mechanics, orthodox quantum theory is invariant under a change in the direction of time.[250]

Physicist Gerald Feinberg also commented on the compatibility between modern physics and precognition:

> Instead of forbidding precognition from happening, [accepted physical] theories typically have sufficient symmetry (between past and future) to suggest that phenomena akin to precognition should occur…. Indeed,

phenomena involving a reversed time order of cause and effect are generally excluded from consideration on the ground that they have not been observed, rather than because the theory forbids them. This exclusion itself introduces an element of asymmetry into the physical theories, which some physicists have felt was improper or required further explanation.... Thus, if such phenomena indeed occur, *no change in the fundamental equations of physics would be needed to describe them.* [251]

Another objection that has been raised is that the existence of psychokinesis would violate the first law of thermodynamics: Energy can neither be created nor destroyed, merely transformed. CSICOP Chairman Paul Kurtz writes:

What would happen to the conservation-of-energy principle if PK were a fact? *How can a mental entity cause a physical change in the state of matter?* Comparing the alleged evidence for PK with the need to overthrow a basic, well-documented principle of physics is questionable. [252]

An identical objection has been raised by the philosopher Daniel Dennett as a basis for arguing that *dualism* is a physical impossibility.*[253] Physicists Rosenblum and Kuttner disagree:

Some theorists deny the possibility of duality by arguing that a signal from a non-material mind could not carry energy and thus could not influence material brain cells. Because of this inability of a mind to supply energy to influence the neurons of the brain, it is claimed that physics demonstrates an inescapable flaw of dualism. However, no energy need be involved in determining to *which particular* situation a wavefunction collapses. Thus the determination of which of the physically possible conscious experiences becomes the actual experience is a process that need not involve energy transfer. Quantum mechanics therefore allows an escape from the supposed fatal flaw of dualism. It is a mistake to think that dualism can be ruled out on the basis of physics. [254]

As physicist-philosopher C.D. Broad pointed out long ago—at a time when quantum mechanics was still in its infancy—even if all physical-to-physical causation involves a transfer of energy, we have no reason to think that such a transfer would

---

* Dennett, 1991, pages 33-39. Dennett completely ignores quantum physics, and writes: "This fundamentally antiscientific stance of dualism is, to my mind, it's most disqualifying feature, and is the reason why in this book I adopt the apparently dogmatic rule that dualism is to be avoided *at all costs*." [page 37].

For effective refutations of the views of Dennett and several other philosophers by quantum physicists, see Wigner, 1961; Firsoff, 1975; Rosenblum & Kuttner, 1999; and Stapp, 1999.

also be required in mental-to-physical or physical-to-mental causation.[255] This, of course, is completely consistent with the point made above by quantum physicists Rosenblum and Kuttner.

The influence of the mental on the physical does not violate the laws of modern physics. Recognizing that a single quantum event may suffice to make a neuron discharge, John Eccles and other neuroscientists have speculated that the mind interacts with the brain by influencing events in neurons at the quantum level. So, if the phenomenon of non-material minds influencing material brain cells at the quantum level would not involve a violation of modern physics, then neither would the influence of minds on Rhine's dice or on Schmidt's and Jahn's random number generators.

At any rate, it should be noted that even in classical physics the theory of the conservation of energy does not *necessarily* rule out interaction between the mental and the physical. When some philosophers object that causation of a physical event by a mental one is precluded by the conservation of energy principle, they mean that such influence would imply that a quantity of energy is introduced into the world; and this would constitute a violation of the conservation principle, which is often expressed with the statement that in a closed system the amount of energy is constant.

However, as philosopher of science Morris Keeton has pointed out, the proposition that energy is conserved in the material world is not known, either *a priori* or empirically, to be true without exception.[256] The principle of the conservation of energy, or of mass-energy, is in fact only a *conjecture*—a condition that the material world must satisfy *if* it is in fact a wholly, closed, isolated system. When it is asserted that interaction between the mental and physical is impossible because it would violate the "principle" of the conservation of energy, then, as Ducasse remarks, "the very point at issue is of course whether or not the material world *is* in fact a *wholly* closed, isolated system."[257]

Some critics, such as George Price, CSICOP chairman and co-founder Paul Kurtz, and the philosopher Antony Flew[258] place great emphasis on what Broad has called the "basic limiting principles" of science. Unlike Kurtz, Price and Flew admit that they cannot think of any modern scientific law that would be violated by the existence of psi. Back in 1955 Price wrote: "It is sometimes asked: with what scientific laws does ESP conflict? But the conflict is at so fundamental a level as to be not so much with named 'laws' but rather with basic principles."[259] Thirty years later Antony Flew wrote: "Certainly it is not easy to think of any particular named law of nature—such as Boyle's Law or Snell's Law or what have you—that would be, or is, as Hume would have it, 'violated' by the occurrence of psi. What that threatens is more fundamental. For the psi phenomena are in effect defined in terms of the violation of certain 'basic limiting principles,' principles that constitute a framework for all our thinking about and investigation of human affairs, and principles that are continually being verified by our discoveries."[260]

As formulated by Broad in 1949, these "basic limiting principles" include: (a) a person cannot know the contents of another person's mind except through the use of normal senses or inferences from them (would be violated by telepathy); (b) we cannot gain information about a distance point in space without information transmitted to our normal senses (would be violated by clairvoyance); (c) we cannot have knowledge of future events not based on inferences from current events (would be violated by precognition); (d) we cannot modify the state or motion of any objects without the use of our limbs or tools (violated by psychokinesis); and (e) minds cannot exist apart from brains (violated by the evidence for survival).

But as Stokes has pointed out, Broad's basic limiting principles are not in fact derivable from the known laws of science, but are merely restatements of the impossibility of the various forms of psi phenomena. With the possible exception of some forms of psychokinesis, none of the known laws of physics are violated by the various psi phenomena mentioned here. In fact, as we shall see, many of the theoretical explanations, especially the observational theories of Schmidt and Walker, are explicitly constructed in terms of quantum physics.

Psi is a property of conscious, living organisms, and the scope of present day physics is limited to dealing only with inanimate objects. Some may argue with justification that this is its proper scope, but *could* physics be extended to deal with conscious living organisms? Perhaps, but Eugene Wigner believes that this extension would require radical changes: "It will have to be replaced by new laws, based on new concepts, if organisms with consciousness are to be described. ...in order to deal with the phenomenon of life, the laws of physics will have to be changed, not only reinterpreted."[261] This opinion is echoed in a remark made by Nobel laureate physicist Brian Josephson in response to an interview question from Halcomb Noble of the *New York Times*:

> You ask whether parapsychology lies within the bounds of physical law. My feeling is that to some extent it does, but physical law itself may have to be redefined. It may be that some effects in parapsychology are ordered-state effects of a kind not yet encompassed by physical theory.[262]

Currently, physics does not deal directly with variables such as consciousness, intent, and values: They are outside of its scope. But these variables are crucial to any explanation of psi, and so it does not seem likely that parapsychology will be reduced to paraphysics any time soon. As we have seen, an important fact that emerged from the early work of the experimental psychologists was the total absence of any systematic relationships between psi effects and any known physical variables; the operation of psi appears to be unaffected by distance or the presence of barriers. Of course, with the modern concept of non-locality, this theoretical objection of the classical physicist is overcome, but what weak relationships can be derived from the data indicate the relevance of psychological variables such as attitude and certain aspects of personality. Physics currently deals only with the world of inanimate matter, in which nothing, we may safely say, happens in order to fulfill some objective. In contrast, psi phenomena, appears irreducibly goal-directed in character. John Beloff summarizes the dual nature of psi:

> Psi phenomena are problematic precisely because they involve events in the real world and thus become candidates for a physical explanation, yet at the same time they are critically bound up with certain states of mind. Thus they cross the dividing line between objectivity and subjectivity which normal mental phenomena do not.[263]

Parapsychology deals with the interface between the mental and the physical; it straddles the boundary between psychology and physics as it studies the interaction of mind and matter. It should be remembered that psychology is *not* the parent discipline of parapsychology, and so the term "parapsychology" is really a misnomer. However, it is doubtful that we can ever have a purely physical explanation of psi, that is, one that does not include key references to purely mental concepts such as intent, meaning, and belief. Consciousness appears essential in any explanation of psi, for two reasons: 1) results in experiments seem to depend to a large extent on the beliefs, personality factors, and mood of the participants and experimenters, and 2) case studies from the field (or anecdotal reports, if you prefer) seem to strongly indicate that it is *meaningful, useful* information that is usually detected via telepathy or clairvoyance, not random noise. PK similarly appears to be goal-directed. So, we are dealing both with aspects of mind (the subjective) and events in the real world (the objective). Since explanations of psi need to incorporate both the mental and the physical, the contributions of both psychology and physics are crucial. As we have seen, some experiments have strongly suggested that consciousness can not only collapse the state vector, but also bias the outcome. We have also seen that psi seems unaffected by distance or barriers, suggesting that psi phenomena may exploit non-locality. Perhaps the required bridge between psychology and physics will be built on the concepts of the observer effect and non-locality.

The objection that the existence of psi would conflict with physics has been raised far more frequently by psychologists than by modern physicists. Gardner Murphy, former president of the American Psychological Society and later the American Society for Psychical Research, described the state of mind of many psychologists, and predicted a slow but steady change:

> Psychologists may be a little bewildered when they encounter modern physicists who take these phenomena in stride, in fact, take them very much more seriously than psychologists do, saying, as physicists, that they are no longer bound by the types of Newtonian energy distribution, inverse square laws, etc., with which scientists

used to regard themselves as tightly bound. ...psychologists probably will witness a period of slow, but definite, erosion of the blandly exclusive attitude that has offered itself as the only appropriate scientific attitude in this field. The data from parapsychology will be almost certainly in harmony with general psychological principles and will be assimilated rather easily within the systematic framework of psychology as a science when once the imagined appropriateness of Newtonian physics is put aside, and modern physics replaces it.[264]

13

Towards a New World View

Despite what several of the prominent skeptics claim, it should be clear now that the existence of psi *is* consistent with the new metaphysics of science, especially with its acceptance of non-locality, emergent properties, and the causal role of consciousness. Unfamiliarity with the new metaphysical implications of science explains the dogmatism we so often find regarding psi—if a person's *a priori* conviction is that the existence of psi phenomena would render most of modern science obsolete, then almost *any* normal explanation, no matter how improbable or convoluted, will be preferable to an explanation involving psi.

We are in a better position now to understand the resistance of some mainstream scientists to accepting the reality of psi. The main reasons for their resistance would seem to be: 1) lack of awareness of the experimental evidence; 2) fear of ridicule because of the rhetorical campaigns of some skeptics; 3) adherence to an outmoded metaphysics of science; and 4) the inability to explain psi with the generally accepted theories of biology and psychology. The rhetorical arguments of the skeptics derive most of their influence from ignorance of the experimental evidence. As for the third reason, we have seen that adherence to an outmoded metaphysics of science seems much more prevalent among psychologists than physicists. Skeptics such as psychologist Susan Blackmore are fond of saying that the existence of psi is incompatible "with our scientific worldview," but with *which* scientific worldview? Psi is certainly incompatible with the old scientific worldview, based on Newtonian mechanics and behaviorist psychology. It is not incompatible with the emerging scientific worldview based upon quantum mechanics and cognitive psychology.

The case can now be made that the concept of the "paranormal" is an anachronism and should be abandoned. The term is usually used to imply that psi phenomena operate outside of nature, in a parallel realm not subject to the rules of nature as we currently understand them. The term arose within the context of Newtonian physics, and its primary effect has been to create an artificial schism between psi researchers and the rest of the scientific community. As Honorton has written,

> A more empirically fruitful conceptualization is that parapsychology involves the study of currently anomalous communication and energetic processes. This approach guides the efforts of most of the parapsychological researchers I know, who work on the assumption that they are dealing with unexplained—anomalous, but not unexplainable—natural processes.[265]

The current inability to explain psi within mainstream physiology and psychology probably explains the greater resistance to psi found among some members of the scientific community than among laypersons. Most of the latter are not strongly committed, intellectually and emotionally, to the *completeness* of a particular set of explanations regarding perception and action. So, most laypeople are not greatly troubled by reports of experiences that cannot be explained by the currently conventional theories. This also helps explains the acceptance of telepathy, precognition, and so forth among our pre-scientific ancestors, and also among members of so-called "primitive" cultures in modern times. Thomas Kuhn, in his classic book, *The Structure of Scientific Revolutions,* argued that science progresses with the discovery of anomalies, or findings that are not predicted or explained by a currently accepted theory, which he called a "paradigm." According to Kuhn, without a paradigm, there are no anomalies: "Anomaly appears only against the background provided by the paradigm."[266]

Kuhn presents some case histories showing that when scientists are intellectually and emotionally invested in a particular paradigm, some scientists will label as "impossible" many *logically possible* phenomena that cannot be explained within the paradigm. It is important to remember that many of the phenomena mainstream science accepts today were once ridiculed and considered impossible. The idea that rocks could fall from the sky (what we now call meteorites) was strongly resisted. The idea of continental drift was ridiculed for decades, simply because no known mechanism could account for it.[267] This resistance to change seems common among scientists when confronted with anomalies. Even X-rays were considered by some to be an elaborate hoax.[268]

But it is highly unlikely that the current generation of skeptics will ever change their minds. No matter what evidence the psi researchers may present, there is a natural human reluctance to admitting that one was wrong all along. As Kuhn pointed out, to some extent science progresses through warfare between different generations of scientists, with the older generation showing greater resistance to new ideas. It is a grim fact that progress in science is sometimes marked by a funeral.*

---

* One of the two original founders of quantum mechanics (along with Einstein) was the great physicist Max Planck, who sadly remarked in his autobiography "a new scientific truth does not triumph by convincing its opponents and making them see the light, but rather because its opponents eventually die, and a new generation grows up that is familiar with it."

In terms of the scientific worldview due to classical physics, psi phenomena can certainly be considered anomalous in the Kuhnian sense: That is, they may be considered awkward facts that violate, in particular, the physical principle of localism and the metaphysical hypothesis that mind can play no causal role in nature. In terms of the newly emerging scientific worldview described above, however, it is questionable whether psi phenomena may be considered anomalous at all. If they still may be, then it is only in a much weaker sense, namely, that we currently cannot provide a satisfactory explanation of their operation given our current understanding of physiology and psychology. But this is true of many phenomena involving the mind, such as hypnosis, dreaming, the role of optimism in healing, and the placebo effect. Largely, this is the case because we currently have no tenable theories of even ordinary consciousness, let alone its exotic variations.

Scientific revolutions have led to profound changes in our metaphysical theories, and it may be that we are on the verge of another profound change as the phenomenon of consciousness and its effects on the world are increasingly incorporated into mainstream science. Psi phenomena do *not* call into question the newly emerging scientific worldview, but they do illustrate the *incompleteness* of our current understanding. Future historians may look back on the 19th and 20th centuries and shake their heads at the arrogance with which many of our scientists and philosophers dogmatically dismissed experiences people in all cultures have reported for thousands of years.

Part III
Is Parapsychology a Science?

Psychical research, or parapsychology, has its genesis in the myths, the folklore, the magic and mysticism of pre-civilization. There is an unbroken historical continuity observable between superstitious occultism and the more sophisticated occultism which flourishes at the present time.

D.H. Rawcliffe
Illusions and Delusions of the Supernatural and the Occult

Chemistry was largely born out of alchemy, and astronomy out of astrology. Shall we flout the science and art of medicine for the hotbed of superstition in which it was nurtured? So Psychic Research is not so very lonely. It is a science, later to develop, like the others, order and discrimination in the midst of chaotic and heterogeneous materials.

Walter Franklin Prince
Is Psychical Research Worth While?

14

The Impoverished State of Skepticism

Over the past twenty years, Hyman, Blackmore, and other critics have tried very hard to show that the results of psi experiments were either not statistically significant, or that they were dependant upon methodological flaws in the experiments. Having failed on both counts, they have been forced to admit that parapsychology has demonstrated anomalous effects that need to be explained, and also to admit that they have run out of plausible counter-explanations.

The current state of skepticism is impoverished. Blackmore has thrown in the towel, Wiseman denies the fact that he has almost perfectly replicated a psi experiment, and Hyman, instead of presenting arguments based on logic and evidence, now offers only a variety of rhetorical arguments designed to persuade us that parapsychology's status as a normal science is somehow questionable.

For instance, Hyman has written that a "serious challenge to parapsychology's quest for scientific status is the lack of cumulativeness in its database. Only parapsychology, among the fields of inquiry claiming scientific status, lacks a cumulative database."[269]

As mentioned earlier, in 1940 J.B. Rhine published his landmark book *Extra-Sensory Perception after Sixty Years* that summarized all quantitative experiments since the founding of the Society for Psychical Research in 1882. How can we reconcile Hyman's claim that parapsychology "lacks a cumulative database" with the existence of this book, considered a classic of experimental parapsychology?

And if a cumulative database for psi experiments does not exist, then how could Radin and Nelson have performed their meta-analysis of RNG PK experiments conducted between 1959 and 1987? How could Radin and Ferrari have conducted their meta-analysis of PK dice experiments using results of experiments dating back to the 1930s? Meta-analysis is *by definition* the analysis of cumulated experiments.

The evolution of the ganzfeld experiments provides an excellent counter to Hyman's charge that psi research lacks cumulativeness. As we saw earlier, the ganzfeld experiments were inspired by both anecdotal and experimental evidence suggesting that the operation of psi is facilitated by the altered states of dreaming, meditation, and hypnosis. This evidence led Honorton to postulate that psi may operate as a weak signal that is normally masked by the stronger signals constantly besieging us from our conventional sense organs, and the early ganzfeld was an attempt to recreate the state of physical relaxation, alertness, and reduced sensory input that is common to dreaming, meditation, and hypnosis. The design of the ganzfeld was based upon several lines of previous research, and was considered as an improvement upon the earlier dream studies at the Maimonides Medical Center. In turn, the automated ganzfeld was an improvement over the earlier ganzfeld experiments, following from criticisms of the earlier work and the guidelines agreed upon by Honorton and Hyman.

Another one of Hyman's criticisms involves the use of statistics in parapsychology experiments:

> Parapsychology is unique among the sciences in relying solely on significant departures from a chance baseline to establish the presence of its alleged phenomenon. In the other sciences the defining phenomena can be reliably observed and do not require indirect statistical measures to justify their existence. Indeed, each branch of science began with phenomena that could be observed directly.[270]

This is indeed an odd criticism. Parapsychology, like the other branches of science, also began with phenomena that could be observed directly—in this case, the reports from all of recorded history, some of which we covered earlier. Parapsychologists have been mostly confined to their laboratories since the 1920's because the skeptics considered these reports "anecdotal" and "extraordinary", and so have demanded experimental evidence. Is Hyman *now* willing to treat these reports as serious evidence?

The 1988 report *Enhancing Human Performance* that Hyman contributed to goes to great lengths to debunk personal reports of paranormal phenomena. Shortly after the report, Colonel Alexander wrote:

> In private conversation with Ray Hyman, I mentioned a display of PK that I, along with numerous other highly skilled observers, had witnessed at close range…. While this had not been conducted according to the strict protocols of a 'scientific' experiment, nonetheless careful and critical observers all agreed the event had occurred as described.
>
> Hyman's response to me on this occasion was that, while many credible people may have truthfully reported such anecdotal experiences, he does not feel obliged to deal with any findings not appearing in the formal journals, no matter how impressive the reports.

The Colonel also described an event witnessed under laboratory conditions:

During an official visit by the entire EHP committee, this time to the Cleve Backster laboratory, a significant anomalous event occurred while all were watching. The event was the production of an electromagnetic signal reflecting the emotional state of a speaker, who was in another room some distance from the sensor. Although there was no direct link-up between the speaker and the sensor, a dramatic and clearly visible shift was recorded. While Hyman found the tracing of interest at the time, no mention of the event appears in the report.[271]

Statistics is widely used in science whenever there is difficulty separating signal from noise. This difficulty is found in physics and chemistry, but much more often in biology and the social sciences, due to the greater random variability found in living systems. With psi we seem to be dealing with what is usually a rather weak effect, and so the statistical analysis of large samples is necessary to detect it amid all of the noise. But parapsychology is hardly unusual in this regard. The link between smoking and lung cancer was first proposed by physicians who noticed that patients who were heavy smokers seemed more likely to contract the disease. But not everyone that smokes gets cancer, and not everyone with lung cancer smoked. Statistical analysis of large numbers of individuals was necessary to conclusively establish the link.

A more recent example from biological science is the even weaker link between high exposure to unusually strong electromagnetic fields and health. An article is *Science* reported that "After spending nearly a decade reviewing the literature on electromagnetic fields (EMFs), a panel of the National Council on Radiation Protection and Measurements (NCRP) has produced a draft report concluding that some health effects linked to EMFs such as cancer and immune deficiencies appear real and warrant steps to reduce EMF exposure.... Biologists have failed to pinpoint a convincing mechanism of action."[272] In other words, statistics has been used to demonstrate an effect, and biologists are now seeking a mechanism, just as in parapsychology.

Finally, Hyman attempts to convince his readers that parapsychological research is somehow suspect with the following remarks:

> Parapsychology is the only field of scientific inquiry that *does not have even one exemplar that can be assigned to students with the expectation that they will observe the original results!....* This is another way of saying that the other domains of inquiry are based upon robust, lawful phenomena whose conditions of occurrence can be specified in such a way that even novices will be able to observe and/or produce them.[273]

As an example of an experiment any student can perform, Hyman offers the example of splitting a beam of white light into its component colors. But apart from simple experiments such as this, students cannot be expected to do a simple experiment and observe the same result regarding a *number* of well-established phenomena. Examples would include the connection between aspirin and reduced heart attacks, or the connection between smoking and lung cancer.[274] The problem with these more complicated phenomena is, of course, that many other factors influence the probability of heart disease or cancer, and so the use of statistics is necessary to isolate the influence of one factor from among many. Not everyone who smokes will get lung cancer, and not everyone who attempts a psi experiment will obtain positive results. However, in both cases, we can predict the proportions that will with a high degree of confidence.

Parapsychology does have its exemplar experiments, such as the autoganzfeld and the RNG PK experiments. However, to be reasonably assured of a successful outcome in these experiments requires hundreds of trials in the former, and thousands of trials in the latter. One can sense the exasperation statistician Jessica Utts must have felt when she wrote:

> As I have repeatedly tried to explain to Professor Hyman and others, when dealing with a small to medium effect it takes hundreds or sometimes thousands of trials to establish "statistical significance." In fact, the physicians Health Study that initially established the link between taking aspirin and reducing heart attacks studied over 22,000 men. Had it been conducted on only 2,200 men with the same reduction in heart attacks, it would not have achieved statistical significance. Should students be required to recruit 22,000 participants and conduct such an experiment before we believe the connection between aspirin and heart attacks is real?[275]

At any rate, Hyman's remarks are now somewhat dated and obsolete. In recent years, experiments have been designed that can be assigned to students with the expectation that they will observe the original results. The best examples today are probably the telepathy experiments designed by Rupert Sheldrake, and available on his website (along with instructions for teachers). These experiments can be performed with only a handful of participants and completed in less than 20 minutes. In many cases the effects have been robust enough to capture without requiring hundreds or thousands of trials. But thousands of trials *have* been completed, in schools and by private parties, and the results compiled via the internet. As described on the website, the odds against chance for these positive results are quadrillions to one.

15

The Nature of Science

Arguing over whether an anomaly is pseudo-science, and appealing to science as the arbiter of truth, serves to make the nature of science a common theme in these arguments, one about which wide ignorance and confusion are then displayed: over whether science is a quest, or the application of a defined method, or a body of reliable knowledge; over how reliable scientific knowledge actually is, especially when laws or theories are applied under novel circumstances.

Henry Bauer

Debates about the nature of science, and about the scientific status of parapsychology have characterized the history of parapsychology. Since Hyman and other critics have spent so much time and effort questioning the scientific status of parapsychology, it seems appropriate here to discuss the nature of scientific inquiry. But before we examine the philosophic arguments, consider this brief episode in the history of parapsychology's struggle for legitimacy.

In 1961 the Parapsychological Association (PA) applied for affiliation with the American Association for the Advancement of Science (AAAS), but was rejected "on grounds that at present, parapsychology is not firmly or generally accepted as a science."[276] It was rejected again in 1963.

The PA applied for membership again in 1969. Just before the votes were cast, the renowned anthropologist Margaret Mead made the following statement:

> For the last ten years, we have been arguing about what constitutes science and scientific method and what societies use it. We even changed the By-Laws about it. The PA uses statistics and blinds, placebos, double blinds and other standard devices. The whole history of scientific advance is full of scientists investigating phenomena that the establishment did not believe were there. I submit we vote in favor of this Association's work.[277]

Following her speech, the membership voted five-to-one in favor of granting affiliation. But this was not the end of the struggle. Ten years later physicist John A. Wheeler launched a campaign to get the PA disaffiliated from the AAAS. As part of a speech titled "Drive the Pseudos out of the Workshop of Science," Wheeler made the following statement:

> There is nothing that one can't research the hell out of. Research guided by bad judgment is a black hole for good money.... Now is the time for everyone who believes in the Rule of Reason to speak up against pathological science and its purveyors."[278]

The campaign failed. Parapsychology did not experience any stunning break-throughs or notable setbacks between 1961 and 1979, so this brief history shows that social factors have played an important role in determining the recognition of parapsychology as a science. But philosophers have long contemplated the nature of science, and we must examine their work to see if parapsychology qualifies as a science according to rational (as opposed to sociological) criteria.

The Nature of Science

It is generally recognized that science is concerned with theories, but in a scientific context the word *theory* has a somewhat different meaning than it frequently does in ordinary conversation: In the latter it is often used loosely to mean any degree of speculation. In police work, for example, it often means a provisional explanation of what happened in the commission of a crime. But scientific theories are not meant to be explanations of isolated events: They are meant to apply to a class of events that are similar in some crucial respects. So, a scientific theory of crime will not attempt to explain how or why a *particular* crime occurred, but will attempt to explain some *class* of crimes.

This *universal* property of scientific theories cannot be stressed enough. A scientific theory cannot be merely speculation about a particular fact. The ancient Babylonians kept highly precise records of daily observations, and were able to use these records to make highly accurate predictions about the movements of heavenly bodies. But the Babylonians did not engage in science, for although they gathered facts, they did not propose theories to explain *how these facts fit together*. When Isaac Newton proposed that a planet and the sun are attracted by a gravitational force that is directly proportional to the product of their masses and inversely proportional to the square of the distance between them, he offered a *relation* between masses and distances—a relation that of course became celebrated as the Newtonian theory of gravity.[279]

But what makes a theory *scientific*? How do we distinguish between scientific and nonscientific theories? Traditionally, the answer has been that science is distinguished from pseudo-science, and from metaphysics, by its empirical method, which is essentially *inductive*: Theories are inferred from observations, and in turn these theories are *confirmed* by further observations.

But many theories purport to be based on, and confirmed by, observation. Astrology, for instance, is thought by its supporters to be confirmed by extensive empirical evidence based on observation—on horoscopes and biographical data. Should astrology be considered a science? What is the distinction between true science and other forms of belief that purport to be based upon observation?

The celebrated philosopher of science Karl Popper began pondering this question while a student in Austria during the early years of the twentieth century. As a student he had been exposed to a lot of the revolutionary new ideas that were then gaining wide exposure—most notably Freudian theories of psychoanalysis, Adler's theories of individual psychology, the Marxist theory of history, and Einstein's theory of relativity.

It struck the young Popper how the supporters of Freud's and Adler's psychological theories seemed to find confirmation everywhere they looked. The data always seemed to fit the theories, and it began to dawn on Popper that perhaps this fact—that observations always seemed to be consistent with the theories—might not be their biggest strength, as supporters claimed, but their greatest weakness.

The situation with Einstein's theory was different. Here was a theory very different from Newton's theory in its fundamental outlook, which at that time was utterly successful. But what really impressed Popper was the way Einstein used his theory to make a number of bold predictions, all of which could be tested. Einstein declared that these predictions were crucial: If the results of future experiments did not agree with his theoretical calculations, he would regard his theory as refuted. One of these predictions was that light would be bent by massive bodies such as the sun, and in one of the earliest tests photographs of stars taken by the Eddington expedition during an eclipse provided data in agreement with Einstein's prediction.

Here seemed to be a crucial difference between relativity and the two psychological theories: The former took risks in making predictions that could in principle be wrong. Unlike the theories of Freud and Adler, Einstein's theory was *incompatible with certain possible results of observations*. Or, in other words, it could be *tested*.

This consideration led Popper to the conclusion that a theory that is not capable of being refuted by any possible observation is not truly scientific. One can sum up Popper's famous demarcation between science and non-science by saying that the criterion of the scientific status of a theory is its *falsifiability.* Accordingly, theories that are not falsifiable in principle cannot claim to be scientific, and so belong to metaphysics, ideology, or pseudo-science.

It is important to stress that Popper never thought that metaphysical theories were thereby meaningless, or insignificant, or unimportant. They are simply not testable in the way that scientific theories are. Popper actually thought that what Freud and Adler said was of considerable importance, and hoped that these theories might one day play a role as part of psychological theories that are testable. Metaphysical speculations may inspire programs of scientific research; they also may in time become capable of being tested, and hence attain scientific status. Ancient examples of metaphysical theories that became testable would include the speculations of Aristarchus and Copernicus that the earth revolves around the sun; another example would be the theory of Democritus that the world is composed of atoms.

Popper also noted that the reverse can happen: A theory may start out as scientific, by having testable implications, and then *become* unscientific by immunizing itself against apparent examples of falsification. Thus Popper argued that Marxism started out as a scientific theory: It predicted that capitalism would lead to increasing misery among the masses, and then be overthrown by revolution and replaced by socialism; it also predicted that this would occur first in the most technically developed countries. When the so-called worker's revolution first occurred in then-backward and agrarian Russia, supporters of the theory did not accept this as a refutation: The theory was simply modified so that it became immune to falsification.

According to this scheme, Freud's and Adler's theories were never scientific but belonged in the realm of proto-scientific metaphysics; Marxism started out as a science but became an ideology; and astrology, insofar as it makes vague predictions that are simply irrefutable, belongs to pseudo-science. *

A few further points are necessary to clarify this picture. One is that some metaphysical theories may not be directly testable, but may be implied by scientific theories. They enter into our belief systems on the coat tails of currently accepted scientific theories; but if a scientific theory is refuted by observation, then any metaphysical theories that entered in its wake are also refuted. An example of this would be the metaphysical theory of *determinism* implied by the clockwork universe of Newtonian physics. If Newtonian physics is rejected as false, then determinism should be rejected as well.

Another important point is that Popper's demarcation between science and non-science is rough. As mentioned, what was a metaphysical theory yesterday may become a testable scientific theory tomorrow. And of course, some theories are more testable than others for a variety of reasons: the technology currently available, the ease with which reliable data may be gathered, or the nature of the subject matter. According to Popper, "a theory is scientific to the *degree* to which it is testable."[280]

Finally, it is worth pointing out that Popper was not a simple falsificationist in the manner that many of his critics have assumed:[281] He did not think that theories were automatically abandoned as soon as they are shown to be false, but only when we have a better theory available. One theory may be considered better than a competitor in at least two senses: It may pass tests its competitor fails, and it may

---

* What makes Gauquelin's neoastrological claims so different from traditional astrology, of course, is that they are formulated in such a manner as to be easily tested—that is, they are capable of being *falsified* by the data.

explain everything the other theory explains and more. Popper realized that science often operates as though it aims not at truth but merely at approximations to the truth. In such circumstances, a theory will not be discarded as soon as it is falsified, but only when it is found to approximate the truth less accurately than some rival hypothesis.

Early in the last century, Popper attended a lecture given by the young Albert Einstein, and was greatly impressed. Here was a bold new theory that deviated in its fundamental outlook from Newton's, a theory that up to that time was almost entirely and utterly successful in its predictions. (It failed to predict the orbit of Mercury with complete accuracy, but this did not trouble many). According to Einstein's theory, Newton's theory was an excellent approximation, though false (just as, according to Newton's theory, Kepler's theory is an excellent approximation, though false).

What really impressed Popper were the following two points: first, Einstein used his theory to make several bold predictions, and declared that if the subsequent experiments did not agree with his predictions, he would regard his theory as refuted. But as the lecture continued, Einstein went even further, as Popper recounts:

> Even if they were observed as predicted, Einstein declared that *his theory was false*: he said that it would be a better approximation to the truth than Newton's, but he gave reasons why he would not, even if all predictions came out right, regard it as a true theory. He sketched a number of demands that a true theory (a unified field theory) would have to satisfy, and declared that his theory was at best an approximation to this so far unattained unified field theory.[282]

This lecture led Popper to spend the rest of his life in the philosophy of science. Einstein himself spent the rest of his life trying to achieve his dream of a unified field theory and failed, but the crucial point that Popper eventually concluded from Einstein's lecture was that *truth* does not decide the scientific character of a theory—its *falsifiability* does.*

The Problem of Induction: Are our scientific beliefs irrational?

As mentioned earlier, traditional accounts of science stressed *verification* of scientific theories, and argued that scientific theories differ from non-scientific theories in

---

* Critics of Popper's theories occasionally question whether or not the theory of falsifiability is itself falsifiable. But this question should not be asked, as the theory is not meant to be a *scientific* theory: that is, it does not consist of universal statements about some empirical matter. It is meant to be a methodological or philosophical theory. It is important to remember that falsification is a criterion of *demarcation*, not of meaning.

that the former are based on observations, and in turn are verified by further observations. Thus, it was argued that the scientific method is essentially *inductive*: That is, our scientific laws, expressed as universal laws governing a class of events similar in some crucial respects, are *derived* from repeated observations of events of the type in question.

But as long ago as 1739, the Scottish philosopher David Hume pointed out that induction cannot be logically justified. He held that there were no logical arguments that would allow us to establish *"that those instances, of which we have had no experience, should resemble those, of which we have had experience."* He maintained that we have no logical reason to expect the future to resemble the past, as *"even after the observation of the frequent or constant conjunction of objects, we have no reason to draw any inference concerning any object beyond those of which we have had experience."*[283] In other words, from the fact that every crow we may have seen so far is black the conclusion that *all* crows are black does not *logically* follow. Seeing a white crow would not in any sense be a logical contradiction of the earlier observations.

However, Hume of course noticed that men everywhere, including himself, believe in laws and regularities. But if an inductive inference—an inference from repeatedly observed instances to yet unobserved instances—could not be justified on rational grounds, what could account for its apparent prevalence? Hume concluded that it was nothing more than force of habit. Although there was no rational justification for induction, Hume believed that it was a psychological fact, and that in any case, men needed induction for their very survival. But if this is the case—that all empirical belief is based on nothing more than habit—then this would imply that all scientific knowledge is irrational.

This conclusion greatly distressed Bertrand Russell: He was not willing to abandon the principle of *empiricism*, which asserts that only observation and experiment may decide upon the *acceptance or rejection* of scientific statements, including laws and theories. But he was driven to conclude that if Hume's rejection of the principle of induction is valid, then "every attempt to arrive at general scientific laws from particular observations is fallacious, and Hume's scepticism is inescapable for an empiricist."[284] He wrote that "the rejection of induction makes all expectation as to the future irrational" and that "taking even our firmest expectations, such as that the sun will rise tomorrow, there is not a shadow of a reason, for supposing them more likely to be verified than not."[285] He writes of Hume that, "It is evident that he started out with a belief that scientific method yields the truth, the whole truth, and nothing but the truth; he ended, however with the conviction that belief is never rational, since we know nothing."[286] So, "It is therefore important to discover whether there is any answer to Hume within a philosophy that is wholly or mainly empirical. If not, there is no intellectual difference between sanity and insanity. The lunatic who believes that he is a poached egg is to be condemned solely on the ground that he is in a minority. ...This is a desperate point of view, and it must be hoped that there is some way of escaping from it."[287]

Russell's solution is equally desperate: He maintains that "Hume has proved that pure empiricism is not a sufficient basis for science", and so allows a single departure from his otherwise strictly empirical philosophy, basically concluding that we simply have no choice but to accept inductive arguments if we are going to do science. All we can do, according to Russell, is accept that "induction is an independent logical principle, incapable of being inferred either from experience or from other logical principles, and that without this principle science is impossible."[288]

Russell's solution is essentially to accept Hume's logical refutation of induction, but then to argue that we must accept it as a principle incapable of being justified by logic or experience, or in other words, simply on faith. Otherwise, "science is impossible" and "there is no intellectual difference between sanity and insanity."

Popper's solution was radically different. He denied that induction was needed in order to practice science: He even denied that humans or animals used any sort of inductive procedure at all, calling it "a kind of optical illusion."[289] As evidence against *the reality* of induction, he argued that expectations may be formed after only *one* observed instance; that we may be *born* with certain expectations (such as the expectation of being fed); and that long experience may *not* strengthen our expectations of regularities, but rather make us less rigid and dogmatic. Instead of forming our expectations from observed regularities, Popper proposed that both humans and animals use a method of trial and error that only superficially resembles induction, but is logically very different.

As mentioned, Popper proposed that we all may be born with expectations, expectations that are psychologically *a priori*, that is, prior to all observational experience. One of the most important of these expectations is the expectation of finding regularities.[290] Popper thereby turned the tables on Hume's psychological theory: Instead of explaining our propensity to expect regularities as the result of repetition, he proposed that we hypothesize repetition as a result of our propensity to expect regularities. In other words, instead of passively waiting for nature to impose regularities upon us, we actively try to impose regularities upon the world. We search for similarities, and try to explain those similarities in terms of laws invented by us. These laws may have to be discarded later, should observations show that they are wrong. But according to Popper, *first* we jump to conclusions, and then we test them against observations.

> This was a theory of trial and error—of *conjectures and refutations*. It made it possible to understand why our attempts to force interpreta-
>]tions upon the world were logically prior to the observation of similarities. Since there were logical reasons behind this procedure, I thought that it would apply in the field of science also; that scientific theories were not the digest of observations, but that they were inventions—conjectures boldly put forward for trial, to be eliminated if they clashed with observations.[291]

Popper realized that the problem of the irrationality of all human belief, including scientific belief, is solved if we can obtain our knowledge by a non-inductive procedure. There is no need to postulate an "inductive principle"; even if we think that induction exists as a psychological fact, there is, according to Popper, no need to attempt to justify the unjustifiable.

Hume was right: We are not rationally justified in reasoning from instances of which we have had experience to the truth of the corresponding law. But to this negative conclusion Popper added a second: We *are* justified in reasoning from a single counter-instance to the *falsity* of the corresponding law. Consider the universal statement "All swans are white." Hume demonstrated that neither ten nor ten thousand observations of white swans logically imply that the next swan we see will be white. It cannot be verified by *any* number of observations, because no matter how many white swans we may see, it is logically possible that the next swan we see will be black. Yet the universal statement can be *falsified* by the observation of a single black swan.

Of course, in practice, we would be most reluctant to accept a single counter-instance to a highly successful law: We may question the eyewitness accounts, or suspect that the black specimen before us was not really a swan. But this is beside the point: We are logically compelled to reject even the most successful law the moment we accept a single counter-instance. Empirical observation can never *verify* a theory; but it can decisively *refute* a theory.

Popper demonstrated that science can proceed in a truly deductive manner through a process of conjectures and refutations. As long as we concede that all our scientific theories are held tentatively, not as "truths" but as conjectures that may only be *approximations* to the truth, then Hume's dilemma is resolved. They may be falsified by a deductive procedure, but never verified in any logically valid manner. In other words, scientific theories are not *verified* by observations consistent with them; rather, they are *corroborated* by unsuccessful attempts at refutation.

Popper admitted that it took him several years to realize that the problem of induction is an aspect of the problem of demarcation between science and non-science.[292] In fact, his demarcation solves the so-called problem of induction: The problem that, if our scientific beliefs are based on induction, then they are irrational. Hume's problem of induction, and Popper's solution, imply that all our scientific beliefs are not irrational, merely *conjectural*. Belief would indeed be irrational if by "belief" we meant uncritical acceptance of our laws based upon attempts to verify them through repeated observations. If however, by "belief" we mean only tentative acceptance of our scientific theories combined with a willingness to revise them if they fail to pass crucial tests, then Hume was wrong. There is nothing irrational about such acceptance, nor is there anything irrational about relying for practical purposes upon well-tested theories. There is no more rational course of action available to us.

Hume's rejection of induction means that our universal laws or theories can never be proven correct, and so must remain only conjectures, or hypotheses. But

Popper's demonstration of our ability to *falsify* theories by observation means that we can, on purely rational grounds, prefer some competing conjectures to others. Popper sums it up:

> To put it in a nutshell, Russell's desperate remark that if with Hume we reject all positive induction, "there is no intellectual difference between sanity and insanity" is mistaken. For the rejection of induction does not prevent us from preferring, say, Newton's theory to Kepler's, or Einstein's theory to Newton's: during our rational critical discussion of these theories we *may* have accepted the existence of counterexamples to Kepler's theory which do not refute Newton's, and of counterexamples to Newton's which do not refute Einstein's. Given the acceptance of these counterexamples we can say that Kepler's and Newton's theories are certainly false; whilst Einstein's may be true or it may be false: that we don't know. Thus there may exist *purely intellectual* preferences for one or the other of these theories; and we are very far from having to say with Russell that all the difference between science and lunacy disappears. Admittedly, Hume's argument still stands, and therefore the difference between a scientist and a lunatic is not that the first bases his theories securely upon observations while the second does not, or anything like that. Nevertheless we may now see that there *may be* a difference: it *may be* that the lunatic's theory is easily refutable by observation, while the scientist's theory has withstood severe tests.[293]

Nor does there seem to be any valid exceptions to the conclusion that in empirical matters we can never attain certainty of belief, as Popper reminds us:

> From the point of view here developed all laws, all theories, remain essentially tentative, or conjectural, or hypothetical, even when we feel unable to doubt them any longer. Before a theory has been refuted we can never know in what way it may have to be modified. That the sun will always rise and set within twenty-four hours is still proverbial as a law 'established by induction beyond reasonable doubt'. It is odd that this example is still in use, though it may have served well enough in the days of Aristotle and Pytheas of Massalia—the great traveler who for centuries was called a liar because of his tales of Thule, the land of the frozen sea and the *midnight sun.*[294]

A few final points are in order. First of all, as mentioned, although no amount of observation can prove a scientific theory, a single counter-instance can falsify it. But of course, observations that appear to refute a theory *are themselves fallible.* Experiments may not be performed properly, and mistakes may be made, and of course there is always the possibility of fraud. But the acceptance of a single counter-instance logically refutes a universal theory.

Secondly, as mentioned earlier, the *universal* property of scientific theories cannot be stressed enough. A scientific theory cannot be merely speculation about a particular fact or an isolated event, because nothing new and non-trivial can be predicted from such a speculation. This point has to be stressed, because it has caused a great deal of confusion among philosophers and historians of science. For example, historian and professional "skeptic" Michael Shermer has written:

> Popper's attempt to solve the problem of demarcation...between science and nonscience begins to break down in the borderlands of knowledge. Consider the theory that extraterrestrial intelligent life exists somewhere in the cosmos. If we find out by making radio contact through the SETI program then the theory will have been proven absolutely...But how could this theory ever be falsified? [295]

Shermer's mistake is his categorization of the statement "extraterrestrial intelligent life exists somewhere in the cosmos" as a scientific *theory*. It is no such thing. It is merely speculation about a specific fact, from which no non-trivial predictions follow. [296] It is no more a scientific theory than the statement, "There are white swans somewhere on the lake." Such statements about specific factual matters can indeed be confirmed, even proven "beyond all reasonable doubt." But this is only because they are *not* universal statements. Scientific theories are universal statements about how facts fit together, and from such universal statements follow predictions *about* specific facts. So, from the universal statement "All swans are white" follows the prediction that "The next swans we will see on the lake will be white." The former is a (simple) scientific theory; the latter a prediction about a specific fact that follows from the theory, and that may used to *test* the theory.

Note that Shermer would have formulated his idea as a scientific theory if he had stated it in a universal, testable form, such as: "Life arises quickly wherever there is water and an average temperature above freezing, and given a few billion years, some of this life will become recognizably intelligent." This is a universal statement that relates specific facts to each other, can be used to make predictions about how much intelligent life exists elsewhere in our galaxy, and can be tested (at least in principle) by sending probes to planets in which conditions for life appear to have been appropriate for a few billion years. If intelligent life is not found, then the theory is refuted, and must either be abandoned or modified.

Summary of Popper's philosophy of science

Many consider Popper to be the greatest philosopher of science the twentieth century has produced. This is understandable, since his criteria of demarcation between science and non-science is by far the clearest and most logically consistent that has ever been developed. Popper's ideas have been highly influential among both scientists and philosophers: The list of scientists who have acknowledged a debt of gratitude to Popper would include Noble prize winners John Eccles and Peter Medawar. Einstein endorsed Popper's views, and of late Stephen Hawking has taken falsifiability as the defining characteristic of a scientific theory.

According to Popper, the scientific method in its purest form is a method of trial and error: of conjectures and refutations, of boldly proposing new hypotheses and then subjecting them to the most severe tests possible in an attempt to falsify them. Since induction cannot be rationally justified—no amount of repeated observation can guarantee that a rule inferred from such repeated observation is true—it follows that all our scientific theories and laws are only conjectures, only tentative hypotheses. Popper has shown that there is nothing irrational about scientific belief, as long as we realize that our theories are only conjectures open to revision in the light of new evidence. We can have rational preferences for some beliefs or theories over others: One theory may be preferred over another because it has passed more severe attempts at refutation, or because it has more explanatory power.

Popper's principle of falsification as the criterion of scientific theories thus frees our scientific beliefs from the fallacy of induction, and allows us to learn from our mistakes by providing a means by which false theories may be expelled from science. The requirement that scientific theories be open to falsification provides science with a self-corrective mechanism at its very core.

16
The Scientific Status of Parapsychology

According to Popper's criterion, the scientific status of parapsychology would depend simply upon whether or not the field of parapsychology generates theories that are capable of being falsified in principle. It is to this issue that we now turn.

In fact, there is no shortage of theories of psi. Like many other fields of inquiry, theories have come and gone as times have changed, but the various theories break down into two main groups: the *physical* theories and the *psychological* theories. The physical theories attempt to deal with the problem of how information is mediated between the individual and the environment; the psychological theories deal with the problem of how psi comes to manifest itself in the individual's consciousness in the ways that it does. Most theories have focused on the issue of mediation, which is understandable: If we have no conceptual grasp of the mediational aspect, the experiential aspect may be more easily dismissed as fantasy. So we first turn to the physical theories.

Physical theories of psi
Some of the early researchers, such as J.B. Rhine, were unable to find any physical correlates of psi from the cumulative research, and so concluded that psi was extra-physical. This view is still shared by some researchers, but most in recent years have come to the conclusion that the notion of a non-physical psi is more a reaction to classical than contemporary physics. There has been a growing recognition that there is no intrinsic incompatibility between psi and the modern laws of physics, and this recognition has spawned theories of psi that involve extensions of quantum mechanics.

However, before we examine these attempts, it is worth having a look at some of the attempts to explain psi in terms of electromagnetism.

Electromagnetic theories
In essence, these are extensions of the usual *cybernetic* model of human perception, in which information is conveyed to our sense organs by some sort of carrier signal

(such as sound waves to our ears, light rays to our eyes) where it travels along nerve cells to our brain, where the message is decoded. If we then choose to act because of the information received, our brain sends messages to the muscles. In short, the human organism is portrayed as a receiver and decoder of information, conveyed by classically understood forms of energy.

According to the electromagnetic theories, psi is mediated by some form of electromagnetic radiation, and this radiation affects electrical activity in the brain directly, without going through any recognized sense organ. It is speculated that patterns of electrical activity in the brain can be both transmitted and received; accordingly, PK involves only transmission, clairvoyance only reception, and telepathy functions as a sort of "mental radio."

There are numerous objections to the electromagnetic theories. If psi is mediated by electromagnetic radiation, then its behavior must be subject to the inverse square law: The intensity of an energetic transmission is proportional to the square of the distance between transmitter and receiver. In other words, if the distance between target and percipient is doubled, then the strength of the signal should be attenuated to a quarter of its original strength. But it does not appear that scores in psi experiments decrease with the square of the distance between target and percipient: Successful experiments have been carried out at great distances, reinforcing the popular notion that the operation of psi is independent of distance.*

Another objection is that screening devices against radiation should block the operation of psi. But experiments have been carried out using Faraday cages designed to exclude radiation of specific wavelengths. The electromagnetic theories would predict scores only at chance level under these conditions, but these predictions have not been realized.[297] The distinguished Russian physiologist L.L. Vasiliev discussed in his book *Experiments in Distant Influence* the attempts of Cazzamailli, Kajinsky, and others to explain telepathy in terms of electromagnetic theory. Vasiliev conducted a series of experiments involving telepathic communication between a hypnotist and subjects. During some of these experiments the subject and hypnotist were placed in metal cabinets, situated in separate rooms, which shielded against any electromagnetic radiation in the range of ultra-short, short, and medium wavelengths. The subjects were highly successful in responding to the hypnotist's suggestions, and the use of metal shielding did not diminish the results. Even when the hypnotist and the subject were separated by as many as 1,700, kilometers the subject was still successful at responding to telepathic suggestions. Vasiliev writes:

> Contrary to all expectation, screening by metal did not cause any even faintly perceptible weakening of telepathic transmission. Even under

---

* Apollo 14 astronaut Ed Mitchell took part in a telepathy experiment with colleagues on Earth while in orbit in 1971. The results showed evidence of telepathy, but the number of trials was too small to be statistically significant.

conditions of double screening mental suggestions [telepathy] continued to act with the same degree of effectiveness as without screening.[298]

A final strike against these theories would seem to be the fact that, with current technology at least, the electrical activity of the brain cannot be detected more than a few millimeters from the scalp. It is difficult to see how the brain could generate enough electromagnetic radiation to account for psi phenomena at great distances and in spite of radiation shielding. In short, the experimental evidence appears to leave the electromagnetic theories convincingly falsified.

The Observational Theories

We saw in the last chapter how nothing in quantum mechanics forbids psi phenomena. Costa de Beauregard even maintains that the theory of quantum physics virtually *demands* that psi phenomena exist.[299] Nobel Laureate Brian Josephson has written that, "if psychic phenomena had not been found experimentally, they might have been predicted by an imaginative theoretician."[300]

Various modern physicists have gone even farther, proposing theories of psi based upon quantum mechanics. One obvious attraction of such theories is that they would account for what have been the two most puzzling features of psi—its statistical nature, and its seeming independence of space and time. The most detailed of these theories so far has been due to the work of theoretical physicist Evan Harris Walker. Since Walker's theory of psi is an extension of his quantum mechanical theory of consciousness, it is worthwhile to briefly review his and other quantum theories of consciousness.

All of these theories follow the von Neumann/Wigner interpretation of quantum mechanics, which, as the reader may recall, was first formulated by the mathematician John von Neumann in opposition to the then-orthodox Copenhagen interpretation. According to quantum theory the world before observation exists only as pure possibility; yet when we observe the world at any level we see not a range of possibilities but one actual state of affairs. *Something* is required to collapse the state vectors of pure possibility into one actual result. The Copenhagen interpretation asserts that the presence of any macroscopic measuring device is sufficient to collapse the state vector. But von Neumann, following his rigorous mathematical logic wherever it would go, disagreed: The entire physical world, including measuring devices, must obey the laws of quantum physics. Something non-physical, not subject to the laws of quantum mechanics, must account for the collapse of the state vector: The only non-physical entity in the observation process that von Neumann could think of was the consciousness of the observer.

It is difficult to fault the logic, and decades of experimentation by Nobel-hungry physicists eager to knock quantum theory apart has revealed not a single instance of failure. The results of experiments carried out so far indicate that not a single part of the physical world evades the quantum rules. Yet we are aware of one non-physical entity that carries out observations. Since according to quantum theory the world before observation exists only as pure possibility, von Neumann and his followers—most notably London, Bauer, and Wigner—were led inescapably to the conclusion that it is consciousness (human or otherwise) that brings the universe of possibility into actuality.[301]

This brings us to the crux of the mind-body problem: What is the relationship between the mind and the brain? The brain is a physical entity and we have no reason to suppose that it evades the rules of quantum physics. In 1924, when quantum theory was still in its infancy, biologist Alfred Lotkas proposed the daring conjecture that mind exerts control over the brain by modulating the occurrence of otherwise random quantum events. Since then, our knowledge of both quantum mechanics and the brain has increased immeasurably, and today most quantum models of consciousness place the mechanism of mind-matter interaction at the level of the neural synapse—the tiny gap between the electric tentacles of the nerve cells.

In 1963 Sir John Eccles received the Noble Prize in Medicine and Physiology for discovering how nerve cells communicate with each other: they do it with drugs. The synaptic gap is too wide to be bridged by electrical signals: Instead, when a nerve cell is excited, its extremities emit tiny packets of chemicals—called neurotransmitters—that quickly transverse the gap and cause or inhibit the firing of adjacent nerve cells. As Nick Herbert writes, "to handle the fine details of its vast informational traffic, the human brain employs a veritable pharmacy of exotic transmitter substances."[302] Most mind-altering drugs achieve their effects by altering the transmission of neurotransmitters, which gives us important clues about the consciousness-sensitive areas of the brain.

Eccles has written about how the firing of just one "critically-poised neuron" could have a cascading effect on activity in the brain, and speculates that consciousness affects brain activity by manipulating the way chemicals are released into the synaptic gap. The neural sites where packets of chemicals are released are so tiny that quantum uncertainty may govern whether or not the release mechanisms are activated. Eccles speculates that an immaterial mind controls these microsites in one particular part of the brain—the premotor cortex—in order to produce voluntary behavior.

We should expect quantum uncertainty to play an even larger role in systems smaller than this, and so other quantum theories of consciousness place the mind's role in controlling matter at smaller locations near the synaptic gap. Berkeley physicist Henry Stapp has developed a model similar to Eccles's, but he places the critical juncture between mind and matter at the level of the calcium ion—about a million times smaller than Eccles's synaptic microsites—and essential for the operation of the synapse. But Evan Harris Walker, who has developed the most detailed, comprehensive model of quantum consciousness so far, places the interaction between mind and matter at the level of the electron—almost 100,000 times less massive than the calcium ions.

Briefly, according to Walker's model, when a synapse is excited electrons may 'tunnel' across the synaptic gap connecting an initiating neuron with its neighbor, and because of quantum non-locality, may influence electrons controlling the firing of distant synapses. Walker postulates the existence of a second nervous system operating by completely quantum rules, acting in parallel with the conventional nervous system. The latter handles unconscious data processing, and the former allows an immaterial mind to interact with matter by selecting which second-system quantum possibilities become actualized. In turn, these quantum states act upon the conventional nervous system in order to produce voluntary action. One advantage of his model is that it helps account for the unity of conscious experience we observe despite the fact that the brain activity associated with even simple perception is spread out over different parts of the brain.

These three theories differ regarding the precise location of mind-matter interaction, but it should be noted that they are all clearly dualistic, in the sense that they postulate a non-physical mind that also exerts a real influence in the physical world.* As an adherent of the von Neumann interpretation, Walker believes that:

> Duality is already a part of physics. ...The dualism enters because
> "observation" as it is used in quantum theory must have properties
> that go beyond those that can be represented in terms of material
> objects interacting by way of force fields (which is the way all of
> physics describes physical processes). The reason is that the observer
> is introduced in QM as a way to account for state vector collapse.[303]

Brain scientists have generally ignored Walker's model of consciousness, because it contains what are considered by some to be rather unreasonable neurological assumptions.[304] Nevertheless, it is the most ambitious and detailed attempt so far to relate quantum mechanics to the mind-body problem. In common with the other models, it is based on the idea that the conscious mind may bias the collapse of state vectors of quantum phenomena within the brain, in such a way as to influence brain activity in a desired manner. Walker bases his theory of psi upon his theory of consciousness, and in a nutshell it is this: Consciousness can collapse state vectors to a single desired outcome inside the person's own brain; because of the non-local property of quantum phenomena,[305] it can on occasion instantaneously affect the state of another person's brain (telepathy), another person's body (psychic healing), or a distant physical process (PK).

Walker's theory is thus an extension of the original formulation of von Neumann's interpretation, in which observation collapses state vectors. Von Neumann's original formulation implicitly assumed that conscious observation has

---

* Quantum theories of the mind do not necessarily imply that the mind can exist without a brain to express itself with. This is a separate issue.

no effect on *which specific value* the quantum phenomena actually take upon observation—the actual outcome was assumed to be purely random. But we have seen that the experiments of Helmut Schmidt apparently demonstrate that human consciousness *can* bias the collapse of random quantum systems in a desired direction. Yet we have also seen that the effect with random event generators appears to be weak. Walker speculates that consciousness may exert a stronger influence on quantum events within the brain because of its close and intimate link with this sensitive instrument. This idea seems reasonable. After all, it is hardly surprising that the effect of mind on the fission of atoms in the RNG experiments is very weak. We should rather wonder why there should be any effect at all. Any such effect must inevitably be greater on biological systems, which have presumably evolved to respond to mental influence.

Broadly similar theories of psi have been proposed by others, such as Helmut Schmidt, Robert Jahn and Brenda Dunne, although Walker's is the most detailed so far. All of these theories are referred to as "observational" theories because they require observation of results in order for psi to operate. They have sometimes been criticized on the grounds that "observation" is an ambiguous term. But Walker defines "observation" simply, writing that "observation is the interaction of mind with matter" and that "observation is the same as state selection." One great advantage of these observational theories is that they are formulated in mathematical terms and thus generate precise predictions that, at least in principle, are open to testing.[306]

Evaluation of the Observational Theories

One of the obvious strengths of the observational theories is that they provide solid explanations of what have been, up until recently, two of the most puzzling features of psi: its seeming independence of space and time, and its apparently statistical nature. We now know that the universe allows non-local effects, so reports that the operation of psi is indifferent to distance and barriers can no longer be dismissed as contrary to the known laws of physics. The logically impeccable von Neumann interpretation of quantum mechanics holds that events are not fully real until they are observed; the time-displaced PK experiments support this interpretation, and thereby upgrade its status from a purely metaphysical theory to a testable scientific one. Finally, since according to the observational theories psi only operates on otherwise random phenomena by biasing probabilities, they explain why the operation of psi seems fundamentally statistical in nature.

Theoretical physicists familiar with the experimental evidence from both physics and parapsychology have constructed the observational theories, all within the framework of a logically valid interpretation of quantum physics. Hyman's desperate argument that the acceptance of psi would require that we "abandon relativity and quantum mechanics in their current formulations" is thereby shown to be nonsense. Contrast Hyman's statement with that of theoretical physicist Costa de Beauregard, who has written "relativistic quantum mechanics is a conceptual scheme where phenomena such as psychokinesis or telepathy, far from being irrational, should, on the contrary, be expected as *very rational*."[307]

We have seen that the observational theories result in numerous predictions, several of which appear to be corroborated by the experimental evidence. Walker's theory in particular is the most testable theory of psi to come out of modern physics. It suggests many possible experiments, and makes clear predictions about what should happen. But acceptance or rejection may take some time. Applying the theory involves complicated logic and calculation and requires that some questionable assumptions be made. Having said that, it is fair to say that Walker's theory is a gallant attempt to explain psi by means of concepts consistent with modern physics, and its predictions are consistent to some degree with much of the experimental evidence. As such, the theory appears to be a good first approximation to the truth.

At any rate, this theory is certainly limited in that it has nothing to say about the psychological aspects of psi performance. It is to the psychological theories that we now turn.

Psychological theories of psi

One advantage of the observational theories is that they are formulated in mathematical terms and thereby generate precise predictions that allow us to choose between them. But not all phenomena are amenable to quantification. As mathematician Douglas Stokes has written, "counting is the basis of quantification, and counting requires that the entity to be measured be divided into discrete units or parts."[308] So our reductionist science has proceeded by dissection, and up until recently has largely neglected certain holistic phenomena such as consciousness. But just because physical theories are expressed in mathematics does not mean psychological theories must also be. Bertrand Russell once remarked that our physical theories are mathematical not because we know so much but because we know so little: It is only the world's mathematical properties that we have been able to discover.

The psychological theories are concerned not with physical mediation but rather with the states of mind that are associated with the experience of psi. Accordingly, these theories have been much more inspired by real life experiences of psi than the physical theories.

Many people who have had what they believe to be psi experiences feel that laboratory psi is somehow different. In real life, psi experiences tend to be need-relevant, but what needs are being met by taking part in a psi experiment? The philosopher Henri Bergson and others have proposed that the brain acts as a filter for the mind, filtering out input that is not of immediate survival value. Since psi experiences reported from real life tend to be need-relevant and adaptive, it has been suggested that the reason psi experiences in the laboratory are usually so weak is because they are evoked by merely finding flaws in Bergson's filter, rather than by tapping into an ability that may exist in order to provide a genuine benefit to the organism. Also, in real life, people usually do not make any effort to use psi: it simply happens. This is quite different from most laboratory psi experiments, in which people are asked to make a conscious effort to use psi.

These considerations have led parapsychologist Rex Stanford to formulate a model in which psi is portrayed as both need-relevant and unintentional. His theory is termed the *psi-mediated instrumental response* (PMIR) model, and its central tenet is that psi experiences occur because under certain circumstances the individual has some need for the experience to occur. The "psi-mediated response" is therefore fundamentally goal-oriented. Stanford further proposes that the operation of psi is normally unconscious, and specifically occurs in order to facilitate some need or desire that has been encoded in memory. The PMIR model therefore explicitly accommodates non-intentional psi experiences.

Stanford has taken pains to formulate his model as a series of propositions that are designed to be readily testable, such as, "ESP and PK can be used, without intention or awareness, to fulfill needs." Stanford deliberately leaves "needs" undefined; in later writing he uses the term "disposition," and means this term to include not only biological needs but also the more complex wants and desires arising from life in society.

Stanford and Braud have also proposed an explanation for the psi-conducive nature of altered states of consciousness. As discussed earlier, Honorton used this apparent feature of altered states to design the ganzfeld experiment. Honorton postulated that psi might operate as a weak signal that is normally masked by the stronger signals constantly besieging us from our conventional sense organs. His hypothesis, which became known as the "noise-reduction" model of psi, was that by reducing ordinary sensory noise while keeping the subject relaxed and alert, the subject's mind would become starved for stimuli and thus more receptive to any faint signals that ordinarily would not reach consciousness.

But we have seen that the observational theories do not treat psi as a signal, but rather as the influence of observation on otherwise random quantum events. Stanford's explanation as to why these altered states facilitate psi is completely in line with the observational theories. According to Stanford's account, the "noise" or data from the outside world imposes a structure upon the brain and mind when received and interpreted. On the other hand, brains without strongly structured activities are likely to show increasing unpredictability and randomness, with the result that psi effects are more likely to occur. So, Stanford's explanation does not treat psi as a weak signal that is normally masked by noise: Rather, the reduction of sensory input leads to a reduction in the constraints on the activity of the brain, resulting in greater randomness and hence a greater likelihood of psi effects.

Evaluation and implication of psi theories

The physical and psychological theories seek to explain different aspects of the same phenomena, and they both have their strengths and weaknesses. The physical theories explain the independence of space and time, and account for the apparently statistical nature of psi. On the other hand, the PMIR model seems more consistent with spontaneous psi experiences, and some of its predictions also seem to have passed experimental tests.

As discussed above, the physical and psychological theories account for different aspects of the same phenomena, but they are not entirely consistent. A theory is needed that bridges the psychological and the physical theories. A more complete theory of psi would include not only a theory of physical mediation, but would also include details on neurobiology, and would encompass the psychological conditions conducive to psi performance. The construction of such a full-fledged theory is a monumental challenge, requiring an inter-disciplinary approach between physics, biology, and psychology. But given the twentieth century revolutions in physics and psychology, and our growing knowledge of neurobiology, it now appears to be within the reach of a daring theorist.[309]

Implications for parapsychology as science

Parapsychology meets Popper's criterion for scientific status, since we have seen that modern parapsychology does indeed have theories that entail falsifiable predictions. They are certainly incomplete and only approximately true at best, in the way that Popper would describe *all* our scientific theories as incomplete and only approximately true.[310]

The criticisms of skeptics such as Martin Gardner and Antony Flew have now been met. Gardner has reviewed Walker's theory, calling it "staggering", but then quotes Sherlock Holmes' admonition that "theory making should be delayed until one has data."[311] Flew, on the other hand, writing years later, protests that we should be very suspicious of the data supporting the existence of psi because "no one has been able to think up any halfway plausible theory accounting for the occurrence of any psi-phenomenon."[312] Flew never once mentions *any* of the proposed theories of psi, but instead writes that "a plausible theory relating these putative phenomena to something that undoubtedly does occur would tend both to explain and to make probable their actual occurrence." He then goes on to quote a maxim attributed to Sir Arthur Eddington: "it is a good rule not to put overmuch confidence in the observational results until they are confirmed by theory."[313]*

Flew protests that "this should not seem a lapse into anti-empiricist a priori dogmatism," although that is exactly what it is. Meteorites, continental drift, and

---

* One is reminded of a remark the biologist Ernst Haeckel is alleged to have made: *If the facts do not agree with my theory, so much worse for the facts!*

the energy source of the stars only recently found theoretical explanations; yet for millennia the stones fell, the continents moved, and the stars went on shining, completely indifferent to our lack of understanding. The universe is not held hostage by our ignorance.

And as Walker reminds Gardner,

> The data are there for those who have availed themselves of the facts—the facts of physics and the data of parapsychology. QM is well understood by those educated in physics, and psi phenomena have been elucidated in a thousand experiments. The only thing that has been lacking is a rapprochement between parapsychology and the main body of science.[314]

That is what the physical and psychological theories provide. Like meteorites, continental drift, the stars, and countless other phenomena, psi phenomena also had to wait for science to develop to the point where it was capable of providing a tentative explanation.

17

Hume's Argument Revisited

We are now in a position to properly evaluate the famous skeptical argument of David Hume, an argument that has been used by skeptics over and over again to dismiss the existence of psi as highly unlikely on *a priori* grounds.[315] But in order to do so, it will be helpful to first review the intellectual atmosphere in which Hume lived and wrote.

It must have seemed to be a tremendously exciting time, as though wondrous new vistas were opening up for the human race because of the work of men such as Kepler, Galileo, and Newton. The horrors of the religious wars and of the Inquisition were still fresh in peoples' minds, and the new scientific worldview, spread by men such as Diderot and Voltaire, can be seen partly as a reaction against the ecclesiastical domination over thought that the Church held for centuries. In 1600 Giordano Bruno was burnt at the stake for, among other things, the heresy of expressing belief in the heliocentric theory of Copernicus. It is therefore not surprising that, when Galileo fell into the hands of the Inquisition 16 years later, he played it safe and recanted. But when Newton's *Principia* was published in 1687, it was not suppressed but instead reached a wide audience. The Newtonian system predicted the orbits of the planets with astonishing accuracy, and even reduced comets from portents of disaster to phenomena whose appearance in the sky could be predicted like clockwork. The scientific revolution of the seventeenth century completely transformed the outlook of educated men, so that by 1700 their outlook was no longer medieval but completely modern.[316] By this time the picture of a mechanistic universe governed by inviolable laws had established its hold on the imaginations of educated men and women; now such things as magic, sorcery, and second-sight seemed incredible at best, and vulgar superstition at worse. The new scientific worldview had given birth to a distinction between the "natural" and the "supernatural," between the "normal" and the "paranormal," a distinction that, for better or worse, persists to this day.

Popper describes the atmosphere of Hume's time:

> It is perhaps hard for intellectuals of our own day, spoilt and blasé as we are by the spectacle of scientific success, to realize what Newton's

theory meant for any eighteenth-century thinker. After the unmatched daring with which the Ancients had tackled the riddle of the Universe there had come long periods of decay and recovery, and then a staggering success. Newton had discovered the long sought secret. ...No qualified judge of the situation could doubt any longer that Newton's theory was true. It had been tested by the most precise measurements, and it had always been right. It had led to the prediction of minute deviations from Kepler's laws, and to new discoveries. In a time like ours, when theories come and go like the buses in Piccadilly, and when every schoolboy has heard that Newton has long been superseded by Einstein, it is hard to recapture the sense of conviction which Newton's theory inspired, or the sense of elation, and of liberation. A *unique event* had happened in the history of thought, one which could never be repeated: the first and final discovery of the absolute truth about the universe. An age-old dream had come true. Mankind had obtained *knowledge*, real, certain, indubitable, and demonstrable knowledge— divine *scientia* or *episteme*, and not merely *doxa*, human opinion.[317]

Of course, we now know that Newton's system is not certain and indubitable, but also merely *doxa*. But, this was the intellectual atmosphere of the eighteenth century in which Hume wrote his famous *Inquiry Concerning Human Understanding*. It was G.R. Price who, back in 1955, made the first attempt to deploy Hume's skeptical argument as a challenge to the existence of psi phenomena:

> Now it happens that I myself believed in ESP about 15 years ago, after reading *Extra-Sensory Perception After Sixty Years*, but I changed my mind when I became acquainted with the argument presented by David Hume in his chapter "Of Miracles" in *An Enquiry Concerning Human Understanding*.[318]

Price then goes on to quote Hume's now famous argument: "A miracle is a violation of the laws of nature; and as a firm and unalterable experience has established these laws, the proof against a miracle, from the very nature of the fact, is as entire as any argument from experience can possibly be imagined." Modern skeptics still use this argument to say that the existence of psi should be rejected in a like manner because it conflicts with what normal science takes to be the laws of nature. For instance, we have the philosopher Antony Flew almost thirty-five years after Price repeating Hume's argument, along with complaining of Price that "he had not appreciated the full richness and strength of the argument suggested by Hume" and that "So far, no one seems to have appreciated the full significance for parapsychology of Hume's argument."[319] Flew criticizes Price for being too soft on the parapsychologists with Price's insistence that "what is needed is one completely convincing experiment—just one experiment that does not have to be accepted simply on the basis of faith in human honesty." Like Price, Flew defends the validity of Broad's Basic Limiting Principles, but Flew demands a *repeatable* experiment:

> Any supposedly once-and-for-all decisive yet not-in-practice-repeatable demonstration of the reality of psi phenomena has to be rejected. It has to be rejected in the same emphatic way, and for the same excellent reasons, that critical historians reject stories of what they know, or believe they know, to be physically (or practically or contingently) impossible. So to the objection that there are some rare phenomena that, though not repeatable at will, are admitted by science, the correct and crushing reply should be that these are not phenomena for which we have the strongest or indeed any very good reasons for thinking impossible.[320]

Presumably Flew would have been among those rejecting the existence of meteorites and continental drift as "impossible." Be that as it may, let us examine Hume's argument as it appears in Section X of his 1748 *Inquiry*. Hume begins by writing that "I flatter myself that I have discovered an argument of a nature which, if just, will, with the wise and learned, be an everlasting check to all kinds of superstitious delusion, and consequently will be useful as long as the world endures." He then argues very reasonably that "though experience be our only guide in reasoning concerning matters of fact, it must be acknowledged that this guide is not altogether infallible, but in some cases is apt to lead us into errors." He considers cases in which the evidence seems conflicting, and asserts that in such cases a wise man proceeds with caution and "proportions his belief to the evidence." And if we suppose "that the fact which the testimony endeavors to establish partakes of the extraordinary and the marvelous—in that case the evidence resulting from the testimony admits of a diminution, greater or less in proportion as the fact is more or less unusual."

However, if the testimony of witnesses is in favor of a fact that is not marvelous but truly miraculous, then the situation for Hume becomes very different. It is at this point that Hume asserts that "A miracle is a violation of the laws of nature; and as a firm and unalterable experience has established these laws, the proof against a miracle, from the very nature of the fact, is as entire as any argument from experience can possibly be imagined." Hume was aware that miraculous events were being reported even in his own day, but, like the good philosopher he was, he did not try to make things easy for himself by only challenging reports that were easy to discredit. He was aware, for instance, that shortly before his writing several miracles, mostly concerned with healing, had been reported in Paris, then the undisputed cultural capital of the world. They were all connected with the tomb of Francois de Paris, the revered Jansenist priest who had been buried in the cemetery of St. Medard.

Francois, on account of being a Jansenist, was considered a heretic in the eyes of the Church. Reports of healing miracles at his tomb were therefore considered an embarrassment, which led to an effort by the Jesuits and the authorities to discredit them at all costs; when this effort failed, the authorities simply closed down the cemetery. Hume discusses the reports of these miracles, and writes:

> But what is more extraordinary, many of the miracles were immediately proved upon the spot, before judges of unquestioned integrity, attested by witnesses of credit and distinction, in a learned age, and on the most eminent theater that is now in the world. Nor is this all: a relation of them was published and dispersed everywhere, nor were the Jesuits, though a learned body supported by the civil magistrate, and determined enemies to those opinions in whose favor the miracles were said to have been wrought, ever able distinctly to refute or detect them. Where shall we find such a number of circumstances agreeing to the corroboration of one fact? And *what have we to oppose such a cloud of witnesses but the absolute impossibility or miraculous nature of the events which they relate? And this, surely, in the eyes of all reasonable people, will alone be regarded as a sufficient refutation.*

Problems with Hume's view

It may have occurred by now to the astute reader that there is a conflict between Hume's skepticism regarding universal laws and his rejection of any supposed "violations" of these laws. There is no question that Hume's refutation of the validity of belief based on repeated observation had devastating implications. As Popper so colorfully described it, the eighteenth century was a time when educated men believed they were living in an era that had witnessed "the first and final discovery of the absolute truth about the universe"; that mankind had at last "obtained *knowledge*, real, certain, indubitable." But as we have seen, Hume had taught that there could be no such thing as certain knowledge of universal laws; that all we knew was obtained by the observation of singular instances, so that all of our universal laws were uncertain. Given his earlier expressed skeptical views about the rationality of belief based on observation, he has no right to claim rational support for the "laws of nature." In practice, he cannot maintain his rigorous skepticism, and argues as though the scientific laws of his time were known with certainty, much as many of his contemporaries would have argued. If he is going to be perfectly consistent, then he must maintain that when we assert a law of nature, we are really only expressing a habit of association based upon previous observations.

Nevertheless, he plainly thinks—or at least writes as though he thinks—that the laws of nature are correct and complete, and are not merely habits of association that cannot be rationally justified. In this respect, he seems in his essay "On Miracles" to be very much a typical educated man of his times.[321]

So the force of Hume's argument rests on the assumption that we know the laws of nature with virtual certainty, and so can reject any reported "violation" on *a priori* grounds. But Popper has shown that "Hume's negative result establishes for good that all our universal laws or theories remain forever guesses, conjectures, hypotheses."[322] Although psi may be incompatible with the Newtonian model that was so well entrenched in Hume's time, with the benefit of hindsight we now realize that Newton's model is only a marvelous conjecture, an excellent approximation. As we have seen, there is no reason to think that the existence of psi is incompatible with our modern laws of physics (except perhaps for macro-PK). Indeed, we have seen that some of the leading theories of psi are not only compatible with known scientific principles, but are expressly written in terms of them.

In short, Hume's skeptical argument, applied to the existence of psi phenomena, rests on two assumptions that we have dealt with earlier: that our "laws of nature" are known to be correct and complete, and that the existence of psi would necessarily conflict with them. With the benefit of almost three centuries of hindsight, we can now see that, in the context of the eighteenth century, Hume's argument was wrong on the first count, but correct on the second. But the laws of nature as Hume understood them are now long obsolete, and so is his skeptical argument.

Obviously, it is a good rule of common sense that our acceptance of highly unusual or statistically improbable claims should require more careful investigation than we would apply to claims regarding more mundane occurrences. Otherwise, we would uncritically accept the tabloid headings we read when standing in line at the supermarket ("Space Alien Baby Found!"). And even today the dangers of irrationality and fanaticism that Hume was concerned with still exist, including the danger of blindly accepting accounts of miraculous events by those attempting to promote a new religion, or maintain an old one. But Hume's argument breaks down where he draws a distinction between events that are merely unusual and those that are "violations of the laws of nature," with the former warranting careful investigation before being accepted as genuine, and the latter deserving only dismissal on the grounds that they are simply "impossible." Hume obviously does not have our benefit of seeing in hindsight that the laws of nature are not written in stone and have changed profoundly since his time. But regardless of the fact that the existence of psi is far more compatible with the current "laws of nature"* than the laws of Hume's time, there is of course the constant danger of thinking that one knows the laws of nature with certainty, and of rejecting contrary evidence as unscientific. If all scientists did in fact behave the way Hume expected them to, science would long ago have congealed into dogma, and outmoded theories would never have been overthrown and replaced.

---

* Scientists today speak less often of "laws" and more frequently of "models", in which anything resembling laws are presented as tentative propositions within the model.

18

Paradigms and Parapsychology

As briefly discussed earlier, the historian of science Thomas Kuhn has advanced the thesis that science progresses with the discovery of anomalies, or findings that are not predicted or explained by a currently accepted theory, which he called a "paradigm." According to Kuhn, most scientists spend their careers trying to extend and refine the dominant paradigm of their field. When anomalies inevitably appear, they may at first be ignored. But eventually attempts are made to extend or refine the paradigm in order to accommodate the puzzling phenomenon. Most of the time this "puzzle solving" is successful, and the extension and refinement of the paradigm continues.

However, Kuhn thought that paradigms inevitably encounter awkward facts that resist explanation. As resistant anomalies continue to accumulate, more resources and talent are recruited into an increasingly desperate attempt to assimilate these awkward facts into the dominant paradigm. A crisis ensues, and is only resolved when a rival paradigm is accepted that accommodates the troubling new findings as well as those phenomenon explained by the current champion. The new paradigm is typically resisted at first, but eventually it wins over a majority of scientists, and in turn becomes the orthodox viewpoint.

At that point, the revolution is over, and most scientists return to spending their time trying to extend and refine the new paradigm, or as Kuhn would put it, to "solving puzzles." As long as there seem to be no serious challenges to the validity of the paradigm, its truth is simply not questioned. Kuhn referred to the periods between revolutions as "normal science", and thought that it consisted mostly of a routine of solving minor problems that do not threaten acceptance of the theory.

There does seem to be some truth to Kuhn's theory of scientific progress. There have certainly been anomalies in Kuhn's sense that have resisted explanation until the advent of a new theory. Writing in 1934, C.P. Snow described the sudden success of quantum mechanics in 1925, stating that "anomalies ceased to be anomalies, with this new clue; facts which had puzzled us before now fitted in completely."[323]

But critics have pointed out that many historical cases do not fit Kuhn's model: there have been anomalies, such as X-rays, that did not create crisis, and there have been revolutions that were not dependent on anomalies and crisis.[324]

Another weakness of Kuhn's work is the number of ways "paradigm" is defined: as a scientific theory, a metaphysical view of reality, a common vocabulary, a successful experiment, and so on. As Shapere has written, "The truth of the thesis that shared paradigms are the common factors guiding scientific research appears to be guaranteed, not so much by a close examination of actual historical cases, as by the breadth of definition of the term 'paradigm.'" [325] Another critic has classified *twenty-one* different definitions of the word "paradigm" as used by Kuhn. [326]

Nevertheless, the views of Thomas Kuhn are often thought to be highly relevant to parapsychology's struggle to gain recognition. It is thought that psi phenomena constitute genuine anomalies, and that the resistance of the skeptics is due to a perceived threat to the currently dominant paradigms of modern science.

But the notion of anomalies, or "violations of expectation", is as Kuhn pointed out, a sociological notion as much as it might be a logical one. Obviously, if our expectations differ, than so will our classification of anomalies. We have already seen that several contemporary physicists believe that quantum mechanical theory *implies* the existence of psi phenomena, so *their* expectations are obviously not violated by the reports. Since there is no longer any necessary conflict on a theoretical level between psi research and physics, describing psi phenomena as "anomalous" no longer seems to explain very much.

The multiple ways in which the term "paradigm" is used also weakens the explanatory power of Kuhn's thesis. However, if by paradigm we mean a *metaphysical* theory, then perhaps psi research *is* helping bring about a paradigm change in the scientific worldview. There is an emerging metaphysical (and to the degree it is testable, scientific) theory that treats consciousness as having causal efficacy and genuine explanatory power in the universe. This is all we could really mean when we say that psi research may contribute to a new paradigm. Walker wrote in 1984 that "With the exception of parapsychology, the significance and central nature of consciousness has been omitted from science." [327] This remark is now somewhat dated, as there has been an explosion of new scientific research regarding the phenomenon of consciousness in recent years. Unfortunately, like most of the philosophical work on consciousness, much of it has been carried out within a materialistic, mechanistic framework of assumptions, in fretful ignorance and disdain of the contributions of quantum mechanics and psi research. [328]

There is another important sense, though, in which Kuhn's work has relevance to parapsychology's struggle for recognition and acceptance. It involves Kuhn's conception of what he called "normal science." Kuhn thought that the history of science could be separated into "normal' periods" and "revolutionary" periods, with the former characterized by a routine of puzzle solving, in which the truth of prevailing theories is simply not questioned. Theories are treated as though they are known to be correct, and new entrants into the field are taught the orthodox theories as if they were reality. Kuhn referred to the period between revolutions as "normal science", because he had concluded that this was the norm for most scientists most of the time.

Although Popper rejected much of Kuhn's thesis, he did admit that Kuhn's concept of "normal science" was valuable as a warning because it was unfortunately true of the way science has come to be practiced in some laboratories and universities. However, according to Popper this was neither "normal" nor was it science, and should it ever become routine practice it would signal the *end* of science. Popper stressed that the best scientists (such as Bohr in 1913 and Einstein in 1916) realize the tentative nature of their theories, and expect that their theories will be superseded in time.

Kuhn was primarily concerned about the *cultural* distinction between science and non-science, whereas Popper was committed to identifying the underlying *logical* distinction. Popper even insisted that it would be a major disaster for humanity if we were to accept "the replacement of a rational criterion of science by a sociological one."[329]

Clearly then, Popper's demarcation criterion between science and non-science is the most coherent ever developed. Kuhn's contribution to Popper's viewpoint is primarily his sociological description of "normal science," and its often dogmatic nature. In the absence of serious challenges, Kuhn thought that "normal science" meant the practice and teaching of science as though it were simply dogma. Unfortunately, it is often true that scientific theories are taught as though they *were* reality, not merely tentative models of reality.

CONCLUSIONS

Kuhn's description of "normal" science and his historical accounts of the resistance of many scientists to new ideas do show how scientific and metaphysical beliefs can be clung to with near-religious tenacity. This desire for certainty and finality partly explains the dogmatism of some skeptics of psi phenomena.

We have already seen how the psychologist Hebb rejected psi on a priori grounds:

> Why do we not accept ESP as a psychological fact? Rhine has offered enough evidence to have convinced us on almost any other issue.... Personally, I do not accept ESP for a moment, because it does not make sense.... I cannot see what other basis my colleagues have for rejecting it.... Rhine may still turn out to be right, improbable as I think that is, and my own rejection of his view is—in the literal sense—prejudice.

We have also seen the following remark by the physiologist Helmholtz:

> I cannot believe it. Neither the testimony of all the Fellows of the Royal Society, nor even the evidence of my own senses, would lead me to believe in the transmission of thought from one person to another

independently of the recognized channels of sense. It is clearly impossible.

But such closed-minded thought processes are by no means confined to the reaction of scientists to the existence of psi. Physicist Albert Michelson wrote the following twenty years after his crucial experiment on the velocity of light, which led to the downfall of Newtonian mechanics and the eventual acceptance of the special theory of relativity:

> The more important fundamental laws and facts of the physical universe have all been discovered and these are now so firmly entrenched that the possibility of their ever being supplanted in consequence of new discoveries is exceedingly remote.[330]

Michelson admitted that there were "apparent exceptions" but thought that the known physical laws would be sufficient to deal with them. These statements of his shortly preceded Einstein's paper on special relativity and the development of quantum mechanics.

It seems contrary to human nature to readily adopt Popper's ideal of holding our beliefs only as tentative conjectures, capable of being revised if they are shown to be false.* Remember that most of our great destructive wars have been wars of religion or ideology. If religions and ideologies can compel humans to fight and die for them, then it should not be surprising that scientific theories and the worldviews they spawn should often be clung to with the same dogmatic tenacity. It seems reasonable to speculate that the factors inclining an individual toward scientific fundamentalism are similar to those factors inclining an individual toward religious fundamentalism: a desire for certainty in a world that often appears complicated, confusing, and full of ambiguity.

Arrogance is one of the worst diseases of scientists and it gives rise to statements of authority and finality which are expressed usually in fields that are completely beyond the scientific competence of the dogmatist. It is important to realize that dogmatism has now become a disease of scientists rather than of theologians.

John Eccles

---

* In his autobiography Popper writes about his own early struggles to overcome dogmatic thinking. One of the most important incidents in his life occurred on the day in his youth when he realized with horror that he had embraced Marxism without critical thought: "I had accepted a dangerous creed uncritically, dogmatically." (page 26)

Susan Blackmore has been remarkably candid about her own struggle against dogmatic thinking, writing, as we saw earlier,

> Human beings are not built to have open minds. If they try to have open minds they experience *cognitive dissonance*. Leon Festinger first used this term. He argued that people strive to make their beliefs and actions consistent and when there is inconsistency they experience this unpleasant state of "cognitive dissonance," and they then use lots of ploys to reduce it. I have to admit I have become rather familiar with some of them.[331]

Blackmore entered the field of psi as a fervent believer in psi, out-of-body experiences, the Tarot, and the occult. She describes how it all began in her student days:

> I became hooked on the subject when I first went up to Oxford to read physiology and psychology. I began running the Oxford University Society for Psychical Research (OUSPR), finding witches, druids, psychics, clairvoyants, and even a few real live psychical researchers to come to talk to us. We had Ouija board sessions, went exploring in graveyards, and did some experiments on ESP and psychokinesis.
>
> Within a few weeks I had not only learned a lot about the occult and the paranormal, but I had an experience that was to have a lasting effect on me—an out-of-body experience.[332]

She writes in her autobiography that she "had always wanted to be a 'famous parapsychologist,'"[333] She began to perform experiments, yet concluded that most of these had been failures. Describing the effect these perceived failures had on her state of mind, Blackmore writes:

> I found myself simply not believing in psi anymore. I really had become a disbeliever. Like one of those doors with a heavy spring that keeps it closed, my mind seemed to have changed from closed belief to closed disbelief.[334]

Professor Henry Bauer has written on arguments over anomalous phenomena with considerable insight into the psychology of those holding extreme positions:

> In the rare cases when true believers do happen to recognize their error, they do not then adopt a more balanced or judicious stance, rather they typically go to the other extreme. Arthur Koestler's disillusion

with Communism left him implacably anti-Communist; Whittaker
Chambers coupled that shift with conversion from atheism to
Catholicism. Maurice Burton gave credence to the Loch Ness monsters
for nearly three decades and then became a determined debunker;
Razdan and Keiler (1984-1985) became injudiciously critical after their
own search for the monster was unsuccessful. The switch from believer
to debunker is easier than from either of those stances to uncommitted,
because the extreme positions are so similar to one another, psychologically and (il)logically. Thus, the [true] believers and the debunkers
are equally dogmatic.[335]

Blackmore went from one extreme to the other, but as we saw earlier, holding
the opposite extreme position was also difficult. She still had to face the fact that
others were reporting positive results. One day she was asked to witness a telepathy experiment involving children:

We observed for some time, and the children did very well. They
really seemed to be getting the right picture more often than chance
would predict. I began to get excited; even frightened. Was this really
ESP happening right in front of my eyes? Or was there an alternative
explanation?...Somehow I just couldn't accept that this was psi, and I
was to go on arguing about the method used in future years. Was it
just perversity? A refusal to accept my own failures? A deep fear of
psi? Whatever it was, it led me into constant confusion. I just didn't
seem able to accept that other people could find psi while I could
not.[336]

Finally, she experienced, what was to her, an epiphany:

Now I realized, as though I had never realized it before, that sometimes
you can't know. And you don't *have* to know. You don't *have* to be able
to remember everything. You don't *have* to understand everything. I
just didn't know: this mental construction of a self didn't know some
things.[337]

The inability to tolerate uncertainty, to think of our beliefs as merely conjectures, seems to be deeply embedded in the nature of at least some of the skeptics
(and almost surely in the nature of the uncritical "true believers"). At any rate, Blackmore claims to have officially retired from parapsychology, complaining that "I am
just too tired—and tired above all of working to maintain an open mind."

It seems fitting to conclude this book with a quote from Charles Honorton, pioneer of the Ganzfeld experiments. Shortly before his sudden death at age 46 in

1992, Honorton wrote his classic article on skepticism, "Rhetoric over Substance", which he concluded with these words:

> I believe in science, and I am confident that a science that can boldly contemplate the origin of the universe, the nature of reality 10^{-33} seconds after the Big Bang, anthropic principles, quantum nonlocality, and parallel universes, can come to terms with the implications of parapsychological findings—whatever they may turn out to be. There is no danger for science in honestly confronting these issues; it can only be enriched by doing so. But there is a danger for science in encouraging self-appointed protectors who engage in polemical campaigns that distort and misrepresent serious research efforts. Such campaigns are not only counterproductive, they threaten to corrupt the spirit and function of science and raise doubts about its credibility. The distorted history, logical contradictions, and factual omissions exhibited in the arguments of the critics represent neither scholarly criticism nor skepticism, but rather counteradvocacy masquerading as skepticism. True skepticism involves the suspension of belief, not disbelief. In this context we would do well to recall the words of the great nineteenth century naturalist and skeptic, Thomas Huxley: "Sit down before fact like a little child, be prepared to give up every preconceived notion, follow humbly to wherever and to whatever abysses nature leads, or you shall learn nothing."

Postscript

This book was conceived by accident. One day, while living in the San Francisco Bay area, I stumbled across a website devoted to debunking the belief in an afterlife. Having read several serious books on the subject, I was shocked by the crudity of the author's arguments, and by his utter ignorance of the vast amount of research that has been done on the topic over the last 125 years. I sent him an email - message, trying to get him to reconsider his dogmatic position, and to my surprise, he responded with counter-arguments. For the next few weeks we engaged in a debate via email, and I learned much about the so-called "skeptical" mind-set. I realized that it was based upon a certain set of metaphysical assumptions which were not treated as assumptions, but as incontrovertible *facts*; and that it was also based upon an ignorance of certain facts that cast strong doubt on the validity of those assumptions.

I also realized that nothing I could possibly say would ever change his "skeptical" opinion. He had made up his mind, and that was that.

However, his opinions seemed common among a large minority of the educated public, and were expressed—sometimes with the same vehemence—in scores of books and in at least one periodical. I came to the conclusion that this viewpoint was fundamentally flawed, and that a book was needed to directly challenge these biased, prejudiced opinions on the existence of psi, and on the survival hypothesis: the idea that we survive the death of our bodies.

Alas, the task turned out to be larger than I had anticipated. The final product was mammoth-sized, and no publisher would print it all in one book. What had originally been planned as one book turned into a series. You have just read the first.

The next book will deal with ancient and modern evidence for the survival hypothesis, and will carefully consider the skeptical objections.

Chapter Notes

Notes from the *Introduction*

[1] However, as late as 1807 Thomas Jefferson, as president of the American Philosophical Society, reacted to the theory propounded by two New England astronomers that a meteorite found in Weston, Connecticut, was of extraterrestrial origin, by remarking: *"I could more easily believe that two Yankee professors would lie than stones would fall from heaven."*

[2] It is stated in the *Report of the Experiments on Animal Magnetism,* made by a Committee of the Medical Section of the French Royal Academy of Sciences, 1831: "We have seen two somnambulists who distinguished, with their eyes closed, the objects which were placed before them; they mentioned the color and the value of cards, without touching them; they read words traced with the hand, as also some lines of books opened at random. This phenomenon took place even when the eyelids were kept exactly closed with the fingers."

[3] Milner, 1998, p. 99.

[4] Kaku, Michio, 1994, p. 53.

[5] Bellachini's statement read:

"After I had, at the wish of several highly-esteemed gentlemen of rank and position, and also for my own interest, tested the physical mediumship of Mr Slade in a series of sittings by full daylight, as well as in the evening, in his bedroom, I must, for the sake of truth, hereby certify that the phenomenal occurrences with Mr Slade have been thoroughly examined by me with the minutest observation and investigation of his surroundings, including the table, and that I have *not in the smallest degree* found anything to be produced by means of prestidigitative manifestations, or by mechanical appartatus; and that any explanation of the experiments which took place under the circumstances then obtaining by any reference to prestidigitation, *to be absolutely impossible.*

I must rest with such men of science as Crookes and Wallace, in London; Perty, in Berne; Butlerof, in St Petersburg; to search for the explanation of this phenomenal power, and to prove its reality. I declare, moreover, the published opinions of laymen, as to the 'How' of this subject to be premature, and according to *my* view and experience, false and one-sided. This, my declaration, is signed and executed before a notary and witnesses."

(signed) SAMUEL BELLACHINI

Berlin, 6 December, 1877.

[6] Slade's and Zollner's story after this is not a happy one. Zollner died in 1882 from a brain hemorrhage. Three years later Slade arrived in Philadelphia to be examined by the Seybert Commission, created under the terms of the will of Henry Seybert to make an impartial assess-

ment of the evidence for spiritualism. Most of its members, though, were anything but impartial. Slade was able to produce some phenomena for the Commission, and considered the enquiry a personal success, even writing a thank you note for the Commission, offering to return to give further demonstrations. However, the Commission's report described Slade's phenomena as "fraudulent throughout." No one had caught Slade red-handed, but various members of the Commission claimed to have seen suspicious movements of his hands or feet, and this was all they needed. The report, published in 1877, completely demolished Slade's reputation. A broken man, Slade became increasingly addicted to alcohol and morphine, dying in a Michigan sanatorium in 1905.

The Seybert Commission then set out to discredit Zollner and his colleagues. The Commission's secretary, Professor Fullerton, traveled to Leipzig and subsequently issued a statement declaring that Zollner had been mentally unbalanced at the time of the Slade experiments. The other scientists were dismissed on the grounds of age or physical infirmity, portraying them as a group of infirm old men led by a lunatic. Zollner's friends were infuriated at the suggestion that he was unbalanced, and offered to swear oaths that he had been perfectly sane until the day of his death.

But the campaign to discredit Zollner was highly successful, and today his name is rarely mentioned in science text books. Nevertheless, his theories are echoed today in modern string theory, with its mathematical models of n-dimensional space.

[7] As quoted in Michio, 1994, p. 53.

[8] From a booklet accompanying the Royal Mail Stamps issued on October 2, 2001 to commemorate the centenary of the Nobel prizes.

[9] Robin McKie, *The Observer*, September 30, 2001.

[10] "Royal Mail's Nobel Guru in Telepathy Row", by Robin McKie, *The Observer*, Sunday September 30, 2001.

[11] "Pioneer of the Paranormal", by Edwin Cartlidge, *Physics World,* May 2002, pp.10-11.

[12] "Physicists probe the paranormal", by Martin Durrani, *Physics World*, May 2000.

[13] *The Observer*, October 7, 2001.

[14] Transcript of BBC Radio 4's Today program, October 2nd, 2001.

[15] However, it has been said that Humphrey "pocketed an estimated £75,000 without doing any noticeable research at all." ("Telepathy, Stamps, and Fuzzy Logic", by Guy Lyon Playfair, in The Skeptical Observer, published on-line). During the three years Humphrey held the Research Fellowship he did no psychical research, but instead wrote a book, *Soul Searching,* in which he claimed to have proved on theoretical grounds that phenomena like telepathy were impossible. Few were impressed with his proofs. Even his fellow skeptic, Susan Blackmore, in a review of his book in *New Scientist,* described his dismissal of the experimental evidence for telepathy as misleading and unfair.

Notes from Chapter 1, *Origin of the Debate*

[16] Ducasse, Curt. 1959. Ducasse shrewdly added that "The emotional motivation for irresponsible disbelief is, in fact, probably even stronger—especially in scientifically educated per-

sons, whose pride of knowledge is at stake—than is in other persons the motivation for irresponsible belief."

[17] Bauer, 1989, p. 4-5.

[18] Ibid, p. 5.

[19] Popper, 1970, p. 56f.

[20] Hutcheon, 1996, page 48.

Notes from Chapter 2, *The Modern Critics*

[21] See for instance Price, 1955; Kurtz, 1985, pages xviii-xix; and Flew, 1989.

[22] Bok, Jerome, Kurtz, et al, 1975.

[23] As quoted in Clark, 1990, page 418.

[24] Kurtz, Paul, 1976 (May/June), page 28.

[25] Zelen, Marvin, 1976, page 33 (emphasis added).

[26] Abell, et al, 1976, p. 44.

[27] Zelen, Kurtz, and Abell, 1977, p. 38.

[28] Rawlins, 1981, p. 67.

[29] Rawlins, 1981.

[30] The debate over the existence of a genuine Mars Effect continues to this day, conducted mostly by psychologist Suitbert Ertel and freelance technical writer Geoffrey Dean.

[31] Curry, Patrick, 1982. On the Committee's investigation of the Mars Effect, Curry concluded: "Their work could now best function as a model and a warning of how *not* to conduct such investigations. Rawlins and Gauquelin are in fact the only two major figures to emerge with scientific credibility intact."

[32] Kammann, Richard, 1982. Kammann describes his difficulty believing Rawlins' story when he first read it:

"The trouble with 'Starbaby' on first reading is that the case is too strong, and the cover-up too deep to be entirely believable. Like the other Fellows of CSICOP, I couldn't accept that Dennis Rawlins was the single honest and correct person on a nine-man Council consisting of men of such stature and reputation as Martin Gardner, Professor Ray Hyman, the Amazing Randi and Kendrick Frazier.... After seven months of research, I have come to the opposite conclusion. CSICOP has no good defense of the trio's Mars fiasco and has progressively trapped itself, degree by irreversible degree, into an anti-Rawlins propaganda campaign, into suppression of the evidence, and into stonewalling against other critics." (Part II)

[33] "Policy on Sponsoring Research, Testing Individual Claims, and Conducting Investigations of Alleged Paranormal Powers and Phenomena", *Skeptical Inquirer*, Spring 1982, p. 9.

In part, the statement reads:

"CSICOP, as a body, does not directly engage in the testing of psychics, research on paranormal phenomena, or investigations on related matters.... In other words, CSICOP will try, within the context of its limited resources, to be a catalyst for competent research on the paranormal, but it cannot conduct the actual research itself, nor can it be held responsible for the quality and outcome of the investigation."

[34] Hansen, 1992a, p. 40-41.

[35] Pinch & Collins, 1984, p. 539.

[36] Rawlins, 1981, ibid.

[37] The Sept/Oct 2002 issue reports sales through vendors at 16,635 and mail subscriptions at 34,747.

[38] Hansen, 1992a, p. 24-25. Examples of articles in mainstream scientific journals would include Child, 1985; Jahn, 1982; Radin & Nelson, 1989; Rao & Palmer, 1987; Winkelman, 1982; Utts, 1991a; Bem & Honorton, 1994; Stapp, 1994.

[39] From a CSICOP fund-raising letter of September 18, 1987, as found in Hansen, ibid. p. 41-42.

[40] Frazier, 1981, from the Introduction.

[41] Bauer, 1989, p. 9.

[42] Mayer, Elizabeth, 2007, p. 93.

[43] Hansen, ibid, p. 26.

[44] From Birdsell's unpublished thesis, 1981, as mentioned in Truzzi, 1997, p. 224.

[45] As mentioned in Truzzi, ibid, p. 224.

[46] Truzzi, ibid, p. 224.

[47] Hansen, 1990a, 1990b; Truzzi, 1997, pages 231-234.

[48] Hansen, 1992b, p. 163.

[49] Alcock, 1985.

[50] Alcock, 1981, p. 7.

[51] Gardner, 1983, p. 239.

[52] Hansen, 1992, Table 3.

[53] There is an apocalyptic strain to some of the Committee's writing. For instance, the announcement of the founding of CSICOP stated: *"Perhaps we ought not to assume that the scientific enlightenment will continue indefinitely...like the Hellenic civilization, it may be overwhelmed by irrationalism, subjectivism, and obscurantism."* (Kurtz, 1976)

[54] Harris poll released January 1978, quoted in Clark, 1990, p. 425.

[55] Clark, 1990, p. 425.

[56] Hyman, 1988.

[57] Greely, 1987.

[58] Sagan, 1995, p. 302.

[59] Radin, 1997, p. 3.

Notes from Chapter 3, *The Historical Evidence*

[60] Inglis, 1985, p. 38.

[61] Inglis, 1985, p. 38.

[62] Inglis, 1977, p. 21.

[63] Inglis, 1977, p. 33.

[64] As quoted in Inglis, 1977, p. 34.

[65] in Inglis, 1985, p. 65.

[66] Lamon, p. 116-117.

[67] As mentioned in Radin, 1997, p. 112-3.

[68] Inglis, 1985, p. 53.

[69] From the video *Arthur C. Clarke's World of Strange Powers: Warnings from the Future?* Chicago, Questar Video, 1995.

[70] Rhine, L.E., 1954.

[71] As told to Dean Radin. Radin, 1997, p. 24.

[72] Sheldrake, 1999a, p. 109.

[73] Ibid, p. 110.

[74] Ibid, p. 167.

[75] Ibid, p. 153.

Notes from Chapter 4, *The Early Years*

[76] This remark was made to William Barrett, Professor of Physics in the Royal College of Science in Dublin, and one of the early founders of the Society for Psychical Research.

[77] Utts, 1995a, page 6.

[78] Note that which error we try to avoid depends upon the perceived cost of making that error. The world of scientific research tends to be very conservative in its approach to accepting new ideas, and so there is tacit agreement that the cost of a Type I error is higher than that of a Type II error (that is, it is preferable to mistakenly conclude that there is no effect when there really is one, than it is to mistakenly conclude there is an effect when there really is none). This emphasis on avoiding Type I errors thus tends to put the burden of evidence on

researchers that are making new claims. However, in other situations, such as certain medical investigations, the cost of a Type II error is considered much higher than the cost of a Type I error. In such cases, tentative conclusions may be reached and acted upon before samples of data are available that would be large enough to reject the null hypothesis at the 5% significance level with the effect size observed in the sample at hand.

[79] The "true" result can be thought of in two different ways: in the case of a finite population, it can be thought of as the result of an experiment or survey conducted on the entire population—for instance, a political poll that surveyed the entire country's voting-age population. In the case of experiments that can be conducted over and over, the true result can be thought of as the result we would attain as the number of experiments approached infinity.

[80] Utts, 1991a. See also Stuart and Greenwood, 1937.

[81] Camp, 1937.

[82] Honorton, 1975, page 107.

[83] Hansel, 1966.

[84] Honorton, 1975, pages 109-110.

[85] Hansel, 1980, page 22.

[86] Hansel, 1980, page 21.

Notes from Chapter 5, *Psychokinesis*

[87] Zorab, 1985.

[88] Beloff, 1993, pages 45-57.

[89] As found in Beloff, 1993, page 50. Original source is *Francis Galton: Life and Letters*, by Karl Pearson. See volume 2, 1914.

[90] See Broughton, 1991, pages 141-150.

[91] Radin & Ferrari, 1991.

[92] Radin & Nelson, 1989, pages 1510-1511.

[93] Nelson & Dobyns, 1991.

[94] Dunne & Jahn, 1992.

[95] Herbert, 1993, pages 195-197.

[96] Blackmore, 1987, page 251.

Notes from Chapter 6, *Telepathy*

[97] Prasad & Stevenson, 1968; L.E. Rhine, 1962.

[98] Radin, 1997, pages 70-73; Ullman, Krippner and Vaughan, 1989.

Notes from Chapter 7, *The Great Ganzfeld Debate*

[99] Honorton, 1993, page 206; Bem & Honorton, 1994.

[100] Radin, 1997, page 79.

[101] Blackmore, 1980.

[102] Hyman and Honorton, 1986, page 352.

[103] Honorton, 1985; Radin, 1997, pages 81-82.

[104] Harris & Rosenthal, 1988b; Saunders, 1985; Utts, 1991b.

[105] Saunders, 1985, page 87.

[106] Hyman and Honorton, 1986, page 353.

[107] Scott, 1986, page 349.

[108] Hyman & Honorton, 1986, page 351.

[109] Radin, 1997, page 85.

[110] Hyman, 1985a.

[111] Rosenthal, 1986, page 333.

[112] Described in Broughton, 1991, page 322. Also see News & Comment, 1987, and Druckman & Swets, 1988.

[113] Alexander, 1989, page 12.

[114] Hyman & Honorton, 1986, page 352.

[115] News and Comment: Academy helps Army be all that it can be, 1987.

[116] Harris & Rosenthal, 1988a, page 53.

[117] Harris & Rosenthal, 1988a, page 51.

[118] Office of Technology Assessment, 1989.

[119] Alexander, 1989, (emphasis added).

[120] Bem & Honorton, 1994.

[121] Ibid, 1994.

[122] Utts, 1991a.

[123] Bem & Honorton, 1994. See also: Schmeidler, 1988; Dalton, 1997; Krippner (1962-63); Palmer, 1978; and Honorton, Ferrari, & Bem, 1992.

[124] Hyman, 1991, page 392.

[125] Bierman, 1995.

[126] Morris, Dalton, Delanoy, and Watt, 1995.

[127] Broughton & Alexander, 1995.

[128] Utts, 1995a, page 21.

[129] Milton & Wiseman, 1999, page 388.

[130] Ibid, page 388.

[131] Ibid, page 391.

[132] Radin, 2006, pages 118, 316.

[133] Dalton, 1997.

[134] Hyman & Honorton, 1986, page 361.

[135] Bem, Palmer, and Broughton, 2001, page 208.

[136] Hyman, 1996.

[137] Steering Committee of the Physicians Health Research Group, 1988.

[138] Utts, 1986.

[139] Utts, 1995b, page 3.

Notes from Chapter 8, *The Research of the Skeptics*

[140] Honorton, 1993, page 194.

[141] Gardner, 1983, page 60.

[142] Blackmore, 1996a.

[143] *Skeptical Inquirer*, 13, 1988.

[144] Blackmore, 1987. The title of her article is *"The Elusive Open Mind: Ten Years of Negative Research in Parapsychology."*

[145] Berger, 1989a, page 140.

[146] Berger, 1989a, page 137.

[147] Berger, 1989a, page 137.

[148] Blackmore, 1989, page 71.

[149] Berger, 1989a.

[150] Berger, 1989b.

[151] Blackmore, 1989b., page 145.

[152] Berger, 1989a, page 140.

[153] Blackmore, 1989b, page 152.

[154] Blackmore, 1987, page 250.

[155] Blackmore, 1989a, page 74.

[156] Blackmore, 1996a.

[157] Blackmore, 1996b, page 163, 187.

[158] Blackmore, 2000.

[159] ITV: November 1, 1996.

[160] Blackmore, S. 1999, p. 18.

[161] This is the text from Wiseman's website: "Dr Matthew Smith (Liverpool Hope University) and Prof Wiseman conducted four experiments examining the claim that a Yorkshire terrier named Jaytee could psychically detect when his owner was returning home. The results of these experiments did not support the existence of any paranormal communication between the owner and her pet. This research was widely reported in the media and published in The British Journal of Psychology."

[162] From Sheldrake's website, www.sheldrake.org

[163] Crace, John, *The Guardian*, March 2, 2004. The full quote is: "I've found plenty of evidence of unscientific approaches to data, but have never come across a paranormal experiment that can be replicated."

[164] Honorton, 1993, page 210.

[165] Randi, 1982, p. 211.

[166] From Sheldrake's website, October 2002.

[167] Letter from Jule Eisenbud, in 'The Psi Researcher' No. 5, 1992, page 18.

[168] Personal correspondence, Sept 27, 2002.

[169] Rawlins, 1981, p. 89.

[170] Truzzi, 1998.

[171] Blackmore, 1995.

[172] Hyman, Ray. 1996, page 24.

Notes from Chapter 9, *The Roots of Disbelief*

[173] Hyman, Ray. 1996, page 26.

[174] Evans, 1973; Wagner and Mary Monet, 1979. In the former study 53% of the "ESP is an impossibility" responses came from psychologists, although psychologists made up only 6% of the total sample. Only 3% of natural scientists considered ESP "an impossibility", compared to 34% of psychologists.

[175] Broughton 1991, 75.

[176] Robert G. Jahn, "On the Representation of Psychic Research to the Community of Established Science," in Rhea White and Richard Broughton, editors, *Research in Parapsychology 1983* (Metuchen, N.J.: Scarecrow, 1984), pages 127-138.

[177] James McClenon, *Deviant Science: The Case of Parapsychology* (Philadelphia: University of Pennsylvania, 1984).

[178] Schouten, S.A., (in press). Are we making progress? In *Psi research methodology: A re-examination* (37th Annual International Conference of the Parapsychology Foundation). New York: Parapsychology Foundation Inc.

[179] Marks, D.F. 1986. Investigating the Paranormal. *Nature* 320: 119-124.

[180] Quoted in "Einstein and ESP" by Martin Gardner, appearing in *Paranormal Borderlands of Science*, edited by Kendrick Frazier, Prometheus Books, 1981.

[181] O. Costa de Beauregard, "Quantum Paradoxes and Aristotle's Twofold Information Concept," in Laura Oteri, editor, *Quantum Physics and Parapsychology* (New York: Parapsychology Foundation, 1975), pages 91-102. See also "The Expanding Paradigm of the Einstein Theory", in A. Puharich, editor, *The Iceland Papers* (Amherst: Essentia Research Associates, 1979), pages 161-191.

[182] Brian Josephson speaking on the BBC World Service radio program "The Unexplained," May 5, 1987.

Notes from Chapter 10, *Modern Science versus Classical Science*

[183] Excellent discussions of these issues can be found in Lee Smolin's book, *Three Roads to Quantum Gravity*, (Basic Books, 2001), and in chapter 5 of *Hyperspace* by Michio Kaku (Oxford University Press, 1994). Quantum mechanics describes three of the four fundamental forces of modern physics: electromagnetism, the strong nuclear force (holds atomic nuclei together), and the weak nuclear force (governs radioactive decay). Relativity describes the fourth, gravity. A unified theory would describe all four forces.

[184] A very clear description of this experiment can be found in Bartley, 1978, pages 679-683. Note that in 1978 it was still only a thought experiment, but has since been performed.

[185] Rosenblum and Kuttner, 1999.

[186] Rosenblum and Kuttner, 1999.

[187] Some defenders of the Copenhagen interpretation will assert that the use of a measuring instrument to make a record results in a thermodynamically irreversible event, and so anything that makes a record can collapse the state vector. The problem with this is, as EH Walker writes, that "thermodynamic irreversibility is derived from the basic principles of physics and requires for that derivation the assumption of state vector collapse." (Walker, 1987, p. 345) In other words, a thermodynamically irreversible event requires the state vector to first collapse, so cannot be used to explain it.

[188] Herbert, 1993, page 157. Note that the transistor is a purely quantum mechanical device.

[189] Physicist Henry Stapp writes: "Whereas the Copenhagen approach excluded the bodies and brains of the human observers from the physical world that they sought to describe, and

renounced the aim of describing reality itself, von Neumann demanded logical cohesion and mathematical precision, and was willing to follow where this rational approach led. Being a mathematician, fortified by the rigor and precision of his thought, he seemed less intimidated than his physicist brethren by the sharp contrast between the nature of the world called for by the new mathematics and the nature of the world that the genius of Isaac Newton had concocted." (Stapp, Science and Human Values, chapter 1)

[190] Wigner, Eugene, 1961, "Remarks on the Mind-Body Question", in Quantum Theory and Measurement, edited by John Wheeler and Wojciech Zurek, Princeton: Princeton University Press, 1983.

[191] Euan Squires 1994, pages 68 and 81.

[192] It should be pointed out that the average quantum mechanic is about as interested in philosophy as the average garage mechanic. Theoretical physicist Michio Kaku wrote: "When confronted with sticky philosophical questions, such as the role of 'consciousness' in performing quantum measurement, most physicists shrug their shoulders. As long as they can calculate the outcome of an experiment, they really don't care about its philosophical implications.... Nevertheless, although the average physicist is not bothered by philosophical questions, the greatest of them were. Einstein, Heisenberg, and Bohr spent long hours in heated discussions, wrestling late into the night with the meaning of measurement, the problems of consciousness, and the meaning of probability in their work." (*Hyperspace*, p. 317)

[193] Polkinghorne 1984, page 68. For excellent discussions of these matters aimed at the lay-person I refer the reader to *The Mystery of the Quantum World*, by quantum theorist Euan Squires; to *The Quantum World* by physicist JC Polkinghorne; and to *Quantum Reality: Beyond the New Physics*, by physicist Nick Herbert.

[194] Schmidt, Morris, & Rudolph, 1986, page 3.

[195] Schmidt, Morris, & Rudolph, 1986.

[196] Euan Squires 1994, page 65.

[197] Ibid, page 68.

It should be mentioned that Squires did not seem, at least at the time of this writing, to be convinced of the reality of extra-sensory perception, as he added "Such evidence, however, is perhaps better left out of the discussion until it becomes more convincing."

[198] Ibid, page 68.

[199] Herbert, 1985, pages 226-7; Squires 1994, pages 98-102.

[200] Danah Zohar, 'Why Einstein was Wrong about Light', *Sunday Times*, February 20 1983.

[201] Squires 1994, pages 98-105, and Polkinghorne 1984, chapter 7, page 70-77.

[202] Physicist John Bell derived a simple inequality known today as Bell's Inequality, which must hold if reality is indeed local. A clear description of Bell's Inequality and the experiments that demonstrate violations of it can be found in chapter 12 of *Quantum Reality* by Nick Herbert.

[203] Stapp, 1999, page 150.

[204] Hameroff, S.R. 1994 Quantum coherence in microtubules: a neural basis for emergent consciousness? *Journal of Consciouss Studies* I: 91-118.

[205] Penrose, Roger, 1994, *Shadows of the Mind*, New York: Oxford University Press.

[206] For a somewhat detailed discussion and additional references, see Herbert, 1993, especially chapter 10. These models of quantum consciousness are essentially dualistic; they propose that consciousness collapses potentialities into actualities in the brain, and Walker attempts to account for psi in a similar manner (see Walker, 1974). Speculations on the connection between quantum mechanics and consciousness can also be found in Rosenblum and Kuttner, 1996.

[207] For concise summaries of these theories, see Stokes 1987b, and Rush 1986.

[208] Radin, Dean, 1997, pages 281-285. See also Walker, 1974, pages 544-568.

[209] Anderson, P.W. 1972. More is Different. *Science* August 1972, volume 177: 393-396.

[210] It could be argued that all of life is the end result of downward causation, as all the elements except hydrogen were originally forged in the interiors of stars. Popper describes stars as a pre-biological example of downward causation. Stars may be viewed as machines that put the atoms and elementary particles in their central region under terrific gravitational pressure, with the "result that some atomic nuclei fuse and form the nuclei of heavier elements; an excellent example of downward causation, of the action of the whole structure upon its constituent parts." (Popper and Eccles, 1977, page 20).

[211] Note the self-refuting nature of the first position: If I believe that consciousness does not exist, then how could my belief exist? If it does not, then neither does my belief. And if my expression of belief is just a machine going through the motions, then you have no reason to accept it as correct.

As for the identity theory: if brain states can be described in physical terms (at least in principle), and if thoughts are identical to brain states, then why can't we describe thoughts in physical terms? Unlike brain states, thoughts have no position, mass, charge, and so forth.

[212] Examples are renowned philosopher Curt Ducasse, neurophysiologist and Nobel laureate Sir John Eccles, and the celebrated neurosurgeon Wilder Penfield. It should be pointed out that none of these individuals hold this position as a matter of religious faith.

[213] Sperry, 1985, page 30.

[214] The history and current status of artificial intelligence (AI) research is discussed in a very entertaining manner in chapter 7 of John Horgan's book *The Undiscovered Mind*.

[215] Wigner 1969.

[216] Herbert 1985, page 249.

[217] Sperry, 1985, page 30.

[218] Popper, 1978.

[219] Sperry, 1985, page 36.

[220] Rao, 1994.

[221] Beloff, 1994. Beloff writes: "It says something about the desperation of those who want to dismiss radical dualism that such phony arguments should repeatedly be invoked by highly reputable philosophers who should know better."

[222] Popper and Eccles, 1977, pages 36-38, 176-180. Also, Popper, 1960.

[223] Sperry, 1985, page 40.

[224] Libet, 1999.

[225] Popper, 1978.

[226] Eccles has provided a clear exposition of Libet's experiments (complete with diagrams) in *The Self and its Brain*, by Popper & Eccles, pages 256-259.

[227] Popper and Eccles, 1977.

[228] Radin, 1997, chapter 7.

[229] Radin, 1997, page 284.

[230] Gardner, 1985, page 110.

[231] Sperry, 1987.

[232] MacKay, 1978.

[233] Searle, 1980, 1983.

[234] Morowitz, 1980, page 12.

[235] Morwowitz, ibid, page 16.

[236] Stapp, "Science and Human Values", from the internet, unpublished in print.

[237] Some of my critics are bound to point out that Roger Sperry did not share this view. For instance, shortly before his death he wrote that his account of consciousness leaves for dualism "only abstract arguments like those from Plato and Popper, and observations like those from parapsychology." (Sperry, 1985, p. 93)

[238] Blackmore, 1996a.

[239] Libet, 1999.

[240] Stapp, 1999.

[241] Thouless and Wiesner, 1949. Beloff writes: "Most of our transactions with the world are effectuated through the brain. Paranormal action and paranormal cognition occur when, for some obscure reason, we are able to by-pass the dependence on the brain and allow the mind to interact directly with the outside world." (Beloff, 1976)

[242] Popper and Eccles, 1977, pages 98-99.

[243] Penfield, 1977, page 39.

[244] Ibid, page 47.

Notes from Chapter 11, *The "Extraordinary Claims" of Parapsychology*

[245] Hebb, 1951, page 45.

[246] Honorton, 1993, page 196.

[247] Hansel, 1980.

[248] Kurtz, 1981, pages 13-14.

Notes from Chapter 12, *Psi and Physics*

[249] Hyamn, 1996, page 26.

[250] Squires, 1994, pages 115 and 147, emphasis added.

[251] Feinberg, 1975, page 54-55, emphasis added.

[252] Kurtz, 1981, page 19.

[253] Dennett, 1991, pages 33-39. Despite giving his book the rather pompous title *Consciousness Explained* Dennett of course does no such thing: he ends up simply denying the existence of conscious experience (presumably because of his failure to explain it).

Tracing the absurdity of the views of philosophers such as Dennett on the mind-body problem to an adherence to outmoded physics, physicist Henry Stapp writes: "There is a growing group of physicists who believe almost all thinking on this issue during the past few centuries to be logically unsound, because it is based implicitly on the precepts of classical theory, which are now known to be fundamentally incorrect. Contemporary physical theory differs profoundly from classical physical theory precisely on the nature of the dynamical linkage between minds and physical states." [Stapp, 1999, page 145].

[254] Rosenblum and Kuttner, 1999, page 248.

[255] Broad, 1929, page 103.

[256] Keeton, 1941. Keeton wrote that "It is still within the province of reason to question this great dogma notwithstanding the fact that it is a god at whose feet many scientists worship with blind and jealous devotion." His main point in the article is that the theory of the conservation of energy is not falsifiable by any possible set of observations, and that it can be interpreted to cover *any* observed energy relationships.

[257] Ducasse, 1961, page 107. This was also Karl Popper's position: see Popper & Eccles, 1977, p. 542.

[258] See Price, 1955; Kurtz, 1981, page 6; and Flew, 1985 page 527, 1989 page 314.

[259] Price, 1955, page 360.

[260] Flew, 1985, page 527.

[261] Wigner, 1969, page 99.

[262] Noble, 1988, page 179.

[263] Beloff, "Can there be a physical explanation for Psi?", in *The Relentless Question,* 1990.

[264] Murphy, Gardner, "Psychology in the Year 2000," in Lois B. Murphy, editor, *There is More Beyond: Selected Papers of Gardner Murphy.* Jefferson, NC: McFarland & Co., 1989.

Notes from Chapter 13, *Toward a New World View*

[265] Honorton, 1993, p. 211.

[266] Kuhn, 1962, page 65.

[267] Laudan, 1980, page 293. See also McClenon, 1984, page 55. McClenon rightly considers a mechanical model of nature to be scientistic rather than scientific, and notes how modern physics has outgrown a mechanistic conception of nature. The point is of course that psi is not accepted by some because it resists a mechanistic explanation.

[268] Kuhn, 1970, page 58.

Notes from Chapter 14, *The Impovershed State of Skepticism*

[269] Hyman, 1996.

[270] Hyman, 1996.

[271] Alexander, 1989, pages 15 & 52.

[272] Kaiser, 1995.

[273] Hyman, 1996.

[274] "Replication on demand" is a problem not exclusive to psi research, but found throughout the life sciences. Commenting on experiments in conventional psychology, Seymour Epstein wrote in a prominent psychology journal: "Not only are experimental findings often difficult to replicate when there are the slightest alterations in conditions, but even attempts at exact replication frequently fail." (Epstein, 1980). Sociologist Harry Collins conducted an extensive study of replication in science and concluded: "Experiments hardly ever work the first time; indeed, they hardly ever work at all." (Collins, 1985, 40).

[275] Utts, 1995b, page 3.

Notes from Chapter 15, *The Nature of Science*

[276] AAAS minutes, 1961, as found in McClenon, 1984, page 23.

[277] Dean, 1990, pages 7-8.

[278] Wheeler, 1979.

[279] All his life Newton was somewhat embarrassed by his own theory of gravity, thinking it incomplete and in need of some further explanation. "That gravity", he wrote, "should be innate, inherent, and essential to matter, so that one body may act upon another at a dis-tance…is to me so great an absurdity that I believe no man who has in philosophical mat-

ters a competent faculty of thinking can ever fall into it." [letter to Richard Bentley, 25th February 1693, as found in Popper, 1965, page 106]. He tried hard to explain it further but failed, refusing to invent any *ad hoc* hypothesis (*hypotheses non fingo*).

[280] Popper, 1974b, page 981, emphasis added.

[281] See for instance Putnam, 1974, pages 227-229; and Kuhn, 1996, pages 146-147.

[282] Popper, 1974b, page 980.

[283] Hume, *Treatise of Human Nature*, Book 1, Part III, sections vi and xii. Italics are Hume's.

[284] Russell, 1946, p. 647.

[285] Ibid, p. 641.

[286] Ibid, p. 644.

[287] Ibid, p. 646.

[288] Ibid, p. 647.

[289] Popper, 1974b, p. 1015.

[290] Popper, 1965, page 47.

[291] Popper, 1965, page 46.

[292] See Popper, 1965, page 42; Popper, 1974b, page 1013.

[293] Popper, 1974b, p. 1021.

[294] Popper, 1965, pages 51-52.

[295] Shermer, 2001, p. 216. Shermer's book is an attempt to classify various lines of research into science, nonscience, and "borderlands" science, but he follows no rigorous methodology such as Popper's. Instead, he subjectively classifies various theories, practices, and lines of research into his three categories.

[296] For instance, it does not follow from this that such life would want to contact us, would share our values, would be friendly toward us, and so forth.

Notes from Chapter 16, *The Scientific Status of Parapsychology*

[297] Tart, 1988; Vasiliev, 1976.

[298] Vasiliev, 1976, pages 126-127.

[299] Costa de Beauregard, 1979, p. 182.

[300] See Josephson's 'Forword' of *The Iceland Papers*, edited by A. Puharich, 1979.

[301] The original papers of von Neumann, Wigner, London, and Bauer on the consciousness question have been collected by Wheeler and Zurek in *Quantum Theory and Measurement*.

[302] Herbert, 1993, page 251. Chapter 10 contains an excellent summary of the various quantum theories of consciousness.

303 Walker, 1984, page 279.

304 Concerning the strength of electrical barriers in the synapses. See Herbert, 1993, pages 260-261.

305 Walker considers two possibilities: In the first, consciousness is localized in the brain, and produces non-local effects via non-local correlations between brain states and physical states outside of the brain. In the second, *consciousness itself is non-local*: That is, it extends beyond the spatial limits of the brain: "Instead of just observing its own brain directly, consciousness is also able to directly observe physical objects distant from the brain…. We do not wish to imply that consciousness *always* behaves non-locally, but rather that it is *capable* of non-local behavior." (Mattuck & Walker, 1979, p. 127)

306 The details of these theories are beyond the scope of this book. Interested readers may consult the original sources in the references. The mathematician Douglas Stokes has provided an excellent summary and comparison of the various quantum theories (see Stokes, 1987).

307 1975, p. 101.

308 Stokes, 1987b, page 138.

309 Biologist Rupert Sheldrake has taken some tentative steps in this direction with his novel theory of the "extended mind." His arguments may be found in his book *The Sense of Being Stared At.*

310 Popper, 1974a, page 103. Popper writes:

"Explanation is always incomplete: we can always raise another why-question. And the new why-question may lead to a new theory which not only 'explains' the old theory, but corrects it. This is why the evolution of physics is likely to be an endless process of correction and better approximation."

In a footnote to the above, Popper illustrates his point with a passage from Harald Hoffding's *Den menneskelige Tanke:*

"We have no knowledge going beyond experience; but at no stage are we entitled to look upon experience as complete. Thus knowledge, even at its highest, provides us with nothing more than a segment of the existing world. Every reality, we may find, is itself again a part of a wider reality." (p. 303)

311 Gardner, 1982.

312 Flew, 1989, p. 322.

313 Flew, 1989, page 322. Note that many psychological phenomena are studied without benefit of a full theoretical explanation, such as learning, memory, and hypnosis.

314 Walker, 1984, p. 326.

Notes from Chapter 17, *Hume's Argument Revisited*

315 See Price, 1955; Kurtz, 1985, page xviii; and Flew, 1985 page 526-530, 1989 page 317-325.

[316] For an excellent summary of the rise of science during the seventeenth century, see Russell, 1946, chapter VI.

[317] Popper, 1965, p. 93.

[318] Price, 1955, page 360.

[319] Flew, 1989, pages 317-18.

[320] Flew, 1989, page 321.

[321] To be fair, Hume does admit this difficulty, but seems to imply that he has no choice if he is going to write anything more. "The sceptic still continues to reason and believe, even though he asserts that he cannot defend his reason by reason." (*Treatise of Human Nature*, Book I, part iv, section ii).

[322] Popper, 1974b, page 1021.

Notes from Chapter 18, *Paradigms and Parapsychology*

[323] Snow, 1934, page 172.

[324] Greene, 1980; Popper, 1974b, pages 1144-1153. Greene discusses the Darwinian revolution. Popper discusses the introduction of relativity.

[325] Shapere, D. 1964. "The Structure of Scientific Revolutions", review in *Philosophical Review,* 73, page 363-394. As quoted in McClenon, 1984, page 21.

[326] Masterman, 1970.

[327] Walker, 1984, p. 282.

[328] A fascinating critical overview of mind-science can be found in *The Undiscovered Mind* by science writer John Horgan.

[329] Popper, 1974b, p.1147.

[330] Feuer, 1974, p. 253.

[331] Blackmore, 1987, p. 250-1.

[332] Blackmore, 1987, p. 244-5.

[333] Blackmore, 1996, page 187.

[334] Blackmore, 1987, page 249.

[335] Bauer, 1989, page 7.

[336] Blackmore, 1996, page 88.

[337] Blackmore, 1996, page 242.

Bibliography

Abell, G.O., Abell, A.A., M. Gauquelin and F. Gauquelin, 1976. "A Test of the Gauquelin Mars Effect", *The Humanist* (Sept-Oct 1976), pages 40-45.

Alcock, J.E., 1981. *Parapsychology: Science or Magic?* New York: Pergamon.

Alcock, J.E., 1985. "Parapsychology: the Spiritual Science". *Free Inquiry*, 5 (2), p. 25-35.

Alexander, John A, (Col., U.S. Army, Ret.) 1989. "Enhancing Human Performance: A Challenge to the Report," *New Realities,* 9(4), pages 10-15, 52-53.

Barker, David, 1979. "Letter to the Editors", *The Journal of Parapsychology*, 43, pp. 268-9.

Barrett, William, 1926. *Death Bed Visions*. London: Methuen.

Bartley, W.W. 1978. "The Philosophy of Karl Popper Part II: Consciousness and Physics." *Philisophia*, Isreal 7, 3-4, July, pages 675-716.

Bauer, Henry, 1989. "Arguments Over Anomalies: II. Polemics", *Journal of Scientific Exploration*, Vol. 3, No. 1, pages 1-14.

Beloff, John. "Mind-Body interaction in light of the parapsychological evidence." *Theoria to Theory*, Vol 10, 1976.

Beloff, John. 1990. *The Relentless Question.* North Carolina: McFarland & Co.

Beloff, John. 1988. "Parapsychology and Physics: can they be reconciled?" *Theoretical Parapsychology*, Vol. 6, pages 23-29.

Beloff, John. 1993. *Parapsychology: A Concise History.* London: The Athlone Press.

Beloff, John. 1994. "The Mind-Brain Problem." *The Journal of Scientific Exploration*, Vol. 8, No 4.

Bem, D., and Honorton, C., 1994. "Does Psi Exist?", *Psychological Bulletin*, Vol. 115, No. 1, pages 4-18.

Bem, D., Palmer, John, and Richard Broughton, 2001. "Updating the Ganzfeld Database: a victim of its own success?", The Journal of Parapsychology, Vol. 65, September, pages 207-218.

Berger, Rick, 1989a "Discussion: A Critical Examination of the Blackmore Psi Experiments" *Journal of the American Society for Psychical Research*, Vol. 83, April 1989, pages 123-144.

Berger, Rick, 1989b "Reply to Blackmore's 'A Critical Response to Rick Berger'" *Journal of the American Society for Psychical Research*, Vol. 83, April 1989, pages 155-157.

Bierman, Dick J., 1995. "The Amsterdam Ganzfeld Series III & IV: Target clip emotionality, effect sizes, and openness," *Proceedings of the 38th Annual Parapsychological Association Convention*, pages 27-37.

Blackmore, Susan. 1980. "The extent of selective reporting of ESP Ganzfeld studies" *European Journal of Parapsychology*, 3, pages 213-219.

Blackmore, Susan. 1985a. "The Adventures of a psi-inhibitory experimenter." In P. Kurtz (editor), *A Skeptic's Handbook of Parapsychology* (pages 425-448). Buffalo: Prometheus Books.

Blackmore, Susan. 1985b. "Unrepeatability: parapsychology's only finding" In B. Shapin & L. Coly (editors), *The Repeatability Problem in Parapsychology* (pages 183-206). New York: Parapsychology Foundation.

Blackmore, Susan. 1986. *The Adventures of a Parapsychologist*. Buffalo: Prometheus Books.

Blackmore, Susan. 1987. "The Elusive Open Mind: Ten Years of Negative Research in Parapsychology" *Skeptical Inquirer*, Vol. XI, no. 3, Spring 1987, pages 244-255.

Blackmore, Susan. 1989a. "Confessions of a Parapsychologist" In T. Schultz (editor), *The Fringes of Reason: a whole Earth Catalog,* (pages 70-74). New York: Harmony Books.

Blackmore, Susan. 1989b. "A Critical Response to Rick Berger." *Journal of the American Society for Psychical Research*, Vol. 83, April 1989, pages 145-154.

Blackmore, Susan. 1995. "Which Skeptical Position?" *Skeptical Inquirer*, May/June, 1995, page 26.

Blackmore, Susan, 1996a. Reply to "Do you believe in psychic phenomena?" *The Times Higher Education Supplement*, April 5.

Blackmore, Susan, 1996b. *In Search of the Light: the Adventures of a Parapsychologist*, Amherst, New York: Prometheus Books.

Blackmore, S. 1999. "If the truth is out there, we've not found it yet" *The Times Higher Education Supplement*, August 27 1999, page 18.

Blackmore, Susan, 2000. "Into the Unknown" *New Scientist*, no. 2263, November 4, 2000, page 55.

Bok, B., Jerome, L., & Paul Kurtz, et al. 1975. "Objections to Astrology", *The Humanist*, September/October 1975

B.B. Boycott, "Learning in the Octopus", *Scientific American* 212, 1965, pp. 42-50.

Braud, W. G. (1975). "Conscious versus unconscious clairvoyance in the context of an academic examination." *Journal of Parapsychology*, 39, 277-288.

Braude, Stephen, 1986. *The Limits of Influence*, New York and London: Routledge & Kegan Paul.

Broad, C.D. 1929. *The Mind and its Place in Nature*, New York: Harcourt, Brace & Co.

Broad, C.D. 1949. "The Relevance of Psychical Research to Philosophy", *The Journal of the Royal Institute of Philosophy*, vol. XXIV, no. 91, October, pages 291-309.

Broad, C.D., 1962 *Lectures on Psychical Research*, New York: Humanities Press.

Broughton, Richard, 1991. *Parapsychology: The Controversial Science*. New York: Ballantine Books.

Broughton, Richard, and Cheryl Alexander, 1995. "Autoganzfeld II: The first 100 sessions," *Proceedings of the 38th Annual Parapsychological Association Convention*, pages 53-61.

Burt, Cyril, 1975. *ESP and Psychology*. London: Weidenfeld and Nicolson.

Camp, B. H. 1937. (Statement in Notes Section.). *Journal of Parapsychology* 1 305.

Cerf, Christopher; Navasky, Victor, 1984. *The Experts Speak: the Definitive Compendium of Authoritative Misinformation.* New York: Pantheon Books.

Child, Irvin, 1985. "Psychology and Anomalous Observations, The Question of ESP in Dreams." *American Psychologist*, November 1985, pp. 1219-1230.

Clark, Jerome, 1990. "Skeptics and the New Age" in J. Gordon Melton, Jerome Clark, and Aidan Kelly, *New Age Encyclopedia.* Detroit: Gale Research, 1990, p. 417-427.

Collins, H.H., 1985. *Changing Order: Replication and Induction in Scientific Practice.* Beverly Hills, CA: Sage.

Costa de Beauregard, Olivier, 1975. "Quantum Paradoxes and Aristotle's Twofold Information Concept," in Laura Oteri, editor, *Quantum Physics and Parapsychology* (New York: Parapsychology Foundation, 1975), pages 91-102.

Costa de Beauregard, Olivier, 1979. "The Expanding Paradigm of the Einstein Theory", in A. Puharich, editor, *The Iceland Papers* (Amherst: Essentia Research Associates, 1979), pages 161-191.

Crace, John, 2004. "Richard Wiseman: fortune teller". *The Guardian*, Tuesday, March 2, 2004.

Crosland, Maurice, 1992. *Science Under Control: the French Academy of Sciences 1795-1914.* Cambridge: Cambridge University Press.

Curry, Patrick, 1982. "Research on the Mars Effect," *Zetetic Scholar*, No. 9, pages 34-53.

Dalton, Kathy 1997. "Exploring the links: Creativity and psi in the ganzfeld." *Proceedings of Presented Papers, The Parapsychological Association 40th Annual Convention*, pages 119-134.

Dean, Douglas, 1990. "20th Anniversary of the PA and the AAAS, Part 1: 1963-1969." *ASPR Newsletter*, Winter 1990.

Dennett, D.C. 1991. *Consciousness Explained.* New York: Little Brown.

Druckman, Daniel, and John A. Swets (editors) 1988. *Enhancing Human Performance: Issues, Theories, and Techniques.* Washington, DC: National Academy Press.

Ducasse, Curt. 1959. *Paranormal Science and Life After Death.* Illinois: Charles C. Thomas.

Ducasse, Curt. 1961. *A Critical Examination of the Belief in a Life After Death.* Illinois: Charles C. Thomas.

Dunne, B., and R. Jahn. 1992. "Experiments in remote human/machine interaction", *Journal of Scientific Exploration*, 6, pages 311-332.

Dukhan, H., and Rao, K.R., 1973. "Meditation and ESP Scoring", in W.G. Roll, R.L. Morris, & J.D. Morris (editors) *Research in Parapsychology* 1972, pages 148-151. Metuchen, NJ: Scarecrow Press.

Eccles, John. 1953. *The Neurophysiological Basis of Mind.* Oxford, Oxford University Press.

Eccles, John. 1970. *Facing Reality: Philosophical Adventures of a Brain Scientist.* New York, Heidelberg, Berlin: Springer-Verlag.

Elitzur, Avshalom; Sackler, Beverly; Sackler, Raymond. 1995. "Consciousness Can No More Be Ignored" *Journal of Consciousness Studies*, **2**, No. 1, pages 353-357.

Epstein, S. 1980. "The stability of behavior. II. Implications for psychological research." *American Psychologist* 35: pages 790-806.

Ertel, Suitbert, 1994. *Testing Sheldrake's Claims of Morphogenetic Fields*, in Research in Parapsychology 1991, edited by Emily Cook and Deborah Delanoy, London: The Scarecrow Press, pages 169-192.

Evans, Christopher, 1973. "Parapsychology—what the questionnaire revealed", *New Scientist*, 25, January 1973, page 209.

Eysenck, H., and Carl Sargent, 1982. *Explaining the Unexplained: Mysteries of the Paranormal*. London: Book Club Associates.

Feinberg, G. 1975. "Precognition—a memory of things future". In L. Oteri (Editor), *Quantum physics and parapsychology*, pages 54-73. New York: Parapsychology Foundation.

Feuer, L. 1974. *Einstein and the generations of science*. New York: Basic Books.

Firsoff, V.A. 1975. "Life and Quantum Physics". In L. Oteri (Editor), *Quantum physics and parapsychology*, pages 109-120. New York: Parapsychology Foundation.

Flew, A. 1985. "Parapsychology: Science or Pseudoscience?", in *A Skeptic's Handbook of Parapsychology*. Buffalo: Prometheus Books, pages 519-536.

Flew, A. 1989. "Evidencing the improbable and the impossible". In Zollschan, Schumaker & Walsh (editors), 1989.

Frazier, Kendrick, editor. 1981. *Paranormal Borderlands of Science*. Buffalo: Prometheus Books.

Gabbard, G., & Twemlow, S., 1984. *With the Eyes of the Mind*, New York: Praeger.

Gardner, M. 1982. "Parapsychology and quantum mechanics" in G.O. Abell & B. Singer (eds) *Science and the Paranormal*. New York: Charles Scribner's Sons.

Gardner, M. 1983. *The whys of a philosophical scrivener*. New York: Quill.

Gardner, Howard. 1985. *The Mind's New Science: A history of the cognitive revolution*. New York: Basic Books.

Gauqulin, Michel, and Francoise Gauqulin, 1977. "The Zelen Test of the Mars Effect", *The Humanist* 1977 (November/December), pages 30-35.

Gordon, Henry, 1988. *Extrasensory Deception*. Toronto: Macmillan of Canada.

Greeley, A. (1987). "Mysticism goes mainstream", *American Health* 7 47-49.

Greene, John, 1980. "The Kuhnian Paradigm and the Darwinian Revolution in Natural History", in *Paradigms and Revolutions*, Gary Gutting, ed. Notre Dame, Indiana: University of Notre Dame Press.

Halgren, E., Walter, R., Cherlow, D, and Paul Crandall, 1978. "Mental Phenomena Evoked by Electrical Stimulation of the Human Hippocampal Formation and Amygdala", *Brain*, 1978, 101, pp. 83-117.

Hansel, C.E.M. 1966/1980. *ESP and Parapsychology: A critical re-evaluation*. Buffalo, NY: Prometheus.

Hansen, George, 1990a. "Magicians who endorsed psychic phenomena", *Linking Ring*, 70 (8), pages 63-65, 109.

Hansen, George, 1990b. "Magicians who endorsed psychic phenomena", *Linking Ring*, 70 (9), pages 63-65, 109.

Hansen, George, 1992a. "CSICOP and the Skeptics: and Overview", *Journal of the American Society for Psychical Research*, vol. 86, January 1992, pages 19-63.

Hansen, George, 1992b. "Magicians and the Paranormal", *Journal of the American Society for Psychical Research*, Vol. 86, April 1992, pages 151-185.

Harman, W. 1988. *Global Mind Change*. Indianapolis, IN: Knowledge Systems.

Harris, Melvin, 1986. *Investigating the Unexplained*. Buffalo, New York: Prometheus Books.

Harris, M., & Rosenthal, R. 1988a. "Human Performance Research: an overview." Washington, D.C.: National Academy Press.

Harris, M., & Rosenthal, R. 1988b. "Postscript to 'Human Performance Research: an overview.'" Washington, D.C.: National Academy Press.

Hebb, D.O. 1951. "The Role of Neurological Ideas in Psychology" *Journal of Personality*, 20: pages 39-55.

Herbert, Nick, 1985. *Quantum Reality: Beyond the New Physics*. New York: Anchor Press.

Herbert, Nick, 1993. *Elemental Mind: Human Consciousness and the New Physics*. New York: Penguin Books.

Heywood, Rosalind, 1961. *Beyond the Reach of Sense*. New York: EP Dutton & Company.

Hines, Terrance, 1988. *Pseudoscience and the Paranormal*. Buffalo: Prometheus Books.

Hippocrates, *On the Sacred Disease*.

Honorton, C., 1975. "Error some place!". *Journal of Communication*, 25, pages 103-116.

Honorton, C., 1993. "Rhetoric over Substance: the Impoverished State of Skepticism". *Journal of Parapsychology* 57, pages 191-214.

Honorton, C., Ferrari, D., and Bem, D.J., 1992. "Extraversion and ESP Performance: Meta-analysis and a new confirmation". In L.A. Henkel & G.R. Schmeidler (editors), *Research in parapsychology 1990*, pages 35-38. Metuchen, NJ: Scarecrow Press.

Horgan, John, 1999. *The Undiscovered Mind*. New York: Simon & Schuster.

Houtkooper, Joop, 2002. "Arguing for an Observational Theory of Paranormal Phenomena", *Journal of Scientific Exploration*, Vol. 16, No. 2, pages 171-185.

Hume, David, 1739. *Treatise of Human Nature*.

Hume, David, 1748. *An Inquiry Concerning Human Understanding*.

Hutcheon, Pat Duffy, 1995. "Popper and Kuhn on the Evolution of Science", in *Book Review*, Vol. 4, No. 1/2., pages 28-37.

Hutcheon, Pat Duffy, 1996. *Leaving the Cave: Evolutionary Naturalism in Social-Scientific Thought*. Waterloo, Ontario: Wilfred Laurier University Press.

Huxley, Aldous, 1954. *The Doors of Perception*, first published by Chatto & Windus Ltd, republished by Granada Publishing, 1984, London, UK.

Hyman, Ray. 1985a. "A critical overview of parapsychology." *A Skeptic's Handbook of Parapsychology* (P. Kurtz, ed.) pages 1-96. Prometheus Books, Buffalo, N.Y.

Hyman, R. 1985b. "The ganzfeld psi experiment: A critical appraisal". *Journal of Parapsychology*, 49, pages 3-49.

Hyman, R., and Honorton, C., 1986. "A joint communiqué: the psi ganzfeld controversy." *Journal of Parapsychology*, 50, pages 351-364.

Hyman, Ray, 1988. "Proper Criticism" *The New York Skeptic*, 1, (Spring 1988), page 1.

Hyman, Ray, 1991. "Comment" *Statistical Science*, 6, pages 389-392.

Hyman, Ray, 1996. "Evaluation of Program on Anomalous Mental Phenomena" *Journal of Scientific Exploration,* 10, pages 31-58.

Hyman, Ray, 1996. "The Evidence for Psychic Functioning: Claims vs. Reality" *Skeptical Inquirer,* March/April 1996, pages 24-26.

Inglis, Brian (1977) *Natural and Supernatural*, London: Hodder & Stoughton.

Inglis, Brian (1984) *Science and Parascience: A History of the Paranormal, 1914-1939*, London: Hodder & Stoughton.

Inglis, Brian (1986) *The Paranormal: an Encyclopedia of Psychic Phenomena*, London: Paladin.

Ingram, Jay (2003) "Why I'm skeptical—even of the Skeptic", *Toronto Star*, Sunday, March 16, 2003, p. A14.

Irwin, H.J., 1999. *An Introduction to Parapsychology*, 3rd edition. Jefferson, NC: McFarland & Company.

Jenkins, Elizabeth (1982) *The Shadow and the Light: A Defense of Daniel Dunglas Home the Medium,* London: Hamish Hamilton.

Josephson, B., and Pallikari-Viras, F., 1991. "Biological Utilisation of Quantum NonLocality", *Foundations of Physics*, Vol. 21, pp. 197-207.

Kaiser, Jocelyn, (editor) 1995. "Major EMF Report Warns of Health Risks", *Science*, Vol. 269, August 18, p. 911.

Kaku, Michio, 1994. *Hyperspace*, Oxford University Press (republished in New York by Doubleday, 1995).

Kammann, Richard, 1982. "The True Disbelievers: Mars Effect Drives Skeptics to Irrationality", *Zetetic Scholar*, No. 10, pages 50-65.

Keeton, M.T., 1941. "Some Ambiguities in the Theory of the Conservation of Energy", *Philosophy of Science*, Vol. 8, No. 3, July.

King, M, 1985. *Being Pakeha: an Encounter with New Zealand and the Maori Renaissance.* Auckland: Hodder & Stoughton.

Krippner, S. 1962-62. "Creativity and psychic phenomena". *Indian Journal of Parapsychology*, 4.

Krippner, Stanley, 1990. *Advances in Parapsychological Research 6.* Jefferson, N.C.: McFarland & Company.

Kuhn, Thomas, 1996. *The Structure of Scientific Revolutions, 3rd edition.* Chicago: University of Chicago Press.

Kurtz, Paul, 1976. "Committee to Scientifically Investigate Claims of Paranormal and Other Phenomena", *The Humanist*, 1976 (May/June), p. 28.

Kurtz, Paul, 1977. "The Mars Effect and the Zelen Test", *The Humanist*, 1977 (November/December), p. 29.

Kurtz, Paul, 1981. "Is Parapsychology a Science?" in *Paranormal Borderlands of Science*, edited by Kendrick Frazier, 1981. Buffalo: Prometheus Books.

Kurtz, Paul, (editor), 1985. *A Skeptic's Handbook of Parapsychology.* Buffalo: Prometheus Books

Kurtz, Paul, 1994. "The Growth of Antiscience", *Skeptical Inquirer*, Spring 1994.

Laudan, Rachel. 1980. "The Recent Revolution in Geology and Kuhn's Theory of Scientific Change." In *Paradigms and Revolutions*, Gary Gutting (editor). Notre Dame, Indiana: University of Notre Dame Press.

Lamon, Ward Hill. *Recollections of Abraham Lincoln 1847-1865,* University of Nebraska Press, Lincoln, Nebraska, 1994.

Libet, B., Elwood, W., B. Feinstein and D. Pearl, 1979. "Subjective Referral of the Timing for a Conscious Sensory Experience", *Brain*, 102, Vol. CII, pages 193-224.

Libet, Benjamin. 1999. "Do We Have Free Will?" *Journal of Consciousness Studies,* 6, No. 8-9, pages 47-57.

Libet, B; Freeman, A.; Sutherland, K, editors. 1999. *The Volitional Brain: towards a Neuroscience of Free Will.* Thoverton: Imprint Academic.

Masterman, Margaret, 1970. "The Nature of a Paradigm", in *Criticism and Growth of Knowledge,* Imre Lakatos and Alan Musgrave, eds., Cambridge: Cambridge University Press, 1970.

Mattuck, R., and Evan Harris Walker, 1979. "The Action of Consciousness on Matter: a Quantum Mechanical Theory of Psychokinesis", in A. Puharich, editor, *The Iceland Papers* (Amherst: Essentia Research Associates, 1979), pages 111-160.

Mayer, Elizabeth, 2007. *Extraordinary Knowing: Science, Skepticism, and the Inexplicable Powers of the Human Mind.* New York: Bantam Dell.

McClenon, James. 1984. *Deviant Science: the Case of Parapsychology.* Philadelphia: University of Pennsylvania Press.

McCullagh, Peter, 1993. *Brain Dead, Brain Absent, Brain Donors.* Chichester, England: John Wiley & Sons.

Milner, Richard, 1996. "Charles Darwin and Associates, Ghostbusters", *Scientific American*, October 1996, pp. 96-101.

Milton, J., and Wiseman, R., 1999. "Does Psi Exist? Lack of Replication of an Anomalous Process of Information Transfer", *Psychological Bulletin*, Vol. 125, No. 4, pages 387-391.

Morris, Robert, Kathy Dalton, Deborah Delanoy and Caroline Watt, 1995. "Comparison of the sender/no sender condition in the Ganzfeld," *Proceedings of the 38th Annual Parapsychological Association Convention*, pages 244-259.

Murchison, Carl (editor) 1927. *The Case For and Against Psychical Belief.* Worchester, Massachusetts: Clark University.

Murphy, Lois, 1989. *There is More Beyond: Selected Papers of Gardner Murphy.* Jefferson, NC: McFarland & Co.

Myers, Frederic, 1891-2. "One the Evidence for Clairvoyance", *Journal of the Society for Psychical Research,* 1891-2, Vol. 7, pp. 30-99.

Myers, Frederic, 1903. *Human Personality and its Survival of Bodily Death.* Volumes I and II. New York: Longmans, Green, and Co.

News & Comment, 1987. "Academy Helps Army Be All That It Can Be", *Science*, Vol. 238, 11 December 1987, pages 1501-1502.

Nelson, R.D., and Y.H. Dobyns, 1991. "Analysis of Variance of RNG experiments: Operator intention, secondary parameters, database structure", *Technical Note PEAR 91004*, Princeton Engineering Anomalies Research, Princeton University, School of Engineering/Applied Science, December 1991.

Nigro, Georgia, & Neisser, Ulric, 1983. "Point of View in Personal Memories", *Cognitive Psychology* 15, pp. 467-482.

Noble, H.B. 1988. *Next: the coming era in science.* Boston: Little, Brown.

Office of Technology Assessment (1989). Report of a workshop on experimental parapsychology. *Journal of the American Society for Psychical Research,* **83** 317-339.

Oteri, Laura, 1975 (Editor). *Quantum physics and parapsychology.* New York: Parapsychology Foundation.

Palmer, John, 1978. "Extrasensory Perception: Research findings", in S. Krippner (editor), *Advances in parapsychological research* (Vol. 2, pages 59-243). New York: Plenum Press.

Penfield, Wilder, 1952. *The Cerebral Cortex of Man.* New York: The MacMillan Company.

Penfield, Wilder, 1955. "The Role of the Temporal Cortex in Certain Psychical Phenomena", *Journal of Mental Science*, Vol. 101, No. 424, pp. 451-65.

Penfield, Wilder, 1958. *The Excitable Cortex in Conscious Man.* Liverpool: Liverpool University Press.

Penfield, Wilder, 1975. *The Mystery of the Mind.* Princeton: Princeton University Press.

Pinch, T.J, & Collins, H.M., 1984. "Private Science and Public Knowledge: The Committee for the Scientific Investigation of the Claims of the Paranormal and its use of the literature." *Social Studies of Science*, 14, 521-546.

Plato, *Phaedo.*

Polkinghorne, J.C. 1984. *The Quantum World.* London: Longman Group.

Popper, Karl, 1959. *The Logic of Scientific Discovery.* New York: First Harper Torchbook, second edition.

Popper, Karl, 1960. Philosophy and Physics, *Proceedings of the XIIth International Congress for Philosophy*, Vol. 2, pages 367-74.

Popper, Karl, 1965. *Conjectures and Refutations.* New York: Harper & Row.

Popper, Karl, 1970. "Normal Science and its Dangers", in *Criticism and the Growth of Knowledge*, edited by Imre Lakatos and Alan Musgrave. London: Cambridge University Press.

Popper, Karl, 1974a. "Autobiography", in *The Philosophy of Karl Popper*, Part I, edited by Paul Arthur Schilpp. Illinois, The Open Court Publishing Company.

Popper, Karl, 1974b. "Replies to my Critics", in *The Philosophy of Karl Popper*, Part II, edited by Paul Arthur Schilpp. Illinois, The Open Court Publishing Company.

Popper, K., and Eccles, J. 1977. *The Self and its brain.* New York: Springer International.

Popper, Karl, 1978. "Natural Selection and the Emergence of Mind" *Dialectica* **22**, 3, pages 339-55.

Price, George, R., 1955. "Science and the Supernatural", *Science* Volume 122, number 3165, August 26, pages 359-367.

Prince, Walter Franklin, 1927. "Is Psychical Research Worth While?" in *The Case for and Against Psychical Belief*, edited by Carl Murchison. Worcester: Clark University.

Puharich, A. 1979 (editor). *The Iceland Papers.* Amherst: Essentia Research Associates.

Putnam, Hillary, 1974. "The 'Corroboration' of Theories", in *The Philosophy of Karl Popper*, Part I, edited by Paul Arthur Schilpp. Illinois, The Open Court Publishing Company.

Radin, Dean, and Roger Nelson, 1989. "Evidence for Consciousness-Related Anomalies in Random Physical Systems", *Foundations of Physics*, Vol. 19, No. 12, pages 1499-1514.

Radin, Dean, and Diane Ferrari, 1991. "Effects of consciousness on the fall of dice: a meta-analysis", *Journal of Scientific Exploration*, 5, pages 61-84.

Radin, Dean, 1997. *The Conscious Universe: The Scientific Truth of Psychic Phenomena*. San Francisco: HarperCollins.

Randall, John, 1982. *Psychokinesis: a study of paranormal forces through the ages.* London: Souvenir Press.

Randi, James, 1982. *Flim Flam! Psychics, ESP, Unicorns, and other Delusions.* Buffalo: Prometheus Books.

Rawcliffe, D.H., 1959. *Illusions and Delusions of the Supernatural and the Occult.* New York: Dover.

Rawlins, Dennis. "Starbaby." *Fate* 34, 10, October 1981, pages 67-98.

Rhine, L.E., 1954. "Frequency of Types of Experience in Spontaneous Precognition," *Journal of Parapsychology*, 18 (2): 199.

Rhine, L.E., 1955. "Precognition and Intervention," *Journal of Parapsychology*, 19 (1), pp. 3-34.

Rhine, L.E., 1962. "Psychological Processes in ESP experiences. I. Waking experiences". Journal of Parapsychology, 26, 88-111.

Rosenblum, B., and Kuttner, F. "Consciousness and Quantum Mechanics: The Connection and Analogies." *The Journal of Mind and Behavior*, Summer 1999, Volume 20, Number 3, pages 229-256.

Rosenthal, Robert, 1986. "Meta-analytic Procedures and the Nature of Replication: the Ganzfeld Debate." *Journal of Parapsychology*, 50, pages 315-336.

Rush, Joseph, 1986. "Physical and quasi-physical theories of psi", in *Foundations of Parapsychology*, by Edge, H., Morris, R., Rush, J., and John Palmer. Boston: Routledge & Kegan Paul.

Russell, Bertrand, 1946. *A History of Western Philosophy*, London: George Allen and Unwin.

Russell, Bertrand, 1956. *Portraits from Memory*, London: George Allen and Unwin.

Ryle, Gilbert, 1968. *The Concept of Mind*. Middlesex, England: Penguin Books.

Sagan, Carl, 1979. *Broca's Brain*. New York: Random House.

Sagan, Carl, 1995. *The Demon Haunted World*. New York: Random House.

Saunders, David, 1985. "On Hyman's Factor Analyses". *The Journal of Parapsychology*, Vol. 49, pages 86-90.

Schechter, E.I., 1984. "Hypnotic induction vs. control conditions: Illustrating an approach to the evaluation of replicability in parapsychology." *Journal of the American Society for Psychical Research*, 78, pages 1-27.

Schmeidler, G.R., 1988. *Parapsychology and psychology: Matches and mismatches*. Jefferson, NC: McFarland.

Schmidt, Helmut, 1974. "Comparison of PK action on two different random number generators," *Journal of Parapsychology*, 38, pages 47-55.

Schmidt, Helmut, 1976. "PK effects on pre-recorded targets," *Journal of the American Society for Psychical Research*, 70, pages 267-291.

Schmidt, Helmut, 1985. "Addition effect for PK on pre-recorded targets," *Journal of Parapsychology*, 49, pages 229-244.

Schmidt, Helmut, Morris, R., and L. Rudolph, 1986. "Channeling Evidence for a PK Effect to Independent Observers", *Journal of Parapsychology*, Vol. 50, March, pages 1-15.

Schmidt, Helmut, 1987. "The Strange Properties of Psychokinesis", *Journal of Scientific Exploration*, Vol. 1, No. 2, pages 103-118.

Scott, Christopher, 1986. "Comment on the Hyman-Honorton Debate.", *Journal of Parapsychology*, Vol. 50, December, pages 349-350.

Searle, John R, 1997. *The Mystery of Consciousness*

Sheldrake, Rupert, 1981. *A New Science of Life*. Los Angeles: J.P. Tarcher.

Sheldrake, Rupert, 1988. *The Presence of the Past*. New York: Times Books.

Sheldrake, Rupert, 1991. *The Rebirth of Nature*. New York: Bantam Books.

Sheldrake, Rupert, 1999a. *Dogs that Know when their Owners are Coming Home*. New York: Crown Publishers.

Sheldrake, Rupert, 1999b. "Commentary on a Paper by Wiseman, Smith, and Milton on the 'Psychic Pet' Phenomenon", *Journal of the Society for Psychical Research*, Vol. 63, No. 857, October, 1999, pp. 306-311.

Sheldrake, Rupert, 2000. "A Dog that seems to Know when his Owner is Coming Home: Videotape Experiments and Observations", *Journal of Scientific Exploration*, Vol. 14, No. 2, pp. 233-255.

Sheldrake, Rupert, 2003. "Testing a Language-Using Parrot for Telepathy", *Journal of Scientific Exploration*, Vol. 17, No. 4, pp. 601-616.

Shermer, Michael, 2001. *The Borderlands of Science*, New York: Oxford University Press.

Shermer, Michael, 2003. "Demon Haunted Brain", *Scientific American*, March 2003.

Sidgwick, Mrs. Henry, 1932. "The Society for Psychical Research: A Short Account of its History", *Proceedings of the Society for Psychical Research*, Part XLI, April, 1932-3, pp. 1-26.

Slade, Peter, and Bentall, Richard. 1988. *Sensory Deception.* Baltimore: John Hopkins University Press.

Snow, C.P., 1934. *The Search*. London: Macmillan and Co. (5th edition, 1963).

Sperry, R.W., 1985. *Science and Moral Priority.* New York: Greenwood/Praeger Publishers.

Sperry, R.W., 1987. "Structure and Significance of the Consciousness Revolution". *Journal of Mind and Behavior* 8, 37-65.

Sperry, Roger, 1994. "Holding Course Amid Shifting Paradigms", in *New Metaphysical Foundations of Modern Science*, edited by Harman and Clark, Sausalito: Institute of Noetic Sciences.

Squires, Euan, 1994. *The Mystery of the Quantum World* (second edition). London: Institute of Physics Publishing.

Stanford, R.G., and Mayer, B., 1974. "Relaxation as a psi-conducive state", *Journal of the American Society for Psychical Research*, 68, 182-191.

Stanford, R.G., Zenhausern R., Taylor, A., and Mary Ann Dwyer, 1975. "Psychokinesis as Psi-Mediated Instrumental Response", *Journal of the American Society for Psychical Research*, 69, 127-133.

Stanford, R.G., 1990. "An experimentally testable model for spontaneous psi events: A review of related evidence and concepts from parapsychology and other sciences." In S. Krippner, (editor), *Advances in Parapsychological Research, Vol. 6* (pages 54-167). Jefferson, NC: McFarland.

Stapp, Henry, 1994. "Theoretical model of purported theoretical violations of the predictions of quantum theory." *Physical Review* A, 50, pages 18-22.

Stapp, Henry, 1999. "Attention, Intention, and Will in Quantum Physics", *Journal of Consciousness Studies,* 6, No. 8-9, pages 143-164.

Stapp, Henry, *Science and Human Values*. (Not yet published at time of writing).

Steering Committee of the Physicians' Health Study Research Group, 1988. Preliminary Report: Findings from the aspirin component of the ongoing Physicians' Health Study. *New England Journal of Medicine*, 318, pages 262-264.

Stenger, Victor, 1990. *Physics and Psychics*. Buffalo: Prometheus Books.

Stenger, Victor, 1995. *The Unconscious Quantum*. Buffalo: Prometheus Books.

Stevenson, Ian, 1987. *Children Who Remember Previous Lives.* Charlottesville: University Press of Virginia.

Stevenson, Ian, 1988. "Comments by Ian Stevenson", *Journal of the Society for Psychical Research*, 55, pages 230-234.

Stevenson, Ian, 1997. *Reincarnation and Biology: Volume 2*. Westport, CT: Praeger Publishers.

Stillings, D., 1989. "Mistuh Kurtz—he dead." Review of *Exuberance: An Affirmative Philosophy of Life*, by Paul Kurtz. *Artifex*, 8(4), p. 38

Stokes, Douglas, 1987a. "Promethean Fire: the View from the Other Side", *Journal of Parapsychology*, Vol. 51, September 1987, p. 249-270.

Stokes, Douglas, 1987b. "Theoretical Parapsychology", in *Advances in Parapsychological Research*, edited by Stanley Krippner. London: McFarland & Company.

Tart, Charles, 1988. "Effects of electrical shielding on GESP performance." *Journal of the American Society for Psychical Research*, 80, pages 163-173.

Thouless, R.H.; Wiesner, B.P. 1949. "The Psi Processes in Normal and Paranormal Psychology" *Proceedings of the SPR*, Vol. 48, pages 177-196.

Truzzi, Marcello, 1997. "Reflections on the Sociology and Social Psychology of Conjurors and Their Relations with Psychical Research", in *Advances in Parapsychological Research 8*, edited by Stanley Krippner. London: McFarland & Company.

Truzzi, Marcello, 1998. "On Some Unfair Practices towards Claims of the Paranormal", in Edward Binkowski, editor, *Oxymoron: Annual Thematic Anthology of the Arts and Sciences*, Vol. 2: The Fringe, New York: Oxymoron Media, Inc., 1998.

Ullman, Montague, Stanley Krippner, and Alan Vaughan, 1989. *Dream Telepathy: Experiments in Nocturnal ESP*, second edition. Jefferson, N.C.: McFarland.

Utts, Jessica, 1986. "The Ganzfeld Debate: a statistician's perspective" *The Journal of Parapsychology*, 50, pages 363-402.

Utts, Jessica, 1991a. "Replication and Meta-Analysis in Parapsychology." *Statistical Science*, Vol. 6, No. 4, pages 363-378.

Utts, Jessica, 1991b. "Rejoinder." *Statistical Science*, Vol. 6, No.4, pages 396-403.

Utts, Jessica, 1995a. "An Assessment of the Evidence for Psychic Functioning." As published on the Internet.

Utts, Jessica, 1995b. "Response to Ray Hyman's Report." As published on the Internet.

Utts, J. M., 1996a. "An Assessment of the Evidence for Psychic Functioning", *Journal of Scientific Exploration*, 10 (1), 3-30. Also in *Journal of Parapsychology*, 59(4), 289-320.

Utts, Jessica, 1996b "Response to Ray Hyman's Report of September 11, 1995, 'Evaluation of Program on Anomalous Mental Phenomena.'" Journal of Scientific Exploration 10(1), 59-61. Also in Journal of Parapsychology, 59(4), 353-356.

Vallee, J., 1990. *Confrontations: a Scientists Search for Alien Contact*. New York: Ballantine Books.

Van de Castle, R.L., 1969. "The facilitation of ESP through hypnosis." *American Journal of Clinical Hypnosis*, 12, pages 37-56.

Vandenberg, Philipp, 1979. *The Mysteries of the Oracles*. New York: Macmillan Publishing Company.

Vasiliev, L.L., 1976. *Experiments in distant influence*. New York: Dutton.

Wagner, Mahlon, and Mary Monet, 1979. "Attitudes of College Professors Toward Extra-Sensory Perception," *Zetetic Scholar*, 1979, 5, pages 7-16.

Walker, E.H., 1974. "Consciousness and Quantum Theory", in *Psychic Exploration*, ed. J. White, New York: Putnam's, pages 544-68.

Walker, E.H., 1974. "Foundations of Paraphysical and Parapsychological Phenomena", in *Quantum Physics and Parapsychology*, ed. Laura Oteri, New York: Parapsychology Foundation, pages 1-44.

Walker, E.H., 1979. "The Quantum Theory of Psi Phenomena", Psychoenergetic Systems, Vol. 3, pages 259-299.

Walker, E.H., 1984. "A Review of Criticisms of the Quantum Mechanical Theory of Psi Phenomena", *Journal of Parapsychology*, Vol. 48, December 1984, pages 277-332.

Walker, E.H., 1987. "Measurement in Quantum Mechanics Revisited", *Journal of the American Society for Psychical Research*, Vol. 81, October 1987, pages 333-369.

Wheeler, John A., 1979. "Drive the Pseudos Out of the Workshop of Science" (Address to the Annual Meeting of the AAAS, January 8, 1979), reprinted in *New York Review of Books,* May 17, 1979.

Wheeler, John, and Wojciech Zurek, (editors) 1983. *Quantum Theory and Measurement*, Princeton: Princeton University Press, 1983.

Wigner, Eugene, 1961. "Remarks on the Mind-Body Problem", from *Quantum Theory and Measurement*, edited by John Wheeler and Wojciech Zurek. Princeton: Princeton University Press, 1983.

Wiseman, Richard, Matthew Smith, & Julie Milton, 1998. "Can Animals detect when their owners are returning home? An experimental test of the 'psychic pet' phenomenon." *British Journal of Psychology*, 89, pp. 453-462.

Wiseman, R., Matthew Smith & Julie Milton, 2000. "The 'Psychic Pet' Phenomenon: A Reply to Rupert Sheldrake", *Journal of the Society for Psychical Research*, Vol. 64, No. 858, pp. 46-49, January, 2000.

Yuille, J., & Cutshall, J., 1986. "A Case Study of Eyewitness Memory to a Crime", *Journal of Applied Psychology*, Vol. 71, No. 2, pp. 291-301.

Zelen, Marvin, 1976. "Astrology and Statistics: A Challenge" *The Humanist*, Jan-Feb, 1976, pages 32-33.

Zelen, Marvin, P. Kurtz, and G. Abell, 1977. "Is There a Mars Effect?" *The Humanist*, Nov-Dec, 1977, pages 36-39.

Zingrone, Nancy, 1997. "Failing to Go the Distance: On Critics and Parapsychology." Published by the Parapsychology Foundation. This paper was presented at a meeting of the Society for Psychical Research in London in 1997.

Zollner, Friedrich, 1888. *Transcendental Physics*. Boston: Colby & Rich.

Zollschan, Schumaker & Walsh (editors), 1989. *Exploring the Paranormal: Different Perspective on Belief and Experience*. Dorset, England: Prism Press.

Zorab, George, 1985. "Review of *The Enigma of Daniel Home: Medium or Fraud*", by Trevor Hall. *Journal of Parapsychology*, 1985, 49, pages 103-105.

Index